FAMILY
BETRAYAL

By the same author

The Spy Who Came in from the Co-op
The Lawn Road Flats
Russia and the British Left

FAMILY BETRAYAL

Agent Sonya, MI5 and the Kuczynski Network

DAVID BURKE

The History Press

First published 2021

The History Press
97 St George's Place, Cheltenham,
Gloucestershire, GL50 3QB
www.thehistorypress.co.uk

British Library Cataloguing in Publication Data.
A catalogue record for this book is available from the British Library.

ISBN 978 0 7509 9660 0

Typesetting and origination by The History Press
Printed and bound in Great Britain by TJ Books Ltd.

Trees for LYfe

'All happy families are alike; each unhappy family is unhappy in its own way.'

Leo Tolstoy, *Anna Karenina*

Contents

Illustrations

All images are courtesy of the author's collection unless otherwise stated. While every effort has been made to trace or contact all copyright holders, the publishers would be pleased to rectify at the earliest opportunity any errors or omissions brought to their attention.

Introduction

The two greatest British secrets of the Second World War were undoubtedly the atomic bomb programme and the breaking of the German codes at Bletchley Park. Hitherto, much has been written about how the Soviets gained the secrets of the atomic bomb, but very little has been written about the Soviet infiltration of Bletchley Park. At the centre of the Soviet campaign to access Britain's wartime secrets was a remarkable family of Communist refugees from Nazism, the Kuczynskis. There were eight family members and five marriage partners either directly active, or in supporting roles, working with Russian intelligence: the patriarch and matriarch Robert and Berta, their son Jürgen, and daughters Ursula, Brigitte, Barbara, Sabine and Renate. They were a family whose work for Soviet intelligence would ensure the success of the Russian intelligence offensive against Great Britain for much of the twentieth century. Their respective careers fitted neatly into Soviet intelligence activity in Britain that targeted Left-wing elements and fellow-travellers. This continued long after any ideological solidarity between the Soviet Union and organised labour in Britain had disappeared from the Labour Party's make-up.

The Kuczynskis were not only a family who spied but also one of the chief channels of leakage of information to the Soviets from a variety of sources. During almost seventy years of intelligence activity the Kuczynski family gained access to high-ranking civil servants in the Board of Trade, Ministry of Information, the British Council, the Ministry of Labour and National Service, the BBC, the Ministry of Power, Ministry of Economic Warfare, the Atomic Energy Research Establishment, RAF Harwell, Members of Parliament and the legal profession; many of their contacts were Communists or fellow-travellers, and at one time they included Arthur Drew, Private Secretary to the Secretary of State for War, who worked closely with a number of prominent politicians, among them Emanuel Shinwell, Sir John Grigg and John Profumo. The Kuczynskis created organic networks: an agent once recruited began recruiting friends from various backgrounds.

One of the most significant spy rings in the early Cold War, the Kuczynski network was targeted on Britain's emerging atomic bomb programme and Bletchley Park. It was, for a time, based in what was one of London's most fashionable buildings in leafy Hampstead – the Lawn Road Flats, a haven for spies. No fewer than seven secret agents for Stalin's Russia lived here in the 1930s and '40s including an Austrian-Jewish Communist, Arnold Deutsch, the controller of the group of spies known as the Cambridge Five – Anthony Blunt, Guy Burgess, John Cairncross, Donald Maclean and Kim Philby. Brigitte Kuczynski, code name 'Joyce', arrived in Britain from Geneva on 26 March 1934 and moved into the Lawn Road Flats on 4 July 1936. From there she recruited two important British spies, Alexander Foote and Leon Beurton, who were sent to Switzerland to work with Ursula Kuczynski, code name 'Sonya'.

Ursula Kuczynski had previously worked as a Soviet spy in Manchuria and was an exceptionally adept encrypter, able to use Morse code faster than any other agent on Soviet military intelligence's books. In London, Jürgen Kuczynski, code name 'Peter', another Lawn Road Flats resident, was the vital link between the Kuczynskis and the 'legal' resident at the Soviet Embassy, and was on friendly terms with the Soviet Ambassador, Ivan Maisky. An important asset, he collected intelligence on schisms within the Labour Party and introduced his sister Ursula to the émigré physicist Klaus Fuchs, who was then working on the joint Anglo-American bomb project. From 1943, Ursula lived under cover as a rural Oxfordshire housewife and mother, while transmitting nuclear secrets to Moscow from an adapted washing line in her garden in the Cotswold village of Great Rollright. She described how she would walk down country lanes with Fuchs – they would affect to be young lovers – while he handed over atomic formulae. She also controlled the atomic bomb spy Melita Norwood until 1944 when Moscow Centre and Beria's NKVD[1] took over the handling of the atomic bomb spies from Soviet military intelligence, the GRU.[2] Following his arrest, Fuchs named Ursula as his controller. MI5, however, got nowhere in their attempts to interview her about her espionage activities, and before the Kuczynski network could be fully unravelled both Ursula and Jürgen had beaten a hasty retreat to East Berlin.

Among Barbara Kuczynski's acquaintances were Margot Heinemann and Guy Burgess, and through Margot, Anthony Blunt and Donald Maclean. Barbara's husband, Duncan Macrae Taylor, a well-connected Lowland Scot, trained as a wireless operator with the RAF and served as an intelligence officer in Cairo before being posted to Bletchley Park. Barbara and Duncan both joined the Labour Party, where they cultivated a number of senior party officials, becoming what one acquaintance of the Taylors called 'social enablers'. The youngest of the Kuczynski daughters, Renate, code name 'Katie', was recruited to Soviet military intelligence in 1939 by her sister Ursula. Working closely with Barbara, she introduced Communist sympathisers and fellow-travellers into the government's Code and Cypher School at Bletchley Park.

How legitimate is spying in defence of a cause? Is it possible to confer the honourable title of anti-Nazi resistance on the Kuczynski family, and have done with it? Or should we condemn the family for its espionage activities on behalf of the Soviet Union that, in the main, targeted Great Britain and the British Empire? As an ideology based on internationalism, Soviet Communism found it relatively easy to recruit outside its borders. Under Stalin's dictatorship, however, that internationalism turned inwards to promote the defence of one nation state above all others. Those spies still acting in what they believed to be the best interests of internationalism succumbed to the blandishments of Stalinism. A vast array of Communist propagandists and fellow-travellers were prepared to accept the Soviet Union 'as if it were, in reality, what it was on paper'.[3]

In 1958, two years after Nikita Khrushchev's speech to the Twentieth Party Congress of the Soviet Union, the British historian Henry Pelling wrote of his fascination with the Communist Party of Great Britain (CPGB), stating that 'there can be few topics more worthy of exploration than the problem of how it came to pass, that a band of British citizens could sacrifice themselves so completely ... to the service of a dictatorship in another country.'[4] In the case of the Kuczynskis, that problem was compounded by an added dimension. As German refugees living in Britain they were not merely prepared to spy for the Soviet Union against Germany, but were prepared to spy against the interests of their adopted country. In some respects, they found this quite straightforward owing to their acceptance by British Communists working for the revolutionary overthrow of their own government. This was further enhanced by the anti-imperialist work of the CPGB, which was actively supported by the Kuczynskis. The underground work of Brigitte with the Director of the CPGB's Colonial Affairs Committee, Michael Carritt, who had at one time served as a British Security and District Officer in the Indian Civil Service, was a good example of this. Ursula's work with the Communist Party of China, too, was directed against both Japanese and British imperial interests in the Far East. Jürgen's openly proclaimed support for the Nazi–Soviet pact was largely based on antipathy towards the British Empire and the growing influence of Wall Street in global affairs. Furthermore, when Sabine Kuczynski's husband, the Communist lawyer Francis Loeffler, defended opponents of the Greek monarchy charged with treason, was he guilty of subversion? The legitimate activities of the Kuczynskis brought them into contact with reformist socialists in the Labour Party, the legal apparatus, government ministries, trade unionists and others in their pursuit of a Stalinist vision of Communism and resistance to Fascism.

Since the fall of the Berlin Wall and the opening of Stasi archives, a more detailed picture has emerged not only of Soviet espionage in Germany, but also of Communist resistance to Hitler in Germany. Communist resistance can be said to have taken place on two levels.

Firstly, there was the opposition of rank-and-file Communists who believed that the defeat of Nazism would be followed by the victory of German Communism over capitalism. Secondly, there was an elite group of German intelligence practitioners who believed that German Communism could only be achieved by guaranteeing the security of the Soviet State. This second group included the Kuczynskis and formed the nucleus of the German–Soviet intelligence secret service operating out of Moscow Centre in both Nazi Germany and the UK. Traditional historiography has, hitherto, shied away from the second group while downgrading the first. By doing so historians have created the erroneous impression that there was no serious opposition to Hitler before 1937 and that when it appeared it came 'almost exclusively from a small minority of churchmen, aristocrats and other conservatives'.[5] Such an approach ignores the contribution of those Communists, like the Kuczynskis, to the defeat of Nazism. Many historians prefer to fall back on a crude reductionism that sees the Communist resistance as another form of totalitarianism comparable to that of National Socialism itself, thereby stripping its activities of heroism.[6]

There is, of course, the question of the German Communist refugees' gratitude to Britain, the country that not only offered the Kuczynskis asylum but also guaranteed their freedom from want. Did the Kuczynskis, at least during the period of the USSR's alliance with Britain and the United States, make a worthwhile contribution to the Allied war effort, while advancing the cause of Communism and Stalin's Soviet Union?

The Kuczynskis' activities on behalf of the Soviet Union can be divided into five distinct periods: pre-Hitler Germany, covering the years from the Russian Revolution of 1917 to Hitler's accession to power in January 1933; Hitler's period in power down to the signing of the Nazi–Soviet Pact and the outbreak of the Second World War in September 1939; Communist opposition to the imperialist war, which covers the period from the outbreak of war on 1 September 1939 to the Nazi invasion of the Soviet Union on 22 June 1941; the period of the Second World War and Great Patriotic War, 1941–45; and finally the Cold War that followed. Throughout, Stalinism as a system influenced events. *Family Betrayal*, therefore, takes as its starting point Stalin and German Communism and the ideological 'progression' of the Kuczynskis until Hitler came to power in January 1933. By linking four main areas of Soviet espionage activity in the UK – the race against time to build a Soviet atomic bomb; the garnering of political intelligence from inside the Labour Party; the penetration of Bletchley Park and the British Civil Service – *Family Betrayal* sheds new light on the Soviet Union's intelligence offensive against Great Britain during the twentieth century and MI5's efforts to both thwart their attacks and to counter subversion.

CHAPTER ONE

Class Against Class

Robert René Kuczynski was born on 12 August 1876 in Berlin, the son of a successful banker. On 1 December 1903, he married Berta Gradenwitz, an artist who was born into a land-owning family on 30 June 1879 in Cottbus.

The Kuczynskis were a comfortable, German bourgeois family of Jewish origin that did not practise any faith. Their large lakeside villa by Berlin's Schlachtensee, 'the gift of a wealthy grandfather',[1] boasted an impressive library bought chiefly from the Hungarian-Jewish Communist writer Arthur Holitscher, described by the Kuczynskis' eldest daughter, Ursula, as a frequent visitor to Schlachtensee and a 'friend of the Soviet Union'.[2] Among the volumes on the shelves were works by Thomas Mann, George Bernard Shaw, Upton Sinclair and John Galsworthy.

In her autobiography, Ursula described the family's economic status in Berlin as barely adequate. Despite their spacious and by all accounts impressive surroundings, Robert's salary from the Statistical Office of Berlin[3] was insufficient to provide more than a 'relatively simple standard of living'.[4] Ursula regarded her father as 'more of an academic than an official' whose modest income would not support his large family made up of one son, Jürgen (b. 1904), and five daughters, Ursula (b. 1907), Brigitte (b. 1910), Barbara (b. 1913), Sabine (b. 1919) and Renate (b. 1923). Nevertheless, the family library was overflowing and Berta was said to be 'frantic over this squandering of money on books'.[5]

Sabine was less damning in her description of the family's economic circumstances and described how she was 'brought up against a well-to-do middle-class background', with 'the tremendous advantage of intelligent progressive thinking parents'. Her childhood, she wrote, 'was spent in an atmosphere where art and books, reading and learning were encouraged'.[6]

Robert in 1919 would probably have described himself as a liberal progressive with strong social democratic beliefs. With widespread food scarcity in Europe, he had joined the Fight the Famine Council (FFC)[7] and assisted, as a statistician, in the 'collection of the facts and suggested remedies' to alleviate the situation in Russia, Finland, Poland, Czechoslovakia, the Balkans and Armenia; serious food shortages in Turkey, Bulgaria and Italy were also dealt with by the FFC. In November 1919, the FFC held its first International Economic Conference at Caxton Hall in Westminster, organised by Charles Alfred Cripps, Lord Parmoor, Sir George Paish, William Beveridge and John Maynard Keynes. All four were leading liberal progressives on the Left wing of liberalism in Britain. In 1921 Robert attended the organisation's International Conference for Economic Reconstruction held at the Caxton Hall between 11 and 13 October, where he first made the acquaintance of Britain's future wartime Ambassador to the Soviet Union, Stafford Cripps, the youngest son of Charles Alfred Cripps, and other progressive notables.[8]

Earlier that year the FFC had published the Soviet government's worldwide appeal for aid, *The Famine in Russia: Russia Appeals to the World*, and in its report on the Caxton Hall conference issued an appeal to world leaders and the League of Nations to address the economic problems that besieged Europe under the title *The Needs of Europe, Its Economic Reconstruction*. The report called for German reparations to be fixed at a level that Germany could afford to pay and appealed for the restoration of production in Russia and renewed trade relations with Moscow.[9] The conference identified two critical factors that it believed were preventing European economic reconstruction and threatening world peace: runaway inflation in Germany and the persistence of economies in Europe dependent on heavy industry. The two together were creating a balance of payments crisis that was fuelling political and social unrest. Militarism, the conference warned, had erroneously been accepted as the most direct way out of the crisis:

The Conference desires to record its conviction that Europe cannot obtain either credit guarantees or the credits themselves until the various nations reduce their military outlays, make a real effort to curtail their governmental expenditure, endeavour to restore the equilibrium to the budget, and thus indicate their intention to stop the issue both of paper currency and of governmental loans for other than productive purposes.[10]

This was the central message that Robert brought back to Germany from London in 1921. The world economic crisis, he argued, was drawing the German working class closer to the Russian revolution. His analysis chimed with the activities of the German Communist Willi Münzenberg, who had established Workers International Relief (WIR) in Berlin, also known as International Workers' Aid (IWA), in September 1921. Münzenberg's organisation, an adjunct of the Communist International, promoted international working-class solidarity by channelling relief from various organisations and Communist parties to famine-stricken Russia. As the first Communist organisation to make inroads into non-Communist circles of workers and intellectuals, it made an important departure from orthodox Communist practice. Under Münzenberg's tutelage, Germany became an important springboard for Agitation and Propaganda ('agitprop')[11] and donations to Russia poured in. Twenty-one shiploads of material left Germany for Russia in 1921, increasing to seventy-eight shiploads in 1922. As the German Communist Ruth Fischer observed, its effect on the economic crisis gripping a country the size of Russia could only have been slight but 'as propaganda the value of these collections was inestimable: everyone who donated his little bit felt tied to the workers' fatherland'.[12]

Münzenberg has rightly been seen as the architect of a scheme to enlist and harness intellectuals worldwide in support of the Communists' Soviet experiment.[13] It was under his guardianship that the phenomenom of the fellow-traveller, a 'sympathiser' capable of promoting the Communist cause without becoming a fully paid-up member of a national Communist party, was created.[14] Robert Kuczynski served as an important link between Münzenberg and liberal–socialist–pacifist circles.[15] In this capacity he was protected from the unending doctrinal disputes and the internal strife within the *Kommunistische Partei Deutschlands* (KPD) that prevented the formation of a united front between the Communists and the *Sozialdemokratische Partei Deutschlands* (SPD) throughout the period of the Weimar Republic. The failure of the leaders of the KPD and SPD to build a united front along the lines ordained by the Communist International (Comintern) in 1922[16] had its roots in the Russian Politburo's response to two key events: the French and Belgian occupation of the Rhine-Ruhr on 11 January 1923[17] and the debacle of the failed 1923 German October Revolution.

According to Ruth Fischer, the Russian Politburo jettisoned the united front policy soon after the KPD had agreed to unite with the SPD leadership in a programme of strict disobedience to the occupation authorities and to fight for a workers' government. However, the tactic was condemned by the Russian Politburo as a 'Right deviation' and at a secret conference in Moscow German Communists were instructed to intensify the struggle for power, particularly in the occupied Rhine-Ruhr region.[18] Following a nationwide general strike in Germany in mid-August, the Russian Politburo 'discussed the question of a German revolution in all its details'.[19] A committee of four was appointed to supervise the preparations; Stalin alone advised caution. In September a small revolutionary committee of German and Russian officers was brought together to direct the uprising. 'Governments of proletarian defence' were formed in Saxony and Thuringia on 10 and 16 October respectively, composed of representatives from both the SPD and KPD.[20] On 20 October the Central Committee of the KPD agreed unanimously to call a general strike and prepared to launch an armed struggle. The absolute refusal of the SPD to endorse the KPD's proposals, however, spread confusion and the revolution was abruptly called off. The following day, the German Army intervened and the coalition governments of Saxony and Thuringia were overthrown. On

2 November SPD members in the Grand Coalition cabinet tendered their resignations, prompting the Central Committee of the KPD to launch an attack on the leaders of the SPD, who they condemned for failing to support the revolutionary aspirations of the German working class.[21] Later that month the KPD was declared illegal.[22]

The lessons of the German October were not lost on Stalin, whose theory of 'Socialism in One Country' – that the building up of the Soviet Union's industrial base and military might must take precedence over the export of revolution abroad – gained widespread support in the Russian Politburo. By 1924 'Socialism in One Country' was the dominant premise. The Nazis, meanwhile, sowed further divisions among Germany's working class by presenting militant nationalism as an alternative to proletarian revolution. Any lingering hopes of a united front between the leaders of the two working-class parties were finally discarded when the Comintern and the KPD denounced the SPD as 'accomplices of Fascism'.[23] In January 1924 the President of the Communist International, Grigori Zinoviev, condemned the SPD for forming 'a life and death alliance against the proletarian revolution' with the Reichswehr.[24] The tactic of 'unity from above', he urged, must give way to 'unity from below':

> The essence of the matter consists in this, that General Seeckt[25] is a fascist like others, that the leaders of German Social Democracy have become Fascist through and through, that they have in fact formed a life and death alliance against the proletarian revolution with General Seeckt, this German Kolchak.[26] That is the reason why our whole attitude towards Social Democracy needs revising … The slogan 'unity from below' must become a living reality.[27]

Zinoviev's instructions could not easily be ignored. At this time the KPD could claim between 125,000 and 135,000 members and was – by German standards – a weak organisation; whereas the apparatus of the Party remained strong largely owing to Moscow's grip over important elements within the KPD:

The Central Committee, its secretaries, editors, technical employees	850
Newspaper and printing plants, including advertising staff	1,800
Book shops, with associated agitprop groups	200
Trade union employees (principally in Stuttgart, Berlin, Halle, Thuringia, Chemnitz)	200
Sick benefit societies	150
International Workers' Aid, with affiliated newspapers	50
Red Aid, including children's homes in Thuringia	50
German employees of Soviet institutions (Soviet Embassy, trade legations in Berlin, Leipzig, and Hamburg, the Ostbank, various German–Russian corporations)	1,000
Total:	4,300[28]

All these employees, Ruth Fischer pointed out, depended upon Moscow for their positions. Swelling their number were the 'invisible undercover agents', roughly amounting to the same number. If these figures are correct, she maintained, 'almost one twelfth of the party membership was in direct Russian pay'.[29]

In 1926 the counter-espionage section of the GRU founded the first Lenin School in Moscow where, in a secret annex on the outskirts of the city, conspiratorial methods were taught. As the revolutionary prospects in Germany faded, the 'invisible undercover agents' concentrated on espionage in various fields of activity. 'Out of the ruins of the Communist revolution,' wrote one of Stalin's principal agents, 'we built in Germany for Soviet Russia a brilliant intelligence service, the envy of every other nation.'[30] A secret apparatus began to dominate the internal life of the KPD – *die Nachrichten* (intelligence) – also known as the N-Group. Between 1926 and 1929 the N-Group, controlled by OGPU[31] men, prepared a complete index of German Communists. The future East German leader Walter Ulbricht became the principal contact between the Russian secret service and the German party and 'Berlin became a second headquarters for Russian agents penetrating the rest of Europe.'[32]

The KPD became less of a political party and more of a pressure group along the lines of their British counterparts in the Communist Party of Great Britain (CPGB). Nowhere was this more evident than in the part played by the Party in the plebiscite to expropriate the Hohenzollerns.

The Kaiser's considerable fortune had been sequestered by Prussia at the end of the First World War. However, confiscation of his entire wealth was postponed indefinitely by a dispute, dragging through the courts and the Reichstag Judiciary Committee, on whether William II should be compensated for his losses. When the SPD proposed a Reichstag Bill to settle the matter, the Communists intervened and demanded that the imperial fortune be confiscated without any compensation whatsoever. Their stand won widespread support among the SPD rank-and-file and other liberal groups and led to the setting up of various liberal–socialist–Communist committees under the leadership of Robert Kuczynski, who expertly cultivated 'unity from below' within the framework of the forgotten united front:

> At that time the Peace Cartel[33] was the influential centre of all specific cultural political movements and groups within the German republic; and if this Cartel once made common cause with the KPD, the SPD could not remain aloof without making itself ridiculous, so within a few days, and with bad grace, it joined the Committee against the Royal Indemnity. The leadership was de facto in the hands of the Communists and a non-party man, naturally Dr. Robert KUCZYNSKI was elected as president, it was the Communist Party's reward to him for his attitude.

The general secretary of the German League for the Rights of Man,[34] the pacifist Otto Lehmann-Ruessbueldt, worked closely with Robert Kuczynski on the Committee. In 1941 he offered this telling character sketch of Robert to the British security service, MI5:

> I have brought up the Royal Indemnity because it is characteristic of Dr. KUCZYNSKI. As a politician he was a popular radical,

courageous and soft to the point of demagogy, officially divided from the Communists, but in actual fact very near to them and because he was not a party member, protected from being drawn into the internal party strife and quarrels. He belonged to the circle of 'bourgeois sympathisers' so painstakingly cultivated by the KPD. I am convinced that KUCZYNSKI has never actually belonged to the KPD himself. However, as he is very vain, he welcomed the honours done to him by a great Party.[35]

Lehmann-Ruessbueldt later claimed that the action taken against the Royal Indemnity (*Fürstenabfindung*) 'was wrecked through Communist-Radical stupidity, and social democratic and left-wing slackness'. Under the deal the government had allowed the royal family to hold on to part of their possessions and to have the use of Cecilienhof, a sprawling neo-Tudor palace in Potsdam.[36] In July 1941 Lehmann-Ruessbueldt, by now an MI5 informant inside London's German émigré community, told the security service that he 'remembered quite clearly what attitude Robert Kuczynski took up at that time':

The President Prof. Ludwig QUIDDE, subsequently a nobel prize winner …, had moved that the wishes of the people should be the basis of the claim; that the former dynasty should be deprived of all their property, except for a capital sum, the interest on which would amount to 1000 RM a month (£50). Respectively: a state pension of 1000 RM per month. This proposal was reasonable. On this basis, a popular majority would probably have been achieved. The Social democrats who at that time held aloof from the movement, would certainly have been won over by these moderate demands, likewise a large number of bourgeois democrats and Catholics, and even certain petit-bourgeois nationalists. In the negotiations which took place with the Communists about this matter, our Peace cartel was represented by the President QUIDDE, Dr. Helene STOCKER and KUCZYNSKI. Dr. STOCKER (at that time one of my closest collaborators) agreed with QUIDDE's proposal; we were revolutionary but not radical (just as I am today). Originally KUCZYNSKI also agreed. The Communists immediately declared that they would not tolerate a compromise. All or nothing. The Royal families must be stripped of everything, not a pfennig must be left to them, only such a decision would be popular etc. etc. Whereupon KUCZYNSKI declared that if this was the opinion of our Communist friends, we must agree to it, because without the KPD the action could not be begun, and it must be begun.[37]

Robert Kuczynski's strident support for the Communists and his ability to marshal the moderates behind the Communists' campaign against the Hohenzollerns encouraged the Monarchists to organise a vigorous counter-campaign. In an open letter, President Hindenburg complained that the 'proposed expropriation was a great injustice, a regrettable lack of tradition, a crude ingratitude' that 'violated the concept of private property on which the Weimar Republic was based'.[38] A preliminary vote to determine whether or not a referendum should be held on the actual question of expropriation was held on 20 June 1926. Twenty million 'yes' votes were required to hold the plebiscite but out of the almost 40 million eligible voters, only 15 million voted. The result was a sweeping victory for Robert and his liberal–socialist–Communist coalition, with 14.5 million voting 'Yes' and 0.5 million registering a 'No' vote. The number of voters, however, fell far below the 20 million required. The nationalists had simply boycotted the vote; Robert's campaign had so seriously disrupted the nationalist Right that they turned away from the Hohenzollerns and began looking towards Hitler and the Nazis for salvation.

In the face of a growing Nazi threat, Robert was reluctant to abandon the tactic of the united front completely, and continued to urge unity with the SPD against Fascism despite Nikolai Bukharin's calls in 1928 for the struggle against the social democratic parties to be intensified under the slogan 'Class against Class'.[39] According to the new policy, social democracy, by securing agreements with the capitalist class, actively strengthened capitalist infrastructure and was, therefore, to be regarded as a greater threat to Communism than Fascism. The 'main task of the party' was 'to break the influence of the social democratic counter-revolutionaries on the masses'.[40] Robert Kuczynski, while accepting the new line, remained reluctant to throw over completely his united-front beliefs. His one-time colleague in the *Fürstenabfindung*, Lehmann-Ruessbueldt, complained at the end of 1928 that the KPD had become 'more left and idiotic' and criticised 'the party openly'. Robert, he recalled, 'refrained from all open criticism and so remained the Communists' whiteheaded boy. ... Intellectual conscience is not KUCZYNSKI's strongpoint.'[41]

In Germany, 'Class against Class' found considerable support following the shooting of unarmed Communist demonstrators on 1 May 1929 by the Berlin police, then under the control of the SPD Police Chief, Karl Zörgiebel. The SPD was roundly condemned as 'the enemy of the working class' and denounced in *Die Rote Fahne* (*The Red Banner*) for its 'Social fascist regime of terror'.[42] At the KPD's Twelfth Party Congress (16–19 June 1929), Ernst Thälmann, chairman of the KPD, described the newly elected coalition government under Hermann Müller (SPD)[43] as 'an essentially dangerous form of Fascist development, the form of Social Fascism [which] consists in paving the way for fascist dictatorship under the cloak of the so-called "pure democracy"'.[44] He insisted that Fascism could not be defeated without first defeating social democracy. It was the wrong speech at the wrong time. Germany in 1929 descended into a spiral of violence with politically motivated brawls, muggings and stabbings commonplace. During these years the National Socialist German Workers' Party (*Nationalsozialistische Deutsche Arbeiterpartei*, NSDAP) grew as the Communists declined. The grave economic crisis that followed the Wall Street Crash of 1929 paved the way for the Nazis' first decisive triumph in the elections of September 1930, when it became the second-largest party in the Reichstag, with 107 seats. The nationalist Right was in the ascendancy and xenophobia was seized upon by Hitler as a path to power. An agreement between the old ruling caste and the Nazi Party ensured Hitler's success. Industrial rationalisation and the great unemployment crisis of 1931–32 caused such distress among the German working class that a new proletariat emerged, responsive to a new national feeling and ready to receive National Socialism as the antidote to the omnipotence of money. Millions followed Hitler. The establishment of the Third Reich on 30 January 1933 created an order of things under which the Nazi Party would be able to impose its domination over the entire German nation, setting up a machinery of power that made resistance all but impossible. In February, an appeal to Communists and Social Democrats to unite against Nazism written by Robert Kuczynski was posted on hoardings across Berlin. As a result his villa was ransacked by the Gestapo and he fled to Czechoslovakia, leaving his family behind in Berlin. From Prague he went to Geneva, where he undertook honorary work for the League of Nations before moving to London on 11 September 1933. He was conditionally granted entry but on 26 October this was cancelled by the Home Office, although he was not deported.

CHAPTER TWO

Jürgen

MI5's knowledge of the Kuczynski family's German Communist activities was based on a long association between the Metropolitan Police's Special Branch and the Prussian secret police, stretching back to the 1920s.[1] The security service opened a Kuczynski file as early as 1928, based on information from MI6 agents working inside Germany. The file was at first simply a KAEOT – 'Keep an Eye on Them' – commonly known as a K file.[2] In August 1930 an informal agreement was reached between Special Branch and the Prussian secret police that 'closer collaboration' between the two intelligence bodies 'in respect of Bolshevik propaganda and intrigue would be helpful'.[3] As a result, Guy Liddell, Special Branch's leading expert on Communist subversion, visited Berlin on 10 October 1930 to meet with his opposite number in Germany. On 30 March 1933, MI5 opened deliberations with their new Nazi counterparts in the Prussian secret police, soon to be renamed the Gestapo. The initiative had been taken by the Germans, who claimed to have discovered documents detailing the Comintern's attempts to spread unrest throughout the British Empire.[4] Liddell, who had been transferred to MI5 in 1931, was given access to official files and made arrangements for relevant documents to be copied and forwarded to London via Captain Frank Foley, the Passport Control Officer at the British Embassy in Berlin. Liddell produced a lengthy report entitled 'The Liquidation of Communism and Left-wing Socialism in Germany', which would form the basis for future MI5 surveillance of German Left-wing refugees from Hitler's terror, including the Kuczynskis. Robert's son Jürgen was of particular interest.

Born on 17 September 1904 in Elberfeld, Germany, Jürgen had received a good education studying philosophy and history in Berlin,

Heidelberg and Erlangen, where he was awarded a doctorate on the subject of 'Economic Value – an economic, historical, sociological and historical-philosophical view'. A high-flyer, he had worked in a Berlin bank in 1925 and between 1926 and 1929 had studied economics at the Brookings Institution in Washington, DC, where he published his first major work, *Back to Marx*, and ran the statistical section of the American Federation of Labor (AFL) in Washington; he also worked for the Bureau of Labor Statistics. He was very close to his father, who between 1925 and 1931 worked six months of the year at the Brookings Institution. In 1928 Jürgen married Marguerite Steinfeld (born in Bischheim, Strasbourg in Alsace, on 5 December 1904), and in 1929 the couple published a joint work, *The Factory Worker in the American Economy*. Marguerite had been living in the USA for seven years before her marriage to Jürgen.

Urbane with the appearance of a courtly diplomat, Jürgen had been brought to the attention of MI5 in 1931, when he wrote to W.H. Williams, Secretary of the Labour Research Department in London, asking for their British Imperialism Series[5] and other books for review in a journal founded by his father in 1919, *Finanzpolitische Korrespondenz*. He was also known to be in touch with Rajani Palme Dutt, the intellectual guru of the CPGB and editor of the British Communist journal *Labour Monthly*. He joined the KPD in July 1930 and following a visit to the Soviet Union later that year was appointed economics editor of the KPD's newspaper *Die Rote Fahne*. From 1931 he was a fervent supporter of the Revolutionary Trade Union Opposition (RGO) in Germany and often attended official parties together with his father at the Soviet Embassy. He was a close friend of Erich Kunik, head of the information section of the KPD Central Committee who brought him into the KPD's inner circle. On 24 June 1931 Frank Foley included Jürgen 'in a list of functionaries of the Communist Central Organisations' sent to MI5.

Toward the end of 1931 Jürgen was introduced to the Hungarian economist Eugen Varga, who was then working at the Comintern office in the Lindenstrasse, Berlin, and again visited the Soviet Union. He edited the book, *Rote Arbeit: der neue Arbeiter in der Sowjetunion* (*Red Work: The New Worker in the Soviet Union*) defending labour conditions in the Soviet Union against accusations by Western countries that inhumane and slave labour conditions were the norm. The book praised Stalin's Five-Year Plan and extolled the efficiency and superiority of the Russian worker and workforce in the early 1930s compared with their Western counterparts during the Great Depression.[6] Ronald Boswell, director of publishers John Lane, discussed publishing an English edition but the project was not completed. *Rote Arbeit* was, nevertheless, an impressive piece of propaganda for 'Socialism in One Country', welcoming the development of heavy industry and the collectivisation of agriculture as essential for the modernising of the Soviet economy.[7] At the time the OGPU's head of counter-intelligence, Artur Artuzov, was in charge of a major disinformation campaign known as 'Operation Tarantella', which aimed to convince the West that 'the industrialisation of the Soviet Union was a huge success'.[8] Artuzov, who was seeking to engage foreign correspondents as propaganda accomplices, had a high regard for Jürgen's ability. Moscow Centre wanted London to believe that the Soviet Union was far stronger than it actually was. This was the message also carried by fellow-travelling foreign correspondents, among them Jürgen Kuczynski.[9]

Jürgen's reputation as a writer was put to good use by the KPD and in 1932 he made the acquaintance of the German Communist propaganda genius, Willi Münzenberg.[10] Later that year he attended the 'World Congress against War' held in Amsterdam on 27–29 August.[11] Two thousand delegates from twenty-seven countries gathered from various workers' groups, many of whom belonged to the Communist Parties or were known to be sympathetic towards Russia. Accordingly, debate centred upon the need to defend the Soviet Union from the reactionary policies of the Western imperialist powers, chiefly Great Britain. Fascism received little attention. However, at the closing session it was agreed to create a permanent body, the 'World Committee against War and Fascism' (WCAWF), with headquarters in Berlin, to co-ordinate the activities of all working-class parties and progressive groups opposed to the rise of Fascism and militarism. The success of the new body was undoubtedly due to Münzenberg. His skills as a publicist convinced many prominent non-Communist pacifists to join the Committee, among them Henri Barbusse, Romain Rolland, Albert Einstein, Heinrich Mann, Bertrand Russell, Havelock Ellis, Theodore Dreiser, John Dos Passos, and Upton Sinclair. Münzenberg's success in bringing together a number of varied anti-Fascist organisations, however, unsettled the Stalinist-dominated Communist International, whose policy of 'Class against Class' adopted at the Sixth World Congress of the Comintern in 1928 had condemned any co-operation with social democracy. Consequently, in October 1932 control of the WCAWF passed from the charismatic architect of the fellow-traveller Münzenberg to the Bulgarian Stalinist Georgi Dimitrov, who would achieve worldwide fame for his defence against Nazi accusations during the German Reichstag Fire trial of 1933.

Three days after Hitler's appointment as Chancellor of Germany on 30 January 1933, the Nazis dissolved the Reichstag and new elections were arranged for 5 March. The KPD, the largest Communist Party outside the Soviet Union with 360,000 members,[12] adopted a policy of wait and see. To many observers it looked increasingly unlikely that the Nazis would obtain a simple majority even in conjunction with its nationalist allies. Then, on the night of 27 February, the Reichstag building went up in flames. One eyewitness described the spectacle:

> We arrived at the scene perhaps half an hour after the show had been officially opened. The big cupola was bursting in flames like a volcano. The wide square in front of the building overflowed with SA men. Many of them for the first time flaunted their armbands as 'Auxiliary Police'. The Berliners openly made fun of them: 'They must have known in advance! They couldn't have come here so fast with their bandy legs!'
>
> Over the portals of the Reichstag there stood, hewn in stone, the inscription: 'To the German People'. We saw these words, expression of parliamentary democracy, disappear in brownish clouds of smoke, then we left.[13]

The fire, 'a highly imaginative act of provocation', was used to 'whip up a wave of panic and anti-Communist hysteria', paving the way for presidential emergency legislation and a surprise attack on the KPD, leading to the arrest of its leading members throughout Germany.[14] With parliamentary democracy in Germany literally succumbing to the flames, the KPD was forced underground or into exile. By the end of 1933, more than 130,000 Communists had been thrown into concentration camps and 2,500 murdered. Systematically destroyed as a mass movement, the direction of Party work in Germany was placed in the hands of a small group of seven or eight Politburo members with Walter Ulbricht,[15] Franz Dahlem[16] and Wilhelm Pieck[17] emerging as the leading figures.

At the end of May 1933, it was decided that the continued presence of its members in Germany was far too dangerous and the Politburo divided itself into two sections: home leadership (*Inlandsleitung*) in Berlin and an external or émigré leadership (*Auslandsleitung*) with its base in Paris. By the autumn of 1933 the position of those in the *Inlandsleitung* was so precarious that it was decided that they too should emigrate and supervision of the underground work was passed to Czechoslovakia. From the autumn of 1933 onwards the entire leadership of the KPD was in emigration, divided between Paris and Prague.[18] Münzenberg had fled to Paris where, following Dimitrov's arrest by the Nazis in connection with the fire, he resumed the leadership of the WCAWF. Under his guidance, a major anti-war and anti-Fascist conference was held at the Salle Pleyel, Paris, in June 1933 with nearly 3,000 delegates in attendance. Münzenberg, meanwhile, had shifted his position. In a clear signal to Moscow, he moved away from the idea that there were no enemies on the Left. He did, however, criticise the Communists for their abuse of the fellow-traveller, which he regarded as counterproductive. At Salle Pleyel the united front was no longer regarded as heresy and an alliance of socialists and Communists created the 'World Committee of Struggle against War and Fascism' (WCSAWF), albeit with the Communists as the dominant partner. The Amsterdam-Pleyel movement, as the alliance was commonly known after 1933, began the construction of a Popular Front coalition[19] in France and, to a lesser extent, in the UK; although it came much too late to heal the cleavages between the KPD and SPD in Germany and in emigration.

That same year Jürgen, who had remained in Berlin, was recruited to Soviet intelligence by Sergei Alekseevich Bessonov, provisional acting head of the second western department of the *Narodnyi komissariat vnutrennekh del* (NKVD),[20] the predecessor of the KGB, and counsellor at the Soviet embassy in Berlin 1933–35.[21] Jürgen regarded Bessonov as 'the "perfect Communist" – educated, cultured, intelligent and a warm friend. He was interested in everything, to the extent that he could hold a half-hour conversation about the preparation of fish with Marguerite.'[22] Once or twice a month he would meet secretly with Bessonov or with the Soviet Ambassador Lev Khinchuk and then his successor, Yakov Surits, submitting reports on the German situation.[23]

At the time Jürgen's Berlin despatches were regarded so highly that they were sent directly to the People's Commissar for Foreign Affairs, Maxim Litvinov at *Narkomindel* (NKID).[24] They were partly responsible for the siege mentality developing in the Soviet Union, with Surits confirming Germany's hostility towards Communism and Hitler's intention to bring about the international isolation of the USSR.[25] Intelligence from Germany – that Hitler was seeking a rapprochement with the West in anticipation of a military crusade against the Soviet Union – led Stalin to seek an accommodation with Hitler. Throughout this period the Soviet Union pursued a two-tier foreign policy – official and unofficial, formal and informal – based on a policy of binding Germany to Russia in a continental bloc against Britain and France. Jürgen's work with Bessonov and the Soviet Embassy in Berlin was very much within this two-tier framework. In 1935 he was invited to Moscow by the Soviet economist Eugen Varga who, under the name E. Pawlowski, had recently published a series of influential pamphlets encouraging Communist collusion with German nationalist elements:

The German worker will work for British and French imperialism under the control of German managers, who will share the profits with their foreign superiors. Thus Germany will be transformed into a colony of British and French imperialism, working as much as India or Indo-China for the profit of the City and the Bourse. Until now colonies have been backward agrarian countries with slight industrial development. The main profit of the British Empire comes from areas forced to accept British-manufactured commodities in exchange for raw materials and agrarian products. Germany will be the first of a new type of colony; its highly developed industry will be incorporated in its entirety into the British industrial system.[26]

While visiting Varga in Moscow, Jürgen established contact with two exiled members of the KPD leadership, Walter Ulbricht and Wilhelm Pieck. They impressed upon him the importance of the KPD maintaining its whole apparatus in exile in readiness to seize power following the downfall of the Nazi regime. He was advised to leave Germany and work with his family in the UK. By this time all the Kuczynskis were in London with the exception of Jürgen's eldest sister, Ursula.

CHAPTER THREE

Ursula

Ursula Kuczynski, nicknamed 'the Mouse' because of her small, pointed face and 'feverish inquisitiveness', joined the Communist Youth League in 1923 before becoming a fully fledged member of the Communist Party of Germany in May 1926 and leader of its Agitation and Propaganda Department (Agitprop) in Berlin's 10th District.[1] Agitprop troupes – small, amateur formations that used few props – were extremely popular in the Berlin of the Weimar Republic, bringing 'a splash of colour' into the otherwise dull routine of working-class life.[2] Ursula, or Ruth as she preferred to be known, was a visible element of Communist theatre, a 'Red' Sally Bowles in a fading Weimar Republic:

> There's been a lot happening recently. A fancy dress party at the Academy of Arts which I enjoyed enormously. Theme: 'Beyond the Pale'. My costume – bright red scanty shorts and tight-fitting shirt with stiff collar. There are those who say I kissed 20 boys, but without counting Rolf it can't have been more than 19.[3]

With the Berlin police denouncing the agitprop troupes as 'the elementary stages of Communism', in 1928 Ursula was dismissed from her job in the archives of the largest liberal publishing firm in Germany, Ullstein Verlag.[4] She travelled to New York to work in a bookshop before returning to Berlin in 1929 to marry her childhood sweetheart, Rudolph (Rolf or Rudi) Hamburger, an architect with Communist sympathies whom Ursula had kissed at the 'Beyond the Pale' costume party. She was 22 years old and Rolf was 26, and they talked constantly 'about seeing more of the world':

We asked Walter, a good friend of Rolf's who represented a large German firm in China, to keep an eye open for us. One day a telegram arrived from Walter; according to a newspaper advertisement the Shanghai Municipal Council was looking for an architect … Rolf telegraphed his application. It was accepted – on condition that he must start at once.[5]

Shanghai in the 1930s was divided between the French Concession, the Anglo-American International Settlement and the Chinese quarter. It had been designated a special city in 1927 and a municipality in May 1930. Practically a state within a state, the merchant class controlled the city, while the rest of China was divided among warlords. The American journalist J.B. Powell described his time there as 'like sitting on the rim of a volcano'.[6] Before Ursula left Berlin she visited KPD headquarters and informed them that she wished 'to become active in China'. Her offer was greeted with some surprise as Shanghai was then in the grip of a 'White Terror' and China itself was close to civil war. Three years earlier a strike of Shanghai workers had been brutally suppressed by a Chinese warlord backed by British and French troops. Two hundred Chinese had been decapitated in the streets, their heads stuck on bamboo poles or displayed on kitchen platters; the Chinese Communist Party had been outlawed. Was she fully aware of the dangers involved? Looking back, she could understand their incredulity:

> The comrades must have found it rather odd that I should bounce in and tell them naively what I wanted to do. So far I had not distinguished myself in any way. They spoke to me about the serious position in China, where party work was strictly clandestine and every communist, even by the smallest action, exposed to extreme danger.[7]

When the ship carrying Ursula dropped anchor in Shanghai she was appalled by the poverty and exploitation she witnessed around her:

Porters, emerging from the bowels of the ship and padding the steep planks to the quay, followed each other so closely that their heavily laden bamboo poles almost touched. Sweat streamed down their bodies; thick veins protruded from necks, temples and legs. A stench of garlic and sweat drifted from the human conveyor belt towards the travellers on deck. Encircling the ship in floating tubs were beggars, moaning cripples with stumps for arms and legs, children with festering wounds, some blind, some with hairless scab-encrusted heads.[8]

Ursula began vomiting daily and losing weight. The doctor put it down to the unsuitable climate until it became obvious that she was five months' pregnant. Her son, Micha, was born in February 1931 and her illegal work as a Communist was hidden by a more 'outwardly bourgeois life-style':

Rolf held a respected position; we were frequently invited to parties and had to reciprocate. Various ladies called and expected me to return the visit – an alien world which I hated, a stark contrast to the life I had led until then. I did not protest; I knew that if I was ever to work here illegally as a communist, an outwardly bourgeois life-style would provide vital cover. Weeks and months passed while I waited for some word from the party.[9]

Her initial contact was the American journalist, Agnes Smedley, a fluent German speaker who had lived in Berlin during the Weimar period. An agent working for the Comintern's *Otdel Mezhdunarodny Sviasy* (OMS),[10] she was the Far Eastern correspondent of the *Frankfurter Zeitung*, and a socialite who ran 'something of a salon in her various homes, providing a rendezvous for other journalists, communists and fellow-agents'.[11] A number of key figures in the world of espionage passed through her circle, among them allegedly the future head of MI5, Roger Hollis, then a young journalist and an employee of British American Tobacco. However, if Hollis had truly struck up a friendship with Smedley, as his detractors have claimed, it would have estranged him from other journalists in the British ex-pat community, who regarded Smedley with some horror. One late spring afternoon in 1931 Smedley opened her copy of the *Shanghai Evening Post and Mercury* and found there 'a double-columned centre-of-the page attack' against her by a Mr Woodhead, president of the British Residents' Association and one of the most reactionary writers in the British Far East.

> The article was interesting, not because it concerned me, but because it was a perfect example of the 'Shanghai mind'. Even in a city and country where ruthless reaction rode roughshod over every man or woman who even mentioned such insidious ideas as the rights of man, it was a masterpiece of gutter journalism, attacking both my political and my personal life.[12]

It was Smedley who first introduced Ursula to the Soviet agent Richard Sorge, code name 'Ramsay', perhaps the most famous of the GRU's 'great illegals'. Tall, well-built and handsome, his face scarred from previous fights, and dressed in a new but already crumpled suit, he made an immediate impression on Ursula. Born in Baku in 1895 to a German father and a Russian mother, and a member of both the KPD and the All-Union Communist Party (Bolsheviks),[13] he worked as an intelligence officer in China and Japan between 1929 and 1941. In Japan he formed the very effective 'Ramsay group' and established himself so securely in the German Embassy in Tokyo 'that his position was second only to that of the ambassador himself. He was an unofficial embassy adviser, with an office in the embassy building and full and free access to all the files.'[14] Probably his most notable achievement was to send a Top Secret report to Moscow with the exact date of the German Army's planned attack on the Soviet Union in June 1941. His other major contribution to Soviet intelligence was the recruitment of Ursula, the only woman ever to be made an honorary colonel of the Red Army. In 1932, he arranged for her to undergo six months' professional training in Moscow, where she was instructed in wireless telegraphy and in the techniques of repairing and constructing 'music boxes' (radio transmitters). She was also given the code name 'Sonya'.[15]

During her time in Moscow, Rolf remained in Shanghai while their 2-year-old son, Micha, was despatched to Czechoslovakia to stay with Rolf's parents. It was deemed far too risky for Micha to accompany Ursula to the Soviet Union as 'he was bound to learn Russian there'.[16] On this point Moscow Centre was adamant. By speaking out in Russian at the wrong time, the child could inadvertently blow her cover.

In Moscow Ursula learnt to build transmitters, receivers, rectifiers and frequency meters. She trained at the espionage school in Podlipki, a suburb of Moscow set up by the director of the Comintern's secret service, Alexander Mirov-Abramov, to prepare foreign Communists for underground work:

> The students at Podlipki were expected to change their names and commit themselves to lifelong secrecy, and the apparatus made it clear that any breach of that secrecy, whenever and wherever in the world it might happen, would be punished by death. Its cover name, behind the barbed wire, was the 'Eighth International Sports Base,' and it gave training to candidates from Korea to Paraguay.[17]

After completing her training, Ursula was sent to Mukden, Manchuria, in February 1934 to work undercover with a German comrade, whom she referred to only as Ernst. She arrived in Shanghai in the first week of April 1934, where she was briefly reunited with Rolf and Micha before announcing, quite unexpectedly, that they were to separate.[18] Rolf would not accept a divorce so Ursula travelled to Manchuria with Micha as the representative of Evans & Co., an American bookshop dealing in educational, medical and scientific books in Shanghai; Ernst travelled independently as a typewriter salesman.

In Mukden, Ernst and Ursula were to establish contact with the groups of partisans fighting Japanese forces in the mountains, small towns and villages of Manchuria and connect them with Moscow Centre.[19] They were assigned to three partisan leaders – Li in Harbin, Feng in Mukden and a comrade in Jilin, 500km from Mukden. It had been agreed in Moscow that Ernst, as the comrade with the highest rank and responsibility, should be protected, while Ursula would make contact with the partisans and see to the transmitting:

> The meeting with Li, in Harbin, was to take place a few days after our arrival in Mukden. After the long journey from Shanghai to Mukden, I did not want to subject Micha to another journey of twice 600 km. His whooping cough had weakened him, and I was doing all I could to build his strength up. Ernst offered to look after him and was given a list of instructions, which included all the tricks which, with any luck, might induce Micha to imbibe his cod-liver-oil.
>
> Of all the cities that I have known in my life, the Harbin of those days was the most sinister … Beggars, pickpockets and prostitutes dominated the scene. People were frightened to walk the streets alone after dark.[20]

Even the choice of meeting place was alarming:

> Someone had hit upon the bright idea that I meet Li late at night by the entrance to an isolated cemetery. Having made my way to this district, which was deserted but for the occasional drunk staggering along, I was frightened – not of the dead but of the living. I waited ten minutes. My fear grew. Twice abuse was hurled at me by passing men. I waited twenty-five minutes. Li did not come.[21]

In Mukden, Ursula lived separately from Ernst, who thought 'it had been a foregone conclusion'[22] that they would live together. She found accommodation in a small garden house in the grounds of a luxury villa, which had at one time belonged to the owner's mistress. There she began transmitting twice a week:

I did not always have news to send but had to report to Centre in case they had a message for us. If there was interference, if either we or they could not be heard, I tried again the following night.[23]

The text that Ursula transmitted or received contained between sixty and 500 groups, each group having five figures; on rare occasions it might be more. She signalled at different times but always at night and could only select one or two frequencies because the transmitter only worked on specific wavelengths. With messages having to be repeated, the transmitter had to be in operation three or even four times a week, thereby making triangulated detection easy.[24] The danger of arrest was ever present:

I could not get wrought up every time about the danger I had to face … If all went well I felt good. My house with its closed shutters was like a fortress. I covered the light so that only a faint glimmer – just enough for reading and writing – fell on the desk. Everything else lay in darkness. Micha was fast asleep in the next room. The town slept. Only I was awake sending news of the partisans into the ether – and in Vladivostok a Red Army man was sitting and listening.

Spying was not glamorous:

But there were often nights when I cursed the alarm clock and the coldness of the room. The coal fire in the stove went out overnight. I sat at the Morse key in my tracksuit, wrapped in blankets, with fingerless gloves on my hands. Aeroplanes circled over the house. One day they were bound to catch me. For a moment I would hope that my partner would not give his call sign. I wanted so much to climb back into my warm bed. But then I would only have to get up again the following night.[25]

Apart from giving guidance to the partisan groups, one of Ursula and Ernst's most important tasks was to obtain explosives for the groups' sabotage activities against the Japanese. They would visit chemists and general stores in Mukden and neighbouring towns to buy chemicals that, while not dangerous in themselves, would produce explosives in combination. Micha would be taken along on these shopping expeditions to allay suspicion:

> Ernst did not speak Chinese so I went with him, and Micha came along to make it all look as harmless as possible. We found a shop where they had ammonium nitrate in stock. I wondered whether to take two pounds or more; after all, it was used in large quantities in agriculture. I asked for ten pounds. The shopkeeper misunderstood and brought out a hundredweight. Overwhelmed but happy, we took a horse-cab to transport the purchase to my home.
>
> If I remember correctly, a kilo of ammonium nitrate mixed with about 20 per cent sugar or aluminium powder or permanganate was enough to cause an effective explosion if it was packed against a rail. Then again, maybe this was what we mixed with the potassium chlorate, another basic ingredient that we were able to buy quite easily. We may have used something else to ignite the ammonium nitrate. We also bought Sulphur, hydrochloric acid and other chemicals whose names I have forgotten, but we left it to the groups to mix them and pack them into shells.[26]

Feng, the second of Ursula's partisan contacts, arrived to secretly 'remove the hundredweight of ammonium nitrate' from Ursula's house.[27] 'Tall and strong like many northern Chinese, Feng radiated calm and dignity.'[28] Her third contact, 500km away in Jilin, was not so imposing. Their initial meeting took place in circumstances that 'must surely have been suggested by the Chinese partisans'. It made the failed rendezvous at the 'detested cemetery' in Harbin look like a well-executed plan:

> The trains did stop at Jilin, but there were hardly any people about. I was the only foreigner who got off. I followed a Chinese comrade

who was waiting for me as agreed. No words were exchanged. He took a rickshaw and so did I. The two rickshaws must have jogged along for a good forty minutes over pot-holes and sandy paths. Clouds of dust enveloped us, unfortunately without disguising us altogether. It was obvious that no Westerners, let alone a European woman, had set foot here in years. All heads turned towards us. If the aim had been to make me and my partisan stick out a mile, we could not have done better. At last we stopped in front of a shabby little hut, and before we had a chance to step inside a crowd gathered around us and looked me over in amazement. Tea was brought in and served by the partisan's wife. Under these circumstances I had to perform a veritable conjuring trick to hand over the explosives.[29]

By this time Micha was staying regularly with his father in Shanghai for short periods and when they returned to Mukden, Rolf carried with him badly needed transmitter parts and chemicals. In April 1935, Feng was arrested and explosives were found in his house. Under torture it was feared that Feng would identify Ursula as a Soviet agent and she was ordered to leave Mukden immediately and re-establish her wireless station in Beijing. Four months later she discovered that she was pregnant with Ernst's child. She decided to return to Europe with Rolf, who agreed to accept the child as his own; Ernst remained in Beijing:

Micha was now four years old and I yearned for a second child. In my line of business the time would never be right. If I was separated from Ernst, I might never be with anyone again from whom I would want a child. Now that it was on the way I wanted to keep it.

The timing was particularly opportune. Within a few weeks Rolf, who had now completed five years in China, was to begin his home leave in Europe. His English employers would be paying the fares for the whole family. Centre wanted me to use this opportunity to come to Moscow and discuss my work. Besides, I was glad at the chance to visit my family in London.[30]

Back in Moscow she was given instructions to prepare for an assignment in Poland with Rolf, who was now a fellow Soviet agent. First she went with Micha to London, where she was met at the dockside by her parents, and stayed with them at their 'dowdy three-roomed flat' in Belsize Park.[31] It was the first time that she had seen them since 1930. It was now October 1935.[32]

CHAPTER FOUR

London and Spain

Following Robert Kuczynski's flight from Germany to the comparative safe haven of Czechoslovakia, his wife, Berta, along with his two youngest daughters, Sabine and Renate, had remained in Berlin in order to sell their Schlachtensee villa. When they eventually joined Robert in London on 25 February 1934 their identity documents and passports were marked with the *Auswandererin* stamp.[1] They were accompanied by Olga Muth, the family maid, who had been in Berta's employ for twenty-three years. Following their arrival, Robert was granted permission to remain in the UK for an indefinite period.

Between 1936 and 1938, Robert Kuczynski earned a deserved reputation as a leading academic at the London School of Economics (LSE), where he was appointed the first Reader in Demography in a British university. His appointment was backed by Lancelot Hogben, then director of the short-lived Department of Social Biology, and was supported financially by the Academic Assistance Fund and the Rockefeller Foundation. The fellowship was renewed each year, with Robert concentrating on 'methodological questions and the study of non-European populations while establishing the first population courses at LSE, entertaining an international network of population experts and developing close ties with the statistical organisation of the League of Nations'.[2]

While working at the LSE, Robert made the acquaintance of a number of leading figures on both the Right and Left wings of the labour movement, including the Fabian Graham Wallas and the Marxist Harold Laski. He also made the acquaintance of a young English student, Gerty, the youngest daughter of Gertrude Sirnis and sister of Soviet agent Melita Sirnis.[3] Gerty and Melita's mother,

Gertrude, also befriended Robert. In 1921 she had worked with the Society of Friends (Quakers) on relief efforts during the devastating Russian famine. She, too, was connected with Soviet intelligence and was known to MI5. The Sirnis files show that during the 1926 British General Strike, Gertrude had worked with the head of the Moscow National Bank in London, N.V. Gavrilov, distributing funds for striking miners:

Name	P.F. Number and Name	S.F. Number – Serial
Gavrilov N.V.	PFR 1154. SIRNIS	(32A)(36A)(37A)[4]

On 18 June 1926 MI5 intercepted a telegram between the Telegraphic Agency of the Soviet Union (TASS) in Moscow and TASS in London stating:

Activity of the Moscow National Bank Ltd., London. Report made by the Chairman of the Board [N.V. Gavrilov] PFR 1154 Sirnis on the activity for the bank for 1925.[5]

The TASS correspondent in London at this time was Andrew Rothstein, who had recruited the newly wed Melita Norwood (née Sirnis), a secretary working at the British Non-Ferrous Metals Research Association (BN-FMRA), as a spy in 1934. Norwood would go on to work with metallurgists on the atomic bomb programme with Ursula Kuczynski, initially acting as her controller. The Sirnis family were an important cog in the Soviet intelligence wheel in London during the 1930s and '40s with Gertrude Sirnis's home address in Hendon Way, Hampstead, being used as a safe address for communication between Moscow Centre and CPGB headquarters in King Street, Covent Garden.[6] Trainee Comintern wireless operators destined for the Wilson School in Moscow were recruited in this way:

Jack Miller c/o Sirnis 173 Hendon Way, London N.W.2.
Candidate for radio work.

Sending Jack Miller[7] to Moscow giving address for radio work.
Safe address for information from Moscow to London.[8]

It was Gertrude Sirnis, through Gerty, who introduced the Kuczynskis to the Lawn Road Flats, the first Modernist block of flats to be built in London using reinforced concrete. The building, constructed in 1934 became an icon of the Modernist movement and soon filled up with a number of well-known artists and writers, German and Austrian refugees from Fascism, including the Bauhaus's Walter Gropius, Marcel Breuer and László Moholy-Nagy, and a clutch of Soviet spies including Brigitte and Jürgen Kuczynski and Arnold Deutsch, recruiter of the Cambridge spies Anthony Blunt, Guy Burgess, John Cairncross, Donald Maclean and Kim Philby.[9] A regular visitor to both Deutsch and the Flats was the Austrian Communist Edith Tudor-Hart, who regularly passed on intelligence from Philby, Burgess and Blunt to Bob Stewart, a trusted member of the CPGB, who in turn would arrange their transmission to Moscow.[10]

On 17 October 1938 Robert applied for naturalisation and references were taken up from A.M. Carr-Saunders, the Director of the LSE; Sir William Henry Beveridge; Charles Roden Buxton, a barrister and former Member of Parliament; and T.H. Marshall, sociologist, in support of his application. Buxton had known Robert since 1921 and wrote his reference from the position of both friend and colleague:

I first became acquainted with the applicant in Berlin in 1921 when I was endeavouring to re-establish friendly relations with Germany. I have maintained the friendship ever since. I may say that he is one of my best friends, and, like all those who know his work, I revere him as one of the great men of science. I know all his family and he knows all mine … Dr. Kuczynski, as you probably know, is perhaps the greatest authority in the world on the problems of population. Among all the refugees, he is one of those who would bring the greatest advantage, and reflect the highest credit on our country.

I write because he is a very intimate friend of mine since 1921.[11]

Despite these references, Robert's application for British citizenship was turned down owing to his Communist associations and insecure financial position.[12] Fervently anti-Nazi and a founder member of the German Freedom Party, formed in 1937 by a number of exiles of different political persuasions, the Home Office regarded him as suspect; while the following year, as Jews, the family's assets in Berlin were declared the property of the Reich. By this time Robert's position as a leading figure among the German exiles, capable of uniting Social Democrats and Communists, had passed to his son, Jürgen.

By this time, Jürgen was reporting back to Moscow on a regular basis and was able to influence the German exile community and fellow-travellers among his acquaintances in the British labour movement along Communist lines. Writing under the pseudonym Peter Forster, he contributed to a number of papers that were then smuggled into Germany. These included the organ of the Comintern *Inprekorr* (International Press Correspondence), the weekly Communist paper *Rundschau* (Review), edited from Moscow, and the *Deutsche Volkszeitung*, the central organ of the exiled Central Committee of the KPD.[13]

In London, Jürgen cultivated a number of Left-wing members of the Labour Party, including the cousin of the Bloomsbury Group writer Lytton Strachey, John Strachey, and his Communist wife, Celia, whom Jürgen quipped was 'the better man of the two'.[14] Jürgen's collaboration with Strachey began in 1934 when he called at Strachey's 'house at the wish of his Soviet friends' who wanted to 'establish contact'.[15] Strachey, the wealthy son of the owner and editor of the *Spectator*, introduced Jürgen to a host of what might today be called 'enablers' and fellow-travelling talent, among them the Left-wing Labour MP G.R. Strauss, who had visited Moscow with Strachey in 1930. Strachey, an old Etonian, was a most unlikely fellow-traveller. His stock answer for dear old ladies asking him to explain why he had become a Communist was, 'from chagrin, Madam, from chagrin at not getting into the Eton Cricket Eleven'.[16]

Like many fellow-travellers, Strachey, accepting the advice of the Communist Party's intellectual guru, Rajani Palme Dutt, that 'he could do more for the party if he were not a paid-up member', never formally joined the CPGB.[17] Undoubtedly, the power, as well as the conspiratorial character, of international Communism excited Strachey. He positively revelled in the world of 'secret messages, hurried journeys, and ruthlessness' and perhaps even 'the Jesuitical argumentation of Communism delighted him'. But he was a Communist, as his biographer Hugh Thomas pointed out, 'because he felt nothing else would, or could, save what was best in western civilisation'.[18]

His associates included the very effective Hungarian Soviet agent, the 'illegal' resident Theodore Maly, who operated now and then from an office next door to Strachey's London office of the British branch of Münzenberg's 'World Movement against Fascism and War'.[19] From this citadel Strachey organised a huge demonstration in Hyde Park against the British Union of Fascists on 9 September 1934. Fighting broke out and large detachments of police were deployed to keep the two sides apart. Strachey later condemned the leader of the BUF, Oswald Mosley, for his 'attempt to overcome London with his fascist thugs'.[20] Strachey recruited a number of well-intentioned labour and liberal anti-Fascists to the Amsterdam-Pleyel 'Committee for Coordinating Anti-Fascist Activities', including the chief Labour whip of the House of Lords, Dudley Aman, 1st baron Marley, who would write the introduction to Münzenberg's *The Brown Book of the Hitler Terror and the Burning of the Reichstag*.[21]

Strachey's close friendship with Jürgen was important on a number of accounts, not least an introduction to the publisher Victor Gollancz and the Left-wing Labour MP Harold Laski, who together united the various strands of British anti-Fascism under the umbrella of the Left Book Club (LBC) in May 1936. Laski, Professor of Political Science at the LSE and a colleague of Robert Kuczynski's, was appointed the LBC's commissioning editor. Many Left Book Club authors, such as Clement Attlee, Sir Stafford Cripps, Phillip Noel-Baker, Ellen Wilkinson, Konni Zilliacus and G.D.H. Cole, were prominent members of the Labour Party.

Gollancz courted and lived on the fringes of Soviet intelligence throughout the 1930s and '40s and published the work of a number of

Soviet agents working in Britain. In 1933 he collaborated with Stalin's formidable Czech secret agent Otto Katz and Münzenberg in publishing *The Brown Book of the Hitler Terror and the Burning of the Reichstag*, which exposed the Nazi Party's responsibility for the fire of 1933. Katz met up with Gollancz in London in December that year when he attended a session of the Counter-trial – more accurately the Reichstag Fire Enquiry – designed to expose the calumnies and falsehoods of the official trial being held in Leipzig. In April 1934 he visited London again, this time with the Hungarian actor László Löwenstein, better known as Peter Lorre. In September 1935, Katz journeyed to the United States and remained there until the end of May 1936. He paid two further short visits to England in 1936 and 1937, meeting with Jürgen both times. In 1937 Gollancz published *The Nazi Conspiracy in Spain*, a collection of documents edited by Katz establishing German assistance to General Franco during the Spanish Civil War.[22] The LBC's publication of Katz's exposé of Franco's dealings with Hitler introduced him to the work of the National Joint Committee for Spanish Relief and the Spanish Medical Aid Committee, and led to Ellen Wilkinson's and Phillip Noel-Baker's[23] condemnation in Parliament of the British government's non-intervention policies, which, they insisted, worked on the side of General Franco.

On the eve of the Spanish Civil War, Jürgen had returned to Berlin travelling on a German passport issued at Berlin-Zehlendorf on 13 July 1936; unlike many German-Jewish refugees, he was not stateless and had retained his German nationality. In the summer of 1936, he visited Prague, Warsaw and Danzig on KPD business and met with his sister Ursula in Poland. An arranged meeting with Bessonov in Copenhagen did not take place, a non-event 'which he later believed spared his life'.[24] The Great Terror that followed the murder of Sergei Kirov, Leningrad Party chief and Politburo member, in December 1934, had led to the arrest and prosecution of Nikolai Bukharin and the former head of the OGPU, Genrikh Yagoda, in the Trial of the Twenty-One in 1938. Among the accused were the former Soviet Ambassador to Germany, Nikolai Krestinsky, and Sergei Bessonov.[25]

Arriving back in England on 29 July 1936, Jürgen immediately began putting his English affairs in order, registering with the police at Bow Street on 11 November 1936 under the 1919 Aliens Restriction Act. On 25 March 1937 an MI5 informant, known as 'M.S.M.', reported that Jürgen was in touch with the Soviet Embassy and in contact with the Soviet Ambassador, Ivan Maisky, using the name 'Karo'.[26] Jürgen was now operating in much the same way as he had been doing in Berlin: evaluating military, economic and political affairs, and sending reports to Moscow via the Ambassador. He was also exchanging information with Josef Gerasimov Lazian, a Russian official employed as a statistician by the Russian Wood Agency. But it was Spain and not the garnering of British secrets that determined the future direction of Jürgen's intelligence activities in Britain. During the Spanish Civil War he began monitoring the political views of German exiles living in London.

Spain provided the backdrop not only for the international struggle between Fascism and Communism, but also for the struggle between the rival supporters of Stalin and Trotsky. The campaign against Trotskyites[27] as 'agents of fascism' that preceded the Trial of the Twenty-One in 1937 became a fully fledged policy during the Spanish Civil War, which lasted from 17 July 1936 to 1 April 1939. A coalition of the Left in Spain, the *Frente Popular* (Popular Front), consisting of Communists, socialists, the supporters of the Left Republicans, the Republican Union of Martinez Barrios and Lluis Companys' Catalan Left nationalists, had won a resounding victory in the Spanish elections of February 1936. The Right, Centre and outright Fascist parties lost a total of 147 seats. Fascist provocations followed. Drive-by shootings, American gunman style, became popular among the Fascists, creating the feeling that the People's Front government could not maintain law and order. By the middle of June it became clear that matters were reaching a crisis. *Mundo Obrero,* the official organ of the Communist Party of Spain, denounced the efforts of the Fascists and Trotskyites to rupture the People's Front, warning that 'under no circumstances must the united action of the Left Republicans and the proletarian parties be broken'.[28]

The British government, fearing that the Fascist powers of Italy and Germany would intervene openly in Spain, refused supplies to the elected Spanish government and became the principal architect of the non-intervention agreement with the French. Leon Blum's Popular Front government, having secured a substantial majority over the parties of the Right and Centre at the general election of April–May 1936, had reluctantly agreed to enter into a non-intervention pact on the understanding that the Fascist powers would also agree to a policy of non-intervention. The Soviet Union followed the same line as the Popular Front government in France. Britain and France continued to refuse supplies, however, while the Fascist countries continued to pour in munitions of war and soldiers. The Soviet Union sent counter-supplies, and help also came from the International Brigades organised and directed by the Comintern, with headquarters in Paris. The British Labour Party initially supported the Conservative government's policy of non-intervention before shifting its position to medical aid for Spain (but not intervention) in June 1937.[29]

Between 1936 and 1 April 1939, some 3,500 men and women from Great Britain volunteered to fight or perform medical service with the International Brigades in Spain. However, the disturbing activities of the NKVD and GRU in Spain in hunting down Trotskyites and anarchists drove a wedge between the Communists and other groups on the Left. The notorious activities of the German Communist Hans Kahle, Commander of the XI International Brigade (Thalmann), on behalf of the Soviet secret service in Spain impacted negatively on Jürgen's intelligence activities in Britain following Kahle's arrival in the UK in 1939, on the eve of General Franco's final victory over the Popular Front in Spain.

Kahle, the model for General Hans in Ernest Hemingway's *For Whom the Bell Tolls*, was living proof of that 'spirit of youth, adventure, and camaraderie' that Hemingway's Spanish Civil War novel took as its unifying theme. A 'handsome and charming man', Kahle was 'the masculine, romanticised, individualist image of the war'.[30] In reality, his career in Spain was marred by reports of torture and the assassination of political opponents. In Catalonia, fighting between the anarcho-syndicalist CNT in alliance with the Trotskyist-aligned Marxist Workers' Unity Party (POUM) left 500 dead.[31] The POUM was subsequently purged and many of those arrested were interrogated and tortured by German and Russian Communists. Kahle had successfully camouflaged his position as NKVD chief in Madrid by working as the Director of Spanish Workers' Radio and was never connected with these events by British intelligence. Consequently, after the defeat of the Republican forces and the dispersal of the International Brigade he was allowed into the UK on 23 February 1939 travelling on a Spanish identity document as the guest of Ellen Wilkinson and future Labour Prime Minister Clement Attlee. He was granted permission to stay for six months and initially stayed with the British-Indian scientist Professor J.B.S. Haldane, a leading member of the CPGB and an expert in the study of physiology, genetics, evolutionary biology and mathematics.

CHAPTER FIVE

Ursula and Brigitte

On 27 February 1936, Ursula and Rolf, along with Micha and the family maid, Olga Muth, moved into the ground-floor flat of a house in Anin, a suburb of Warsaw. Six weeks later, Ursula's daughter, Janina, was born. In the winter of 1936, Ursula with her two children were transferred to the officially 'free city' of Danzig (present-day Gdansk), a semi-autonomous city state, predominantly German-populated. There she established contact with the Danzig Group, a cell of six Communists reporting on the shipment of arms to the Fascist insurgents in Spain, German U-boat construction and Nazi organisation in the shipyards. Her husband Rolf, who was working as an architect, remained in Warsaw.

In Danzig, Ursula built her wireless set and began communicating with Moscow Centre. Her neighbours, who began experiencing interference on their radio sets, gossiped that somebody must be transmitting from their building. Initially, little more than rumour at this stage, her fears magnified when the Nazi husband of a neighbour told her that he had informed the relevant authorities of their suspicions that there was an unknown broadcaster among them. The increased danger of triangulated detection forced Ursula to cease transmitting and she moved her transmitter, concealed in a gramophone, to the house of a comrade from the Danzig Group before returning to Rolf in Warsaw. In summer 1938, she was recalled to Moscow to hone her wireless skills and was taught how to build 'a more complicated transmitter, of a "push–pull" type'. In Moscow she was promoted to the rank of major in the Red Army and remained there for three months, while Micha, Janina and Ursula's maid, Olga, stayed with Rolf's parents in Czechoslovakia; Rolf continued working in Warsaw.[1]

In Moscow, Ursula attended a school that specialised in training partisans as well as intelligence agents. There she was taught how to handle explosives, assemble detonators, mix incendiary compounds and construct clockwork mechanisms. A decision was taken to send her to Switzerland, where she was to establish a small group of anti-Fascist activists 'prepared for illegal, dangerous work inside Germany'.[2] She insisted that she be allowed to draw her recruits from members of the International Brigade's British Battalion already trained in sabotage techniques, and spent three months in England preparing for this work. Englishmen, she argued, were very well-suited for the task that lay ahead:

> It was not unusual for the odd well-to-do Englishman to travel the world and settle for a while wherever he happened to feel like it, and if he felt inspired to choose Germany, then this was not at all out of keeping with the continental image of the eccentric Englishman. Centre agreed to my plan, but reiterated what I already knew: no contact with the British party. I kept to that.[3]

This was not strictly true. When Ursula arrived in England in late 1938 she approached the Austrian-Czech Communist and ex-Brigader Fred Uhlmann and asked him to recommend two English recruits for a Soviet intelligence sabotage group.[4] He approached the CPGB's national organiser Dick Springhall, who recommended another ex-Brigader, Alexander Foote; either Uhlmann or the British Communist Fred Copeman then interviewed Foote and dangled before him the prospect of a 'secret and dangerous' job abroad. His biographical details were subsequently passed to Ursula, who signalled them to Moscow Centre. His recruitment was approved and Ursula was advised to make contact with Foote before leaving for Switzerland. Foote, however, was taken ill and the proposed meeting never took place. British Communist Party headquarters in King Street then advised Foote to make contact by telephone with Ursula's sister, Brigitte, a member of the St Pancras Branch of the CPGB, who was then living in the Lawn Road Flats.

Brigitte invited Foote to lunch at the Flats, where he was struck by the apparent incongruity of his surroundings and the call to proletarian revolution. He was told that he had been given a special assignment in Germany and was presented with a £10 note along with instructions on how to meet Ursula in Geneva:

> 'You will proceed to Geneva. There you will be contacted and further instructions will be given you.' The voice of my *vis-à-vis* was quiet and matter of fact and the whole atmosphere of the flat was of complete middle class respectability. Nothing could have been more incongruous than the contract between this epitome of bourgeois smugness and the work that was transmitted in its midst.[5]

Foote's meeting with Ursula took place at the end of October 1938 in Geneva, and was remarkable for the two sisters' insistence on bizarre amateur introductory identification marks:

> Wear a white scarf and carry a leather belt in your hand. Sonya will be carrying an orange in one hand and a shopping net containing a green parcel in the other.[6]

When Foote finally established contact with Ursula he was immediately impressed by her cool and calm demeanour. He was instructed to take lodgings in Munich, study German, 'keep his eyes and ears open' and 'establish connections with the Messerschmitt aeroplane factory'.[7] Ursula was also impressed by him and asked if he knew of others in Britain who would be willing to undertake anti-Nazi work. He suggested a rather quiet young man, Leon Charles Beurton, who had served alongside him in the International Brigade. Foote, however, was lax when it came to security and later conveyed his Munich address to Brigitte by a secret ink message concealed in a book.[8] This was undoubtedly risky behaviour and tinged with the romanticism of espionage that Foote craved throughout his career; Foote later claimed that he and Brigitte had been lovers.

In the spring of 1939, Beurton met Brigitte for lunch in the Lawn Road Flats, where he too received a payment of £10 and instructions to rendezvous with Ursula outside the Uniprix shop in Vevey, Switzerland. It was love at first sight:

> I met Len for the first time in January or February 1939 … He was then twenty-five years old, had thick brown hair, eyebrows that met and clear hazel eyes. He was lean and athletic, strong and muscular. Half shy, half-aggressive, he gave the impression of boyish immaturity. Len was seven years younger than I was. Unlike Jim [Foote], he was not interested in material things and again in contrast to Jim, he was extremely sensitive. When I told him that he had been chosen for dangerous work in Germany his face lit up … Len was to settle in Frankfurt am Main and to make contact with personnel at the I.G. Farben works.[9]

Foote and Beurton often travelled to Switzerland from Germany to meet with Ursula and receive instruction in elementary sabotage techniques. She would then ask them for a list of suitable targets in Germany. On one occasion Foote, half-jokingly, suggested Adolf Hitler. He told her of a time when he, along with Leon, had dined at Hitler's favourite restaurant in Munich in the hope of catching a glimpse of the Führer. As luck would have it he turned up:

> 'We didn't have to give the salute because we were British subjects, but we stood up like the rest!' At the moment of Hitler's entrance into the main restaurant BEURTON, who was facing him standing, put his hand inside his jacket to take out his cigarette case, but in appearance as though he were going to draw a revolver. F. said his heart was in his mouth and he thought that he and BEURTON would be shot down by Hitler's escort. However nothing whatever happened and F. commented to Sonya that if there was all this feeling against Hitler it was a wonder no one tried to bump him off considering the lack of precautions taken on these informal occasions. He had

pointed out, for example, that it would have been easy to put a bomb in a suitcase beneath the coats and hats which hung on the partition wall separating Hitler from the main restaurant. Then, said Foote, what did Sonya do but turn on me and say, what an excellent idea![10]

Ursula rented a small renovated farmhouse nestling 'in the mountains of French Switzerland at a height of about 1,200m, near the village of Caux'. Far below on the plain stretched Montreaux, Lake Geneva, and the blue ribbon of the Rhône.[11] It was agreed that Rolf would stay there until she had settled in and her transmitter, which now had to bridge a distance of over 2,000km, was operating:

> My room had a built-in linen cupboard, and below the boards at the bottom there was a cavity. Rolf and I built the transmitter into this space, replaced the covering boards and stood my shoes on top. The set remained in place during operation. When it was not in use, the two holes bored for the banana plugs were stopped with pegs which looked like knots in the wood grain.[12]

Ursula, once more the happily contented mother of two children, complete with attentive nanny, resumed the cover of bourgeois respectability:

> Our idyllic, little house, the 'young mother with two little children' and the 'old nanny who used to nurse the mother' provided us with a respectable middle-class image.[13]

Rolf, who wanted to return to China, now made preparations for his departure and enrolled at a training school for radio operators in Marseilles. He was to work under Ernst, who had recently visited them at Caux and met his daughter for the first and only time. 'Janina was three years old and was lovely to look at, lissome and high-spirited. Although I kept in touch with him, Ernst never asked about her again. Although I was glad to see Ernst, neither could I understand him.'[14] The departure of both men from Caux was 'hard to bear'. War was imminent and Switzerland threatened with invasion. 'There was scarcely any hope that a war could be avoided,' Sonya recalled later, 'Austria and Czechoslovakia were occupied by Hitler; would it be Switzerland's turn next? Would the war begin in our corner of Europe? … the atmosphere was terrible. Any emigrant with a valid passport did everything possible to leave the country quickly.'[15] A British passport now became a necessity. The departure of Rolf and Ernst, both dramatic and sad, left her vulnerable:

> Although I had chosen the separation from both of them I did not regret my decision, I thought in my despair: war will break and the only people who would do everything to help me and the children are leaving for good. I stood on the platform and watched the little blue mountain train until it had disappeared round the bend.[16]

Moscow Centre had decided some time before Rolf and Ernst's departure from Switzerland that Ursula should divorce Rolf and enter into a pro-forma marriage with an Englishman in order to obtain a British passport. With war in Europe imminent, she recalled Beurton and Foote to Switzerland to train them as wireless operators; it was also decided that Foote, being the eldest, should marry Ursula. Foote, however, was uneasy with this proposal and suggested that Ursula might consider Beurton as an alternative. Beurton happily agreed and the couple married on the 23 February 1940, Red Army Day:[17]

> Armed with our marriage certificate, I visited the British Council in Geneva to apply for a passport; his response was distinctly cool. Ten weeks later, on 2 May, 1940, I held the precious document in my hands, much envied by other German refugees.[18]

CHAPTER SIX

Turning Hitler Eastwards

In 1938 Lawrence & Wishart published Jürgen's *Hunger and Work*, a study of the poverty, hunger and general distress of a large section of the British population at the height of the depression from 1931 to 1937, which he called 'Seven Lean Years'. In 1940 it was reviewed favourably in *Science and Society: A Journal of Marxist Thought and Analysis* as an 'original treatment of the available statistics on income, employment, and earnings'. According to Jürgen, 'British workers had improved their position in terms of earnings only negligibly' in comparison 'with huge increases in dividends and profits':

> The workers' slice of cake grew larger, but the cake itself became so much bigger that the larger piece the workers get is a much smaller part of the whole. The actual improvement was due not so much to an increase in the rate of pay as to a decline in part-time work, an increase in overtime and the absorption of some of the unemployed.[1]

The book was a tribute to the work of the social analyst Seebohm Rowntree, and a major indictment of the economic policies implemented by the Labour Prime Minister, Ramsay MacDonald, and his Conservative successor, Stanley Baldwin. To assess the depth of British poverty, Jürgen used what was known as the 'Rowntree standard', the subsistence standard for a worker's family enabling them to just maintain their physical efficiency for future employment.[2] The National Government's plans for further cuts to the amount allocated for unemployment relief and social services was roundly condemned. Baldwin, having taken control of the National Government in 1935, had presided over acute distress in the country. His successor as Prime

Minister in May 1937, Neville Chamberlain, came up with no effective programme to combat poverty, while his policies against the threat of Hitler were non-existent. Appeasement, which led to the signing of the Munich Agreement and the annexation of the Sudetenland by the Nazis, aroused cross-party hostility. The Left Book Club issued a one-page leaflet pleading against the destruction of Czechoslovakia and condemning Chamberlain's policy as a barely disguised cover for an anti-Soviet Union policy that aimed at turning Hitler eastwards; neither Czechoslovakia nor the Soviet Union were consulted before the agreement was signed between the four European powers, Great Britain, France, Italy and Germany, on 30 September 1938:

> If we stand firm we, the French, and the Russians even at this eleventh hour, and say we will not let Hitler destroy Czechoslovakia by armed might, will he fight? Most improbable, for the superiority of the three of us *now* is enormous. And if he were mad enough to challenge us, he would certainly be defeated.[3]

The following month, Jürgen secured his position in the UK when MI5 approved his permanent residence. In December 1938 he helped establish the *Freier Deutscher Kulturbund* (Free German League of Culture, hereafter *Kulturbund*), with its aim of preserving and advancing Free German culture in the face of Nazi barbarism.[4] His control over the *Kulturbund* allowed him to harness, often by disguised means, a number of leading German cultural figures to fellow-travelling activities. These included the refugee lawyer and painter Fred Uhlman, the artist Oskar Kokoschka, drama critic Alfred Kerr, author Stefan Zweig and film director Berthold Viertel. By staging a number of cultural and artistic events, the *Kulturbund* was able to enlist the support of a broad spectrum of Left-liberal, culturally and politically progressive opinion and weld it into an anti-Fascist alliance under the control of the KPD. It was a strategy inspired by Münzenberg's Amsterdam-Pleyel movement and closely mirrored Communist tactics inside the Popular Front. Overt political activity had been barred to German refugees in Britain and the *Kulturbund*'s cultural activities served as 'the continuation of politics by other means'.[5] Not surprisingly, there were a number of impressive Communist functionaries and fellow-travellers among its leading members, including Johannes Fladung,[6] Kurt Hager,[7] Wilhelm Koenen[8] and Professor Alfred Meusel,[9] as well as Jürgen and Robert Kuczynski.

In March 1939 the Left Book Club (LBC) published Jürgen's *The Condition of the Workers in Gt. Britain, Germany & The Soviet Union 1932–38*, a comparative statistical history of labour conditions. Jürgen, as one might expect, presented a roseate picture of labour conditions in the Soviet Union while exposing the degradation of labour in democratic Britain and Fascist Germany. However, a main theme of the book was its damning indictment of the role played by finance capitalism, whether by reactionary or democratic methods, in the rise and consolidation of Fascism:

> The Soviet Union is a socialist society; Great Britain and Germany are finance capitalist countries. But between Great Britain and Germany, too, there is a significant difference: Great Britain is ruled by finance capital as a whole and by democratic methods, Germany is ruled by the most reactionary section of finance capitalism, the heavy industries, the armaments industries, and by dictatorial methods. In Great Britain the whole of finance capitalism, the heavy industries, the export houses and banks, the textile industries, and so on, rule the country; finance capitalism, 'pure and simple', in fact reigns. In Germany the interests of the armaments are decisive: Fascism rules.[10]

The economic drift to war formed an essential part of Jürgen's condemnation of Fascism:

> Preparation for war means relatively increasing employment in the iron, steel and engineering industries, and relatively decreasing employment in the consumption goods producing industries such as textiles, and the food, drink and tobacco manufacturing industries.[11]

The Fascist economy, he warned, 'is directed towards ever-increasing armament production. It tries to keep down the production of consumer goods as much as possible; for every increase in the production of consumption goods means that less raw materials, less foreign exchange, less money, a smaller labour force, and so on, are available for armament production.'[12]

In March 1939, following the Wehrmacht's occupation of the remainder of Czechoslovakia and its incorporation into the Reich, the LBC issued a leaflet entitled 'Save Peace!', calling for a collective security agreement between the Soviet Union, Britain and France. Hitherto, Gollancz's LBC had been firmly behind the Soviet Union's policy of supporting collective security through an alliance with the Western democracies. The architect of collective security, Maxim Litvinov, was regarded as central to the Soviet Union's anti-Fascist foreign policy. In 1934, the year the USSR became a member of the League of Nations, Jürgen's intelligence reports from Berlin on the destruction of Communism and the application of anti-Jewish laws in Germany were being sent directly to Litvinov at the Commissariat. Litvinov, one of the most vociferous spokesmen at the League, condemned Hitler's bellicose policies and threats to the peace of Europe as a result of the intelligence he was receiving from his agents in Berlin. In 1934, the German Ambassador in Moscow, wishing to bring about an improvement in relations between the Soviet Union and Nazi Germany, had focused his wrath on Litvinov. He reported that the Jewish factor and not the suppression of Communism was creating tension between the two countries and claimed that Litvinov, in particular, was responsible for the Soviet Union's antagonistic attitude towards Nazi Germany:

> We have in the past assumed that the reason for the tension was particularly the resentment of the Soviet people toward National-Socialism as the suppressor of communism. Doubtless chagrin at the destruction of communism in Germany and irritation over the race theory do play a very important role in that connection and Litvinov in particular, who in any case is not very fond of us, is evidently the main advocate of this resentment.[13]

Litvinov's replacement by Vyacheslav Molotov on 3 May 1939 was seen by Hitler as a sign that Jewish influence over the Soviet leadership was diminishing, his downfall going some way to removing a barrier to a bilateral agreement between Germany and the Soviet Union. On his appointment, Molotov received orders from Stalin to purge the Commissariat and to bring it more closely under central control:

> Stalin said to me 'Purge the ministry of Jews.' Thank god for these words! Jews formed an absolute majority in the leadership and among the ambassadors. It wasn't good. Latvians and Jews ... and each one drew a crowd of his people along with him. Moreover they regarded my arrival in office with condescension and jeered at the measures I began to implement.[14]

According to Hitler, 'Litvinov's dismissal was decisive.' In his address to army commanders on 22 August 1939, he boasted, 'I brought about the change of attitude towards Russia gradually. In connection with the commercial treaty we got into political conversation.'[15] The following day, 23 August, Molotov and Ribbentrop signed the Nazi–Soviet Pact. Its effect on the Communist movement was devastating. In France, twenty-one Communist deputies out of a total of seventy-two resigned from the *Parti Communiste Français* (PCF) because of the Pact. The KPD Central Committee, on the other hand, issued a statement on 25 August welcoming the Pact as 'a step towards peace' and called on the German people to continue the fight against the Nazi dictatorship. It referred to Germany's 'plans of imperialist aggression', and said the Pact showed that Germany could get what it wanted by peaceful trade.[16] Jürgen, who had been vocal in his support for the Popular Front, was said to be 'flabbergasted and quite unable to account for it'.[17] Many German refugees accused the USSR of betraying the cause of anti-Fascism; others, misinterpreting the Pact as a purely political alliance, feared a convergence of Fascism and Communism. Gollancz, out of despair, refused to take up a position altogether; Strachey, on the other hand, made an open declaration that his faith in Communism had been shaken severely: 'If the Soviet Union were to go into benevolent neutrality toward Germany, my whole position would be shattered. I should have to reconsider everything.'[18]

Eleven days after the signing of the Pact, Britain was at war with Germany despite Molotov having reassured the British Ambassador to Moscow, Sir Stafford Cripps, that the Pact was not designed as an act of hostility towards his country:

> He [Molotov] gave me an explanation as to the Russo-German pact, saying that they felt themselves obliged to enter into some agreement on the west in order to avoid the danger of being drawn into the war, and that the French and British missions quite clearly did not intend to make any reasonable arrangement. At the same time as the Germans changed their anti-Russian policy, Russia felt herself obliged for her own safety to enter into an agreement with Germany. I rather gathered from this part of his explanation that he intended to point out that the German agreement was not in any way an act hostile to Gt. Britain.[19]

On 1 September 1939 Germany invaded Poland from the west. Two days later Britain and France declared war on Germany. In the UK, Harry Pollitt, General Secretary of the CPGB, wrote a pamphlet entitled 'How to win the War', equating the war against Fascism with the centuries-old struggle against capitalism: 'To stand aside from this conflict, to contribute only revolutionary-sounding phrases, while the fascist beasts ride roughshod over Europe, would be a betrayal of everything our forebears have fought to achieve in the long course of long years of struggle against capitalism.'[20] Four days later Stalin informed Dimitrov, General Secretary of the Comintern, what he expected from foreign Communist parties: 'They should denounce their governments' war plans as imperialistic and reduce anti-Fascist propaganda.'[21] On 17 September the Soviet Union invaded Poland without a declaration of war. Following Warsaw's capitulation on the

27th, Molotov and Ribbentrop signed the German–Soviet Treaty of Friendship, Cooperation and Demarcation, which defined in detail the limits of their respective occupations of Polish territory. In a joint declaration the two governments claimed that they had 'definitely settled the problems arising from the collapse of the Polish State and have thereby created a sure foundation for a lasting peace in Europe'.[22] Britain and France were called upon to recognise the boundary changes and to stop prosecuting the war for imperialist aims.

Pollitt, who would soon be replaced as General Secretary of the CPGB by a 'troika' led by Rajani Palme Dutt, received a short, written thesis from the Communist International outlining Moscow's position:

> The present war is an imperialist and unjust war for which the bourgeoisie of all the belligerent states bear equal responsibility. In no country can the working class or the Communist parties support the war. The bourgeoisie is not conducting war against fascism as Chamberlain and the leaders of the Labour Party pretend. War is carried on between two groups of imperialist countries for world domination.[23]

Any lingering doubts about the wisdom of the Nazi–Soviet Pact were quickly dispelled. Initially, the KPD Secretariat in Paris was inclined to see the war as one of national defence on the part of Britain and France, and therefore as an anti-Fascist struggle deserving of support. Within the space of two weeks they were propagating the Soviet view that the war, in the main, was a conflict between two groups of imperialist powers for a new division of the world. MI5 reported that Jürgen Kuczynski, once said to be 'flabbergasted' by the whole affair, now held 'perfectly definite views on the matter, and these were the official views of the Communist party'.[24] He was denounced, along with his father, by the German Catholic writer and anti-Fascist activist, Karl Otten, who expressed his surprise to an MI5 agent embedded in the German émigré community, an eccentric and ambitious informer known as 'M/S':

that KUCZYNSKY, Senr. and Jnr., are allowed to continue their activities unhampered. It is considered that KUCZYNSKY Senr. is by far the more dangerous because through his chair at the London School of Economics he is doing his best to spread defeatism by running down everything British and praising everything Russian. Incidentally, he is telling everyone that the war should be stopped at once.[25]

On 14 October 1939 the head of SIS's Section V (counter-espionage),[26] Valentine Vivian, received a request for information about Robert Kuczynski, claiming that he was involved in 'running the G.P.U. espionage system in this country'.[27] This was an extraordinary claim and, if true, of momentous importance. This piece of intelligence had made its way to MI5 via M/S.

M/S was the British journalist and translator of German texts Claud Sykes, who had been recruited by MI5's Maxwell Knight in the mid-1930s to infiltrate German refugee circles. A former professional actor with a colourful past, Sykes had befriended the Irish author James Joyce in Zurich in 1917 and had typed out the first three episodes of *Ulysses* from Joyce's handwriting. In the spring of 1918, together with Joyce, he founded The English Players, a theatre company to perform plays in the English language. Sykes styled himself as producer and director while Joyce served as business manager.[28] Their first production was Oscar Wilde's *The Importance of Being Earnest*, which was performed in Zurich at the Theatre zu den Kaufleten on 29 April 1918. Sykes's actress wife, Daisy Race, became friendly with Nora Joyce and the two women appeared in J.M. Synge's one-act play *Riders to the Sea* a month later. The English Players continued to perform until late 1919. Syke's literary credentials and his work as a translator gave him 'a very plausible pretext for contacting German refugee authors in Britain' and he reported directly to MI5's B Branch/Division.[29] At this time Sykes was striving to become a fully-fledged MI5 officer and his intelligence was often exaggerated. Vivian found no substantial evidence to support Sykes's claim.

CHAPTER SEVEN

Spying on Fellow Exiles

On 5 October 1939 Sykes had reported that the Spanish Civil War veteran Hans Kahle was running a Soviet espionage system at Bloomsbury House with the help of Jürgen Kuczynski and Professor Alfred Meusel.[1] Bloomsbury House, the former Palace Hotel on Bloomsbury Street, had been taken over by the Jewish Board of Deputies and the Quakers in March 1939 to offer refugees, predominantly Jewish, shelter, financial support and assistance in finding employment. It was the headquarters for around eleven organisations working under the umbrella of the Central Co-ordinating Committee for Refugees, whose chairman was Sir Malcolm Hailey, formerly Governor of the Punjab. These organisations were of a diverse nature and included the Catholic Committee for Refugees from Germany, Friends of Germany Emergency Committee, German Jewish Aid Committee, International Student Service, and the Movement for the Care of Children from Germany. The KPD and the *Kulturbund* did not have an open presence at Bloomsbury House. The Austrian Centre in nearby Westbourne Terrace, W2, where Jürgen's wife, Marguerite, organised a library for refugees, however, had a very well-organised Communist presence under the very able Eva Kolmer, who, in early 1939, had received Home Office permission to take up the post of secretary of the Austrian Centre at a rate of £2 a week. Marguerite had taken up employment with the *Kulturbund* in August 1939 and her library posting assured a Kuczynski presence in the Austrian Centre.[2]

Despite the absence of a Communist presence at Bloomsbury House, the reach and nature of the 'Soviet espionage system' operating inside had a dramatic impact on the lives of the German and Czech émigré communities in London who depended upon it for their welfare. The monitoring of who was living with whom was of particular interest to Jürgen, Kahle and Meusel, raising concerns about the encroachment of the Communists into the 'lives of others' during the Second World War. John Green's recent biography of the Kuczynski family has defended this by suggesting that in such 'turbulent times' the distinction between the personal and the political cannot always be drawn. The KPD in exile 'of necessity became involved in every comrade's personal life', trying 'to ensure that everyone found work, accommodation and had sufficient income to survive'. Anticipating Stasi methods, this unfortunately 'involved monitoring who was living with whom and discouraging couples from having children under such circumstances. It was a sad occurrence, but also had security implications, when marriages fell apart or when men (it was usually men) changed their partners too often.'[3]

Jürgen's sisters, Brigitte and Ursula, as exceptions to this men-only rule, must have caused Jürgen, Kahle, and Meusel considerable anxiety.[4] Brigitte had three husbands and a string of lovers, while Green has described Ursula as 'very much a red-bloodied woman … determined to live life to the full, have lovers and bear children, which she did in the most adverse of circumstances'.[5] Moreover, Jürgen was having difficulty living up to the Party's standards himself. A second son, Peter,[6] having been born in August 1937 increased Marguerite's domestic work and, according to Green, adversely affected her work for the *Kulturbund* and the Austrian Centre; at the same time Jürgen's political work increased:

Despite [the] advice given to others and the inauspicious and unstable circumstances both on the political and personal fronts at this time, Marguerite herself gave birth to their second child, a son, at the end of August 1937. He was called Peter. Now with two small children to feed and clothe, she was fully occupied with domestic chores and had to take a back seat while her husband continued his hectic political work.[7]

And hectic it certainly was. On 5 November 1939 MI6 reported to MI5 that Jürgen had connections with the *Deutscher Freiheitsender 29,8* (German Freedom Station 29.8), the GFS,[8] a short-wave radio transmitter run by the KPD, first in Republican Spain in 1937 by Kahle and later in the Soviet Union. MI5 commented that the Fabian Society's Beatrice and Sidney Webb, the Liberal MP Geoffrey Mander and Strachey's Labour Party colleague, G.R. Strauss,[9] were supplying messages to the Freedom Station, via Jürgen, for propaganda purposes. Jürgen wrote a very well-received book on the GFS entitled *Freedom Calling. The Story of the Secret German Radio*, financed by the *Kulturbund*, with a jacket designed by Helmut Herzfeld, better known as John Heartfield, the pioneer of photomontage. Herzfeld was a founder member of the KPD and of the Dada movement in Berlin. He had been identified to MI5 by Walter Krivitsky 'as an OGPU man who had come originally from the Fourth Department (GRU)'.[10] *Freedom Calling*, almost an intelligence handbook, was a much-needed reaffirmation of the KPD's condemnation of Fascism in the wake of the Nazi–Soviet pact and dismemberment of Poland. The war was still to be opposed as an imperialist war; but so too was Nazism as an ideology. *Freedom Calling* encouraged passive resistance, sabotage and whispering campaigns inside Germany. It called for the setting up of resistance groups and explained how to pass on information. Messages between groups were to be kept short and simple and watchwords were to be used. It also contained detailed instructions on how to detect spies operating against the resistance. Jürgen had been very well trained, and if he knew how to detect spies in the resistance then he also knew how to avoid detection in Britain. The Ministry of Information gave the book its whole-hearted support.[11]

Jürgen was a prolific speaker and addressed a number of groups and societies on the subject of the war, ranging from the Imperialist Bristol Branch of the Royal Empire Society (formerly the Royal Colonial Society),[12] and Dick Sheppard's Peace Pledge Union.[13] As a propagandist Jürgen was persuasive, and he was able to put across the Soviet Union's position on the war to a variety of audiences.[14] Dissension among non-Communist German and Czech refugees, however, was not so easily contained, with the veteran pacifist, Otto Lehmann-Ruessbueldt, writing to Jürgen on 5 December expressing his horror of Stalin and the Soviet Union's seizure of Polish territory:

> The Russian world pursues national power politics or rather power politics of the intelligentsia. It is historical materialism. A vast body, having escaped the consequences of the Great War, again goes along the path which Lenin avoided when he did not succeed against Poland. Men like Stalin cannot tolerate near themselves any but subaltern people. Otherwise he would not have the bad taste to allow himself to be presented to the world as the 'great and wise Stalin.'[15]

Jürgen's continued defence of Stalin in the face of such criticism was further evidence that the Comintern's new line condemning the war as 'imperialist and unjust' was in danger of degenerating into a conspiracy theory. Jürgen sent the following text to *Freedom Calling* in a 'leaflet ... cleverly camouflaged inside a packet of postage stamps':

> ... You understand that there is a fascist plot against the peoples of the world, and that the British Government is assisting the plot. A very unpopular set rules in England; it does not even represent the bourgeoisie but merely protects the interests of the very rich and their fascist supporters. The favourite of these people is Hitler. They need him, and they wish him to remain in power. They, and they only, permit him to have all his successes and without them he would achieve nothing ...
>
> England allowed the occupation of Austria – she made as though she believed that it was really a liberation of German brethren when Hitler behaved in Vienna with his accustomed cruelty. Then the overlords of England gave him Bohemia – not just the Sudeten Germans but the whole of Czechoslovakia – all under the same pretext. Chamberlain and his group know, of course that Bohemia never belonged to Germany and that Austria had never been a German province ...

> A war of destruction against the Soviet Union is the aim of the
> ruling clique in England, the old aim of World capitalism.[16]

The Home Office expressed concern and MI5 concurred, suggesting that
Jürgen was 'little deserving of this country's protection'.[17] Following the
introduction of internment on 28 September 1939, enemy aliens had
been divided into three categories: Category A, to be interned; Category
B, to be exempt from internment but subject to the restrictions decreed
by Special Order; and Category C, to be exempt from both internment
and restrictions. Jürgen's habitual attacks on British imperialism and
his failure to condemn German Fascism as the main architect of the
war led to his appearing before the internment tribunal under Category
A on 20 January 1940 for the following reasons: 'I think that this alien
is a communist, and/or works in sympathy with that movement.'[18]
Marguerite was arraigned under Category B.

During his tribunal hearing Jürgen was questioned 'about the
mysterious espionage system at Bloomsbury House', and answered 'that
he had no connection with it' – implying that he knew of its existence
while not being directly involved with its activities. 'That doesn't
answer the question,' the judge told him. 'You might be connected
with someone who was connected with the espionage system.'[19] The
offending leaflet unearthed in a pile of postage stamps had first surfaced
in the file of his alleged co-conspirator, Hans Kahle, who was interned
on 16 May 1940. Jürgen was interned in January and sent to Warner's
Internment Camp, Devon.

Berta and Robert Kuczynski were placed in Category B by the
internment tribunal on 23 January 1940, despite the LSE 'warmly
testifying to KUCZYNSKI's character, reliability and loyalty'.[20]
On 15 February the Population Investigation Committee called for
the removal of all threats of 'possible internment of KUCZYNSKI,
on grounds that his work is of national importance'.[21] In July the
Society for the Protection of Science and Learning came to Robert's
aid, stating, quite firmly, that as an economist writing for the Colonial
Office on population problems, he should not be interned.[22] The

LSE, which had recently been evacuated to New Court, Peterhouse, Cambridge, complained that Robert was required by the Home Office to apply to the local police for permission to travel to Cambridge and stay overnight. The restrictions were preventing him from fulfilling his academic duties at the LSE and they were subsequently removed on 6 January 1941.

Meanwhile, a campaign to secure Jürgen's release was organised by D.N. Pritt, a Left-wing Labour MP and barrister. A number of leading politicians and high-ranking individuals became involved, among them the future Labour Prime Minister, Clement Attlee, and 'the Red Dean of Canterbury', Hewlett Johnson. Despite his insistence that 'a very unpopular set' ruled Britain and was plotting to protect 'the interests of the very rich and their fascist supporters', royalty intervened when a first cousin of Queen Elizabeth The Queen Mother, Lilian Bowes-Lyon,[23] approached the Under-Secretary of State, Robert Vansittart, on Jürgen's behalf to apprise him of his anti-Fascist activities. In view of the great pressure being brought to bear on the Home Office from a number of high-ranking Establishment figures, MI5 was put on the spot and asked whether their investigation into Jürgen's activities had produced any incriminating results. Alexander Maxwell, Permanent Under-Secretary of State to the Home Office, received a non-committal reply from MI5's Milicent Bagot[24] that, 'Our investigations are not yet complete.'[25]

In a letter to the Home Office concerning the activities of the Communist-controlled Committee of the Friends of the German People's Front, MI5 linked Jürgen's name with two refugee Communist publications, *Inside Nazi Germany* and *Die Frau*, published by the *Kulturbund*'s I.N.G. Publications Ltd. Two other names were linked with the Committee, Jürgen's fellow Bloomsbury House spy Professor Alfred Meusel and Rose Schechter, a 'prominent British Communist'. Schechter, who was 'British born of Russian parents', was said to be 'practically in charge of the [*Kulturbund*] office'.[26] As she was also employed at the Soviet Embassy she served as a direct link between the Committee and Embassy officials.

In January 1940 I.N.G. Publications Ltd had been given a permit by Sir John Reith's Ministry of Information to export its publication, *Inside Nazi Germany*, subject to a copy of each issue being first submitted to the Press and Censorship Bureau.[27] However, owing to the fact that the company was entirely staffed by Germans, with the exception of Rose Schechter, a permit could not be given without prior consultation with MI5. An investigation of the company showed that Jürgen was listed on the letter-heading as a patron. On 20 February MI5 received the following report from Claud Sykes (Source M/S):

> EICHLER spoke with glee of the internment of KUCZYNSKI, whom he told me was a thoroughly bad lot and a direct agent of Moscow. He thought the British authorities had done a very good stroke of work by interning him.[28]

Willi Eichler, a member of the SPD's Executive, had been in London since 1939.[29] In early 1940 he secretly drew up a blacklist of Communists inside the German refugee community, which he passed to Sykes. MI5 believed that Syke's identification of Jürgen as an 'agent of Moscow' would secure his internment for the duration of the war. However, it was at this point, that Alexander Maxwell began pressing the Home Office for Jürgen's release:

> The only reason given by the Tribunal for interning this refugee is that he is believed to be a Communist, but this is not in itself a reason for internment. Unless MI5 have some information beyond what appears in these files, KUCZYNSKI ought to be released without further delay. Ask MI5 to let S. of S. [Secretary of State] know what is the nature of their present information.
> 16.3.40.
> A. Maxwell. [30]

Meanwhile, Jürgen had become a notorious figure at Warner's Internment Camp, having set about converting the Nazi inmates to

Communism; or at least to that dangerous current in German Marxism referred to as National Bolshevism: [31]

> No sooner was he settled down in the internment camp than he began a course of lectures to the Nazi internees. At his first lecture he had an audience of about ten; at the second this was doubled. At the third and subsequent ones every Nazi in the camp attended. [Kuczynski] gets hold of the prisoners of war converting them into the most dangerous class of all, namely Nazi Communists. [32]

As a result, the camp's commandant wrote to Marguerite on 3 April informing her that all privileges had been withdrawn and that her visit scheduled for the 6th had been revoked. A scribbled note from an MI5 officer investigating the case pointed out that Alexander Maxwell, as Permanent Under-Secretary of State to the Home Office, had greater direct influence over the Director-General of MI5, Vernon Kell, than the Home Secretary, Sir John Anderson, and that Jürgen should be released immediately:

> Please see attached letter to Mrs. KUCZYNSKI from Colonel BLIMP! KUCZYNSKI is a Communist who was put in by one of the Tribunals. Pritt and goodness knows who else are agitating for his release and Sir A Maxwell has said that as he has been put in qua Communist he must be released immediately! [33]

On 9 April 1940 MI5's Source 'H' inside the *Kulturbund*, who knew Jürgen 'personally', agreed with this sentiment. He suggested that while 'KUCZYNSKI might be described as a Communist intellectual ... a sincere believer in Communism' he was 'only a fellow traveller with Moscow'. Jürgen, H maintained, could never be a Soviet agent as he was 'too much involved in intellectual pursuits to allow him to be an active agent of his political faith'. [34]

Jürgen was released from internment on 25 April 1940 and joined his wife in the Lawn Road Flats. [35] On his release he was praised as a model internee and a veiled hint was dropped that he might be suitable for intelligence work: 'This man was released yesterday, and if the Director of Enemy Propaganda wants the services of an extremely able man, I think he will find few better than Kuczynski. I venture to suggest that a hint to this effect might usefully be given in the appropriate quarter.'[36]

However, following allegations that Jürgen had secreted KPD funds out of Germany in 1933, MI5 remained hostile and suggested a criminal investigation into his and Marguerite's activities. 'Kuczynski', they pointed out, 'never declared his possession of these funds to the government. If you will remember, an Order in Council or some order, enjoined any resident in this country possessing foreign currency or securities of funds in foreign banks to declare them to the government. If this is the case, Kuczynski has committed a criminal offence.'[37]

A letter from Marguerite to the *Rotterdamsche Bankvereeniging* about a guilder account, dated 15 January 1940, had earlier been intercepted by the postal censor, prompting the Foreign Exchange Control to write to her under the Defence (Finance) Regulations 1939. She replied that the account was held in trust by her on behalf of a US resident and that she, along with her husband, had power to operate the account and to take small sums out. She also disclosed that funds were held in trust in New York. However, the evidence supporting her statements was considered to be insufficient and the guilder funds were surrendered to the Foreign Exchange Control under the 1939 Regulations. The real owner of the account was Dr Hans Gaffron, a Peruvian born of German parents, who had lived in Germany from the age of 12. He was described as 'a man of good reputation, a liberal and an anti-Nazi'. He had been resident in the US since 1937 and had moved to New York in 1938, where his bank account with the National City Bank of New York showed a credit balance of $1,304.81.[38] The Foreign Exchange Control, therefore, permitted the transfer of the currency balance to Dr Gaffron in the United States.[39]

Further information concerning Jürgen and KPD funds was received on 8 May 1940 from Karl Otten. MI6 described him as an unreliable source. Otten had informed MI6 that a friend of his, a former banker, had passed information to him that Jürgen 'had frequently consulted him about investments, etc., but that he had only just discovered from Robert KUCZYNSKI that the money to be invested was Communist funds'. The banker apparently had 'a grudge against the Kuczynski family as a whole, because they had dragged his wife over to Communism'. He had been forced to divorce her and had declared that the sum in question amounted to at least £200,000. MI6 warned MI5, 'you will, of course, bear in mind the source of the information, viz. Karl OTTEN.'[40]

At the time of his internment Jürgen was said to be 'well supplied with funds' and 'to have claimed that his wife had money'.[41] The second part of this statement, MI5 deemed to be inaccurate:

> Kuczynski pretends that the money comes from his wife. That is untrue because we know that she comes from the very poor people. To others he tells stories about German industrialists who gave him the money to speculate at the Stock Exchange. That is simply another smoke screen. Both Professor Kuczynski [Robert] and Professor Meusel are the real directing leaders of the anti-war campaign subsidised by these funds. The four daughters of Professor Kuczynski are doing the same work as innocent little beings, but in truth as very fervent anti-British communists.[42]

According to Otten, 'KUCZYNSKI's wife used to be very poor, and that KUCZYNSKI himself had been making use of K.P.D. money, with which he had speculated successfully.'[43] When he appeared before the enemy alien tribunal, Jürgen had 'stated that he had obtained money from Germany by paying German currency to a Dr. Hans GAFFRON, a Peruvian physicist attached to the Jones Laboratory, University of Chicago, which was transferred to London'.[44] Jürgen's wife had opened a Midland Bank account in June 1936 in the name of Anne Marguerita Madeline Kuczynski with £1,200. Robert Kuczynski had acted as referee and Jürgen had been granted the power to draw money. On 30 April 1940, £625.17.4 was transferred from the *Rotterdamsche*

Bankvereeniging to the Kuczynski's Midland Bank at Haverstock Hill. Rumours were circulating that Jürgen had brought out of Germany the whole funds of the German Communist Party, to the value of about £200,000, and deposited this money in a Dutch bank, where it had been invested in American securities.[45] The £625.17.4, therefore, came courtesy of the KPD.

In June 1940 more details emerged when Claud Sykes informed MI5's Maxwell Knight that Jürgen had secret access to large industrial firms. In this connection his fellow Soviet agent, Hans Kahle, was said to be 'in close touch' with Walter and Ernst Lowenheim, who had recently been arrested on suspicion of military espionage for Russia and Germany. The case of the Lowenheim brothers appears to have shown a unity of purpose not only between German and Russian intelligence officers, but also between German Communists and elements of the non-Communist German Left in Britain. Walter and Ernst Lowenheim were founder members of the KPD but had resigned from the party in 1927 in order to create a Left oppositionist group from former Communists and Left-wing Social Democrats. In September 1933 the Executive Committee of the Social Democratic Party in Exile (SOPADE) published in Prague Walter Lowenheim's pamphlet *Neu Beginnen! Faschismus oder Sozialismus. Als Diskussionsgrundlage der Sozialisten Deutschlands,* (*New Beginning! Fascism or Socialism. A Basis for Discussion by German Socialists*) and the name *Neubeginnen* was adopted by the Lowenheim group. They claimed 1,000 followers and opposed both the SPD and KPD for their failure to understand the true nature of Fascism. In Britain they were supported by Dick Crossman, who was then in charge of German broadcasts at the BBC and the Labour Party's 'Socialist Clarity Group'. Crossman's intervention saw *Neubeginnen* supporters gradually supplant Communists at the BBC. The claim that the Lowenheims were 'in a position to obtain a lot of information which should not be allowed to come their way', was linked to the business interests of Walter; his brother Ernst worked full-time for Gollancz's LBC.[46]

Intelligence co-operation between Jürgen, Hans Kahle and the Lowenheim brothers was a major new twist in the intelligence battles taking place on British soil. Moreover, MI5's B4b[47] claimed to be in receipt of 'reliable information' that the Lowenheim brothers were being backed by certain British MPs: 'they have built, or are building up a machinery business, and thus have access to many of our important factories; the elder brother [Walter] uses the pseudonym of "Dr. BURGER" and both brothers are in touch with the KUCZYNSKI family.'[48]

MI5's Milicent Bagot stepped up her investigation into Jürgen and in January 1941 she sent a note to B5b (Maxwell Knight) asking him whether his information was drawn from more than one source.[49] 'Our information against KUCZYNSKI', she wrote, 'is drawn mainly from you … it is suggested that we should do something about him.'[50] Among Knight's informants was Claud Sykes (now B8c), who in the summer of 1940 had finally achieved his ambition of becoming an MI5 officer.[51]

Knight embedded Sykes in the German refugee community, where a number of *Abwehr*[52] and Gestapo agents masquerading as Social Democrats, Communists or merely anti-Fascists, rubbed shoulders with senior German Communist Party members. Knight, who had been a member of the British Fascisti (BF) between 1924 and 1930, was an eager recipient of such intelligence. Knight had been no ordinary member of the BF. In the same year that he joined the organisation he became their assistant chief of staff as well as their director of intelligence. His first wife, Miss G.E.A. Poole, whom he had married in 1925, was engaged as director of the BF Women Units.[53] Both Knight and MI6 confirmed in January 1941 that Jürgen had been given control of German Communist Party funds.[54] At the same time, Knight informed Milicent Bagot that Sykes had been promoted to B8c: 'he would be the person from whom you can get the names of refugees likely to make statements' against the Kuczynskis, he told her, while he promised to look into Jürgen's Midland Bank account himself.[55]

In February 1941 a new Knight–Sykes informant, Source 'Hi', the writer and founder of the 'Neopathetic Cabaret' in Weimar Berlin, Kurt Hiller, began reporting on the activities of the *Kulturbund*. Arrested by the Nazis in July 1933, Hiller, a pacifist, was both passionately anti-Fascist and anti-Communist in exile.[56]

He became quite friendly with Jürgen and was shocked by his continued support for the Nazi–Soviet Pact, which Jürgen now regarded as the only way of preventing the takeover of Europe by the English in cahoots with the 'financial magnates' of Wall Street:

> Today I got the opportunity in the Coffee Corner of the *Kulturbund* ... to meet Dr. K[uczynski]. A political discussion developed of which I would report the following: The Stalinist Treaty policy with Germany is, according to Kuczynski, the only way of ensuring a new and free Germany for the future. Europe must be prevented, above all, from coming under an English domination. In the same way it must be seen that Europe does not fall completely under the influence of the New York Stock Exchange. It is the duty of every revolutionary Socialist to fight against the dictatorship of the financial magnates not excluding those who hide under the cloak of democracy.[57]

Hiller claimed that Jürgen had been a KPD member since 1927/28, the Economic Adviser to the then Central Committee of the Communist Party and an editorial member of *Inprekorr* (International Press Correspondence), the organ of the Comintern published in Moscow. Hiller regarded Jürgen as an extremely capable and dangerous man:

> Extreme Communist and fanatically pro-Stalin. One of Moscow's most brilliant and dangerous propagandists. From various sources it is claimed that he is an illegal contact with the Soviet Secret Service.[58]

Jürgen's extremism and pro-Soviet propaganda now threatened to undermine his standing with the non-Communist Left in Britain. By the spring of 1940 the three founders of the LBC, Strachey, Gollancz and Laski, had unequivocally condemned the Nazi–Soviet Pact and expressed their disquiet that the Communists were moving away from a straightforward 'revolutionary defeatist' position towards an unequivocal identification of Britain as the real enemy.[59] In February 1941 Gollancz sent Jürgen a copy of a book he had edited and partly written entitled *The Betrayal of the Left*. The book was a well-constructed indictment of Soviet foreign and domestic policy from an ethical standpoint and completely disrupted the moral high ground as a safe haven for the Popular Front.[60] 'You will, of course, dislike it intensely. But if you will read my "Epilogue" on political morality (which you will probably dislike even more than anything else in the book!),' wrote Gollancz, 'you will see the kind of subject matter I have in mind.' He asked Jürgen to submit a 4,000-word article for the next issue of the *Left News*, which was intended as 'a symposium on the question of Socialism and Ethics'.[61]

By the end of 1940, a Kuczynski uncle, Hermann Deutsch, who lived in the Lawn Road Flats, finalised arrangements to bring Ursula (Agent Sonya) to England; thereby uniting the entire Kuczynski clan on British soil. Jürgen, fearing that Ursula's presence in the UK as a Soviet agent would 'compromise the rest of the Kuczynski family in their political work', was angry.[62] At the beginning of 1941 the Soviet Union's London embassy decided to put Jürgen in touch with the NKVD's station in New York; while his work with the London embassy had been ongoing since 1936, the American connection promised great things:

Starting in 1936, K [Kuczynski] established contact with our embassy in London, and in 1941, this connection fell to us, and K began giving various types of informational materials, surveys, and reports, although he was never fully recruited.[63]

On his release from internment it had been suggested that if the Director of Enemy Propaganda required 'the services of an extremely able man' they need look no further than Jürgen.[64] Special Operations Executive (SOE) took an interest in Jürgen and in May 1941 SO2 (PPK), Special Operations Executive, commented on his 'connection with the USSR'; stating that he was receiving 'assistance from the Russian Legation as a man of letters'. They also said that he was 'a typical panic maker who, uninvited, explained to all and sundry that Great Britain would lose the war'.[65]

SO2 was part of the SOE, which had been created in 'deadly secrecy in July 1940' to wage subversive warfare behind enemy lines – to 'set Europe ablaze' in Churchill's famous words. From the outset SOE had been divided into two parts. The 'cloak and dagger' unit SO2 had responsibility for the operational side (sabotage and the fomenting of revolt), while SO1 was engaged in 'psychological' warfare, involving subversion through 'covert' or 'black' propaganda. Under the leadership of the Labour Party's Hugh Dalton, SO2 called upon the services of a number of Communists, including Jürgen, for the simple reason that to organise subversion, a subversive mentality was required. Who, Dalton surmised, understood better the mechanics of labour agitation and strikes than the Communists? It was widely believed at the time that Dalton, a Labour member of Churchill's wartime Cabinet, ran SOE with a strong Left-wing bias. However, anxious to avoid charges of 'organising a Gestapo staffed with members of the Labour Party',[66] Dalton ensured that SO2's 'senior ranks were drawn almost exclusively from the familiar networks of the public schools, the City of London, the business world, the armed forces, and the Secret Intelligence Service (MI6)'.[67] Jürgen had emerged from a similar background in Germany and was comfortable with members of this social class, dining frequently on High Table at Cambridge and Oxford colleges; it was upper-class stuff. Major Thornley of SOE took an interest in the German political refugees and liaised with MI5's W.D. Robson-Scott, who specialised in gathering information about German-speaking political exiles in London. Jürgen's security, of course, was by no means guaranteed and Ursula's entry into Britain threatened to compromise his byzantine activities with Allied and Soviet intelligence.

CHAPTER EIGHT

The Indian Communist Party and the BBC

The German occupation of Belgium and Holland in May 1940 and the capture of France in June left Switzerland completely encircled by enemy powers. Only a narrow corridor near Geneva remained open to the Beurtons. Travellers between Switzerland and the UK were forced to take 'improbable detours' that led them across Marshal Pétain's unoccupied Free Zone, Franco's Spain and the conservative dictator Salazar's Portugal, where a ship or plane could be boarded for England. In late autumn 1940 Moscow Centre, frustrated by the failure of the Beurtons to finalise their travel plans through what was effectively Fascist territory, suggested that Ursula move to England, alone if necessary: 'As a former member of the International Brigade, Len could not travel through Spain and had to stay in Geneva until we could find a different route for him.'[1]

Before her departure for England at the end of December 1940, Ursula trained two replacement radio operators to work with Sandor Radó (code name 'Dora', head of the *Rote Drei*, the Swiss group of the Soviet espionage and spy network in Western Europe, known as the Red Orchestra). One was a long-standing Communist named Edmond Hamel, a 'stocky, tough-looking' Swiss who owned a small radio business and repair shop in Geneva; the other was his wife, Olga, 'an outstanding radio operator' whose 'signaling was fast and faultless'.[2] Foote and Beurton were also transferred to Radó and together they began supplying Centre with a stream of intelligence direct from the German High Command. Until the end of 1943 the *Rote Drei* sent thousands of radio messages detailing information on the Nazi war machine to Moscow. Foote, however, complained that Beurton could not easily make the switch from working with Ursula and German Communist intelligence agents to Radó and the Russians. According to Foote, after coaching Hamel and his wife in wireless telegraphy, Beurton 'showed a disinclination to do any further work for the outfit, even though he was ordered by Moscow to assist'.[3] He hated Radó and was extremely critical of the Russians. Foote would prove far more reliable. Before leaving Geneva, Ursula left instructions for him to transmit the following message to Moscow setting up her initial meetings with the GRU at the Wake Arms public house, near Epping Forest in Essex:

Wake Arms. Epping 1 & 15. G.M.T.3. ... place suggested by Ursula BEURTON (SONYA) for rendez-vous with the Russians on 1st and 15th of each month at 3 p.m. G.M.T. on arrival in the UK in 1941.[4]

It was clear from this message that Ursula was being sent to England to take charge of a specific GRU 'mission'. A note on her MI5 file states: 'It is not clear why Ursula BEURTON left Switzerland as she did at the end of 1940 to proceed to this country, but on the evidence of FOOTE she did so with at least Russian concurrence and the possibility therefore cannot be excluded that she came here with a mission.'[5] According to the GRU, she did not begin her mission 'in an empty place' ('*V Anglii Kuchinski nachala rabotu ne na pustom meste*'), but was helped in her work by her parents, her brother and his wife and her four sisters.[6]

In Britain, Ursula and the Kuczynskis' activities would effectively pave the way for the GRU to take over the Comintern's intelligence apparatus, which, since the recall of Arnold Deutsch and Teodor Maly to Moscow in 1937 and the trial of the Woolwich Arsenal spies in 1938,[7] had failed to reassert itself as an effective intelligence organisation in the UK. The cultivation of spies during the Popular Front period rested heavily on encouraging a belief that they were being recruited into the anti-Fascist struggle and not the intelligence services of a foreign power. By 1938, however, it was clear that the cause the Kuczynskis were working for was not anti-Fascism as such, but Communism *tout court*.[8]

The latter became the lodestar, the guiding principle of those ideological spies (for instance, Melita Norwood and the Cambridge Five) who had been recruited in the early years of the 1930s. Ever since the signing of the Nazi–Soviet Pact the Soviet Union's intelligence services had concentrated on bringing OGPU/NKVD-recruited agents, linked to the OMS, into line with Stalin and the Comintern's broadening of the anti-Fascist agenda to include British and French imperialism. In 1947 the MI5 agent M.F. Serpell produced an insightful document detailing how the Kuczynskis effectively brought the OMS-linked spies into the Comintern and Stalinist fold:

> From this rapid and rather superficial account of the KUCZYNSKI family context there emerges a picture of two circles: the first a circle of Comintern activity and the second of Soviet espionage … Ursula BEURTON [SONYA] appears to represent a point at which these two circles overlapped before the war … it seems likely that the overlap in Switzerland was considerably extended during the war, and it may be found that the war-time necessities brought about the superimposition of the second circle on the first in many places … Jürgen KUCZYNSKI and his wife represent an important segment of the first circle and it is likely that they had a considerable knowledge of the second.[9]

Ursula's movements in England were closely monitored by MI5, who made arrangements as early as 6 December 1940 to keep her under observation:

> As spoken; we cannot refuse to allow this family to come here now, but I am anxious to keep a close eye on them when they do arrive. Could you please arrange for the wife to be put on the Black List, and ask the S.C.O. [Security Control Officer] to notify us when she arrives (by telephone), giving us her destination, description, and the part of the train on which she is travelling. I will then arrange for her to be picked up.[10]

Ursula arrived in Liverpool on 4 February 1941 with her two children, Micha and Janina, and made her way to her parents' address at 78 Woodstock Road, Oxford, a city where Robert was known to be on friendly terms with a number of leading academics and politicians, among them Sir Stafford Cripps, a member of Churchill's War Cabinet.

In Oxford, Ursula's transmitter was put at the disposal of the Kuczynski network, where Robert and Jürgen, despite the latter's initial reticence, would pass intelligence to Ursula for transmission to Moscow. At that time Jürgen was 'preparing economic analyses for the Soviet embassy' and provided Ursula with 'useful information outside the field of economics'.[11] She drew up four to six reports a month from these conversations and commented that Jürgen was aware of the nature of her reports and 'informed' Ursula 'more consciously' than her father did:

> I hoped that Jürgen, and perhaps Father too, would help me obtain information. Father, who was very tactful, had never asked me about my work. Now it seemed right to tell him something about it, but without mentioning its military destination ... I had only to let him know that I was interested in political and economic facts for my work. He nodded and that was all. It hardly had any effect on our conversations since they usually took the form of political discussions in any case. Mostly father mixed with left-wing economists and Labour politicians; at that time many of them had some sort of job connected with the war effort, and Father told me what he heard. But as I said, there were no big secrets, but political talks we would have had anyway.[12]

Ursula's first meeting with her 'illegal' Soviet contact took place in the Wake Arms, Epping, as arranged. Her contact, to whom she referred only as Sergei, underlined the importance of the Kuczynski family as an 'information network' for the Soviets. Sergei 'explained the significance' of their 'work in a country that was at war with the Nazis' that also hosted 'influential reactionary circles ... ready to come to an understanding with Hitler against the Soviet Union. Centre needed news.' Sergei sought information from the family's contacts inside British political and military circles and the date they could expect her transmitter to begin functioning. 'It could be in operation', she told him, 'within 24 hours.'[13]

Ursula's contact inside the legal residency was Nikolai Vladimirovich Apteka, a 'tough-looking man – thick-set and balding, with a big nose and big ears – who could clearly take care of himself in a fight'.[14] His official position was to serve as chauffer and Secretary to the Air Attaché at the Soviet Embassy in London. Apteka had a reputation as a capable agent runner and had built up a number of contacts inside the BBC. The importance of these agents should not be underestimated. He passed control of two of them, 'Freda' and 'Max', to Ursula and throughout the war they supplied her with information detailing the 'effectiveness' of German aerial bombardment on British cities and its impact on civilian morale.[15]

Ursula was in an extremely good position to access 'news', not merely from her father and brother; but also from her four sisters, all of whom were active on the British Left. Her first family recruit, Bridget, recruited to the GRU by Ursula in 1938, was a prominent member of the influential St Pancras Branch of the CPGB.[16] Born in Berlin on 15 July 1910, she had studied at Heidelberg and Basle Universities, obtaining the degree of PhD at the former. She arrived in the UK on 26 March 1934 and registered with the police as a refugee from Nazism. Bridget was no more than 5ft 7in tall, with brown hair and eyes, and was known to have a squint. For a time she worked as a governess at various addresses in north-west London before working for a year as a statistician with Lord William Malcom Hailey in connection with his monumental study *An African Survey: A Study of Problems Arising in Africa South of the Sahara*, often simply known as the African Survey.[17] An experienced statistician, she later worked for three years with the International Committee on Price History under the chairmanship of Sir William Beveridge and two years with the Social Biology Department of the London School of Economics under Professor A.M. Carr-Saunders, Director of the School. An 'exceptionally good linguist',[18] she married Anthony Gordon Lewis, known as Tony, a student six years her junior at the Hampstead (London) Register Office on 4 July 1936 before moving into 4 Lawn Road Flats. Anthony Gordon Lewis, born at Haddenham, Isle of Ely, on 23 September 1913, was the son of a mechanical engineer. Bridget obtained British citizenship through this marriage and was subsequently issued with a British passport on 21 July 1936 valid for European countries, the British Empire, the USA and the USSR. She also anglicised her name, changing it to Bridget.

Bridget had first come to the attention of Special Branch on 4 November 1936 when she interviewed members of the House of Commons about arms for Spain. The CPGB's campaign in aid of Spain called on members to organise meetings, mass demonstrations, vigilance committees at the ports and railway depots, collections of money, care of Spanish children, food ships every week, medical supplies and clothing. Above all, the Communists insisted upon the right of the Spanish government to buy arms in Britain. According to Special Branch reports, she was one of nine women present, 'about 30 Persons' in all, at a St Pancras Branch meeting held on 13 January 1938 at the Fred Tallent Hall, Camden. The meeting discussed the position in Spain and the subject of rent-racketeering in the borough.[19]

In July 1939 Bridget took charge of the industrial section of the St Pancras Branch CPGB and joined the Communist Party Group at the London School of Economics.[20] At the end of the year her intelligence activities caused an abrupt change in her behaviour and she moved to Bristol along with her husband. The couple continued to visit London and they retained their Lawn Road Flats address. She undertook research for her father at the Colonial Office's Library in Downing Street before the withdrawal of her library pass following warnings from Maxwell Knight and Roger Hollis.[21] Hollis informed the Colonial Office that Bridget Lewis was 'an active member of the Communist Party' and was, therefore, not 'a very suitable person to have this privilege. I should be most grateful if you could ascertain for me whether my information is correct and if so for what purpose Mrs LEWIS has been granted the pass.'[22] The reply was straightforward enough: 'Professor Kuczynski, together with Mrs. Lewis and a typist, have been working in our Library on the preparation of a book on demography.' The Colonial Office, however, agreed that official passes to the Library should not have been issued and withdrew them from all three in what appeared to be a petty act of discouragement.[23] However, it later emerged that Bridget was also supplying information gleaned from her work in the Colonial Office Library to the CPGB's Colonial Affairs Committee, which was finding its way to the Party's Colonial Information Bureau.

In connection with this, in November 1940 Indian Political Intelligence (IPI)[24] contacted MI5 claiming that a woman named Bridget was supplying information about Malaya to the CPGB's Colonial Affairs Committee (CAC). This information, which had subsequently appeared in the Communist Party's Colonial Information Bulletin, had been sent to Michael Carritt, Secretary of CAC and the liaison between King Street and the illegal Communist Party of India. Further information from IPI claimed that somebody had been providing a cover address for Michael Carritt.

An unassuming Oxford graduate, Carritt was described by his Oxford friend, Dick Crossman,[25] as 'one of the golden boys'.[26] In 1928 he had joined the Indian Civil Service, where he had been put in charge of the sub-division of the Burdwan District on the western frontier of Bengal Province. In this sub-division (the size of East Sussex) he was effectively the representative of the Bengal government, its Chief Magistrate and Chief Executive Officer with responsibility for law and order and tax collection. Overall, however, Carritt found his time in India 'a sickening experience'.[27] In his autobiography he was quite clear that imperial rule was not merely degrading, but was also demoralising the mother country. He wrote:

It will come as a surprise to many people that up to that time (the 1930s) the Jail Code, which laid down the rules and procedures ... for the treatment of inmates, specifically laid down forms of punishment for minor offences (e.g. cheeking a warder, refusal to obey an order, etc.) that were quite barbaric. These punishments included wall-fetters, chain-and-ball fetters and (worst of all) bar-fetters. I have seen emaciated men, like animals, chained to the wall or dragging around an iron ball chained to one ankle; and most foul of all, the bar-fetters where the flesh round the ankles was torn away and bleeding by the two iron bracelets connected by a rigid bar.[28]

'Repulsed' by the brutality he witnessed and 'the almost unlimited power of the police, the corrupt role of informers and the danger that comes from depending exclusively upon anonymous evidence', Carritt began working with the underground Communist Party of India (CPI) to end British rule in India.[29] In his autobiography *A Mole in the Crown* he describes how he exploited his position as a Special Officer in the Political Department of Government in Calcutta to undermine the working of the Suppression of Terrorism Outrages Act in India.[30] As a Special Officer he received fortnightly 'intelligence' reports about terrorist and other subversive activities in his area and carried around with him a small, black box containing cypher codes, cypher pads and secret files. He was recruited by the GRU and given the code name 'Bashir'; although he always claimed to be a minor cog in the British administrative system in India his timely warnings to labour leaders and members of the Indian Communist Party saved many nationalists from arrest and detention:

> Although I was only a rather subordinate cog in the government's machinery for watching over and trying to contain the political activities of Indian nationalists and the increasing signs of unrest amongst workers and peasants, I did in fact have on my desk the weekly secret reports from police and district officers on their way up to the Chief Secretary as well as all enciphered correspondence with London. I had, therefore access to much valuable information. And I have no doubt that some of the warnings I was able to give and the briefings on the plans for the detention of labour leaders were of marginal value in enabling fugitive agitators to remain at large. And

certainly the information, which I handed on weekly about police interception of letters at 'suspect' addresses, was a useful protection.[31]

Carritt's usefulness increased after his appointment as Under-Secretary to the Imperial government in the Political and Home Department, which necessitated working further underground – 'moles', he explained 'do not like working in the full light of day.'[32]

By this time, however, Carritt was living in constant fear that the 'Mole in the Crown' would be forced to the surface. The Calcutta Police Commissioner's reports to the government 'began to speak excitedly of 'a Moscow Agent, believed to be Russian operating in India and at the moment in Bengal'.[33] In late summer 1938 Carritt handed in his resignation from the Indian Civil Service and later that year left for England. Investigations continued, however, and his identity as a Soviet mole was eventually unearthed. In 1940 he received an official letter from the Secretary of State for India informing him 'of the intended withdrawal of [his] remaining pension on the grounds of behaviour (unspecified) that was not compatible with "approved service"'.[34]

Back in Britain, MI5's Hollis and his two assistants, Miss H. Creedy and Miss W. Ogilvie, were given responsibility for identifying Carritt's accomplice, known only as Bridget. Hollis spoke of a letter from Bridget to Carritt, dated 27 November 1940, sent from 4 Lawn Road Flats containing the communal telephone number of the building, Primrose 2315, with the instruction: 'Our phone does not always function but you could of course try.'[35] Hollis also mentioned that Bridget had been staying at the Lawn Road Flats between 14–16 October and 12–13 November and spoke of a rumoured affair between Bridget and Carritt. The affair, Hollis recounted, could not be conducted at Carritt's luxurious Dolphin Square flat in Pimlico, because his fiancée was living with him:

As I told you orally, Michael CARRITT is rumoured to be engaged to a girl called Marjorie TURNER, who is living with him and his brother Gabriel at their Dolphin Square flat; if this rumour is correct his affair with BRIDGET would seem to be something more than a personal matter and there is undoubtedly something secretive about it, as if she wished, there is no reason why she could not call on him either at his flat or at his office at 58 Theobald Rd.[36] I think, therefore that in view of Michael CARRITT'S position in the C.P.G.B. she merits some further investigation. Possibly the porter at No. 4. Lawn Flats could give some information as to who she is.[37]

Miss Ogilvie, in addition to her work as an MI5 agent, was fortuitously also a colleague of Professor Robert Kuczynski at the LSE, and from the correspondence between Carritt and Bridget she now identified her as Robert's daughter, Bridget Lewis:

> Please see attached report from B.6. from which it seems that Michael CARRITT's correspondent BRIDGET must be Mrs LEWIS, daughter of Professor KUCZINSKI. B.4.b. tells me that the KUCZINSKI's address is now Lawn Rd Flats – actually I believe No.6. Professor KUCZYNSKI is a colleague of mine at the London School of Economics and I knew of his daughter although I did not know her name. It is very likely from what I know of the KUCZINSKIS that she would be a research assistant – this may account for the reference to 'libraries' in her letters to CARRITT.[38]

In an undated letter addressed to Marguerite at No. 6 Lawn Road Flats, post-marked Bristol, 19 November 1940, Bridget had included a cheque for £1 12s 6d made out to Isokon Lawn Road Flats requesting that Marguerite deliver the cheque to the manager 'as she did not want to send it direct, because that would involve us in giving him our address here and I don't want that under any circumstances to happen. If he asks you say please that you don't know it. Please don't forget to look for letters now and then and to post them on.'[39]

Bewildered by the fact that Bridget had left no forwarding address with the management at the Lawn Road Flats, IPI now suggested that MI5 take steps to uncover her address in Bristol:

I wonder could we find out whether she has given a re-direction notice for letters or whether she collects them once a month when she visits London?[40] It seems strange to me that the management of Lawn Road Flats should not have taken her address in case, for one reason or another, she failed to turn up to discharge her obligations![41] Possibly the easiest way to find out what we wish to know would be by consulting the G.P.O. as to the possibility of the re-direction notice and if none has been taken out, by putting on an Observation check. Perhaps you would let me have your views?[42]

In fact, MI5 had already discovered that Bridget had moved to Exeter Buildings, Redland, Bristol, on 14 January 1941 and on 5 February had requested a daily return of correspondence for the next two weeks on her address. A Home Office Warrant (HOW)[43] was requested by Hollis on the 27th and he now switched his attention to Bridget's husband, Tony Lewis, and the BBC.[44]

Lewis was then employed as the Assistant Director of the British Institute of Public Opinion (BIPO) at Aldwych House and had moved to Bristol together with Bridget, where he was engaged for a time on Listeners' Research work – his duties were described officially as follows: 'Research in social statistics, handling mass data, and … controlling daily listening surveys for the BBC'.[45] An interesting cross-reference was made by Hollis, who picked up on a Miss Ellen or Eileen Johnstone, a member of the Association of Women Clerks and Secretaries (AWCS), which was included in the Lewises' KV2 file. 'This woman', he wrote, 'is supposed to have got some work with Imperial Airways at Bristol. This girl was engaged to another Party member with a name like Charles Kairn. This man was supposed to have been in the BBC at Bristol but to have been dismissed.' The AWCS was also the trade union of Melita Norwood, whose family had been on friendly terms with the Kuczynskis since 1934, the year she had been recruited to Soviet intelligence by the TASS correspondent in London, Andrew Rothstein.[46]

On 4 February 1941, the head of MI5's B Division, Brigadier Oswald A. Harker, commonly known as 'Jasper', wrote to Bristol's Chief Constable, C.G. Maby, providing a summary of the Lewises' background and asking for further information:

> Bridget LEWIS first came to my notice in November 1936 as one of a delegation of 13 Communists who interviewed members of the House of Commons about arms for the Spanish Government. In June 1937 she was a delegate from the St. Pancras branch of the Communist Party to the 14th Party Congress. She subsequently became propaganda secretary to St. Pancras branch, and was later in charge of the industrial section of the branch.[47] She was formerly employed as a private secretary to a professor at the London School of Economics. She is a sister of Professor Kuczynski who was interned but has since been released. The only information that I have about her husband is that he is described as a research student in Sociology, and I have been told that he is an underground member of the Communist Party. This information comes from a very delicate source. He is alleged to have obtained employment with the BBC.[48]

A reply was received on 12 March stating that 'continued enquiries' had 'failed to reveal any Communist activities of these persons in Bristol'. Lewis, Chief Constable Maby wrote, had 'informed his neighbours' that he worked in 'Insurance', ... travelled to London 'twice weekly, sometimes remaining away for two or three days. His wife seldom leaves the house, except on the usual shopping expeditions.'[49]

At the request of MI5, Bristol constabulary now conducted a thorough investigation of Tony and Bridget Lewis, reporting back that Lewis, 'and a man named Moss who resides in London, managed a department at BIPO known as the Impartial Fact Finding Organisation'. This organisation supplied 'regular reports to the BBC and the *News Chronicle* on the popularity or otherwise of current broadcasts and newspaper articles'. Lewis's earnings were said to be £10 a week.[50] However, they could find nothing against Lewis, reporting only that 'Mr. Silvey, who was in charge of the Listeners' Research Department of the British Broadcasting Corporation at 20 Elmdale Road, Bristol ... knows Lewis very well and is quite satisfied about his loyalty to this Country. Mr. Silvey knows nothing about Lewis's wife and there was no evidence that they were associating with local Communists.'[51]

Bridget, at this time, was in fact conducting research for the Nuffield College Reconstruction Survey (NCRS) on employment policy and the organisation of industry after the war under the direction of Professor Hamilton Whyte, Department of Economics, at the University of Bristol. In 1941 a decision was taken to exclude Communists from government and private departments engaged on secret work. MI5 began compiling a blacklist of Communists and fellow-travellers, vetting researchers accessing secret information concerning industries involved with post-war reconstruction.[52] Not surprisingly, Bridget's name was flagged as a security risk:

> There had been one or two cases in which members of the Communist Party had been asked by the Nuffield College Reconstruction Survey ... to assist with this reconstruction work. An instance which had come to notice was that of Mrs. Brigitte LEWIS.[53]

The NCRS, launched in 1941, was the brainchild of the socialist labour historian G.D.H. Cole, who sought to foster co-operation between academics and the nation's business and political leaders.[54] Initially restricted to 'the location of industry and the distribution of population, during and after the war', it was expanded under Cole's guidance to include education, local government and social services, thereby laying the foundations for the Welfare State. In the financial year 1941–42 it received a grant of £5,000 from the Treasury and produced a number of reports prepared at the request of government departments.[55] It also contributed to official inquiries such as the Scott Committee, which investigated industrial developments in rural areas.

The Survey collaborated with the Oxford Institute of Statistics and the Royal Institute of International Affairs (Chatham House), and assisted the Beveridge Inquiry.[56] Opposition to the project, however, manifested itself as early as October 1941, when MI5 raised the question of vetting. In November 1941 the Hebdomadal Council of the University of Oxford, to whom the Survey was accountable, passed a motion 'urging the Survey to restrict the scope of its research'. The following year Lord Nuffield expressed his concern at G.D.H. Cole's leading role in the Survey and accused the NCRS of a Left-wing bias.[57] Bridget was removed from her post.

CHAPTER NINE

Barbara and Renate

Bridget's sister Barbara born on 20 November 1913 in Schöneberg, had been resident in the UK since September 1935. Like Bridget and her father, she was initially employed by the LSE, working as a research assistant in Social Biology. Ursula described her as 'intelligent, conscientious and ambitious'.[1] On 12 October 1936 the Home Office granted her permission to remain in the UK for an indefinite period and she married Duncan Macrae Burnett Taylor, a well-connected Edinburgh Scot, on 21 January 1937, at Hampstead Register Office. They had first met at a Quaker summer school in 1936 in Honfleur, Normandy, in a house belonging to a mutual friend, an American Quaker named Mary Kelsey, who had made Robert's acquaintance in the 1920s while engaged on famine relief work with the American Friends Reconstruction Unit. Barbara and Duncan, presumably before their marriage, had worked together on a translation into English of the German social anthropologist Martin Block's book *Zigeuner: Ihr Leben und Ihre Seele* (*Gypsies: Their life and Their Customs*). Block's work, published in London in 1938 with the names Barbara Kuczynski and Duncan Taylor appearing together as translators on the title page, challenged the Nazi view that gypsies were a foreign race in Germany.

From her arrival in the UK Barbara was on friendly terms with several leading female members of the CPGB, particularly the sisters Dorothy and Margot Heinemann and the historian Noreen Branson. The backgrounds of these women were similar in many respects and their friendship centred upon the Labour Research Department and the Hampstead suburb of London. German refugees themselves of sorts, Margot and Dorothy were the daughters of Meyer Max Heinemann, a merchant banker, and Selma Schott, both non-Orthodox Jews from Frankfurt, Germany. Margot, described as 'petite, with a strong handsome face and curly hair', had been educated at Roedean and King Alfred School in London before graduating in English in 1934 from Newnham College, Cambridge, with first-class honours.[2] At Cambridge she fell in love with the poet John Cornford, who was killed in Spain the day after his twenty-first birthday while serving with the International Brigade. 'To Margot Heinemann', a poem he wrote in 1936, was his last love letter to Margot, and probably remains his most moving and memorable work, although less well-known than 'Full Moon at Tierz':

On the last mile to Huesca,
The last fence for our pride,
Think so kindly, dear, that I
Sense you at my side.

And if bad luck should lay my strength
Into the shallow grave,
Remember all the good you can;
Don't forget my love.[3]

A member of the Communist Party since 1934, Margot had been friendly with Blunt, Burgess and Maclean at Cambridge. In 1936 she moved to Birmingham to teach 14-year-old girls on day release from the chocolate factory at Cadbury's Continuation School in Bournville, now Bournville College, before joining Noreen Branson at the Labour Research Department in 1937.

A copy of a letter to Burgess from Margot, unearthed at the Courtald Institute of Art in November 1951, claimed that Heinemann was on close terms with Guy Burgess in 1936 and that she had used his address as a temporary place of residence when applying for a passport. MI5 commented at the time that, 'It is interesting that HEINEMANN should be writing to Burgess at this date, when BURGESS had apparently given up Communism in favour of Fascism.'[4] In the original (undated) letter addressed to 'My dear Guy', Margot complained of ill health due to over-work, and implored Burgess to get in touch with her, suggesting that they meet up in London:

> I would like to know when and where you are in case I am able to put into London next week.
>
> If you are in London at all, you might ring me up some time – I am always in and it only costs 4d after 7 o'clock and I would like to see you.
>
> I could have rung you up, of course, if I hadn't lost the bit of paper I wrote your telephone number down on. But I did, so I couldn't.
> Love
> Margot.[5]

Her sister, Dorothy, a Communist known to Special Branch, was a high-ranking civil servant employed by the Ministry of Labour. Both the Heinemanns and Branson skirted on the fringes of Soviet intelligence, which in the 1930s and '40s colonised much of Belsize Park and Hampstead.

On 17 August 1939 a cryptic message, somewhat fortuitously, fell into the hands of MI5: 'Barbara and Duncan are guarding the future infant in Switzerland.' The message was extracted from a letter addressed to a Mrs H.S. Stanham, Rifugio Principe Umberto, Posta Misurina, Italy, from her daughter, the writer and cook, Patience Stanham, whose *Honey from a Weed*, published under the name Gray, has rightly been proclaimed as 'one of the most important and best-loved cookbooks of the twentieth century'.[6] The letter, dated 17 August 1939, had come into MI5's possession when it was dropped by Patience while she was under observation by B6.[7]

Patience Stanham met all the criteria required for membership of the rather well-heeled and Bohemian Taylor–Kuczynski circle. Born on 31 October 1917 at Michen Hall in the Surrey village of Shackleford, near Godalming, she was the second of three daughters of Hermann Stanham, the son of a rabbi named Warschavski, who had fled persecution in Poland in 1861. Exceptionally bright, she had studied

German and economics at Bonn University and in 1937 took the degree of BSc (Econ) at the LSE, where her tutor was the future Labour leader, Hugh Gaitskell. Barbara, Bridget and their father, Robert, were also at the LSE at this time and they all became close friends:

> Patience also had a lively group of friends at university, including Mary Best and Barbara Kuczynski, whose father, the noted German economist Robert René Kuczynski; was a lecturer at the London School of Economics ... During her final year of college, Patience shared an attic flat with Mary Best in West London; it was rather spare containing a single gas ring, toilet on the landing, and a 'horrible square stone sink.' Best, who had grown up among the landed aristocracy of Dorset and later married a radical trade unionist, introduced Patience to the journalist and writer Nicholas Davenport, and they frequently spent weekends at his estate, Hinton Manor, near Oxford. Davenport was best known for his popular column on politics and economics – he was a good friend of John Maynard Keynes – in the *New Statesman* and then the *Spectator.*[8]

Patience found employment in the Foreign Office, 'furnishing the press with the weekly Foreign Office report, producing "thirteen carbon copies on an antique machine"'. When the European war broke out she was dismissed, however, for extensive travel and 'having too many foreign contacts'.[9] Davenport was warned by a close friend in MI5, Brigadier 'Jasper' Harker,[10] that Patience was a 'suspected person'.[11] Her dismissal came two weeks after the discovery of the Barbara and Duncan Taylor letter by MI5's B6 concerning the wellbeing of 'the future child in Switzerland'. Patience was, apparently, 'happy to leave' the FO as she had recently fallen in love with a married man, Thomas Gray, a Spanish Civil War veteran and a card-carrying member of the CPGB; Gray also claimed to be an artist.[12] Shortly after the declaration of war he had been appointed honorary secretary of the Art and Entertainment Emergency Council (AEEC) with instructions to bring art and culture to the masses. As the group's chairman put it, 'In war time the need for Art and Entertainment is far greater than it is in peace time.'[13] Patience was named secretary and was one of the few members to receive a salary. In 1940, however, Gray was dismissed from his post and began working as an explosives instructor on a clandestine counter-insurgency course for the Home Guard at Hurlingham, London. Patience became secretary of this school, which had been set up to teach civilians new skills 'such as how to make Molotov cocktails'.[14] When Gray was conscripted, Patience was left alone to cope with a son and daughter in a cottage on the South Downs. She took the name Gray by public announcement in the *London Gazette* on 17 January 1941.[15] In December 1941 she became an assistant to the editor of the *Journal of the Free Danes* (*Frit Danmark*), an underground Left-wing newspaper published by the Danish government in exile.[16]

Despite his Communist beliefs, Duncan Taylor viewed himself as patriotic and was a popular schoolteacher at Marylebone Grammar School, where the headmaster, Philip Wayne (affectionately known to the boys as 'Dicky'), had affected a Churchillian manner. A semi-polymath with a love of English and German literature, Wayne was 'brisk in all he did and worked with gusto'. Within a week of the declaration of war the school was paraded every day for a week, while pupils and staff alike prepared for evacuation. Finally, 'they were all marched through a line of weeping parents to Paddington Station where in locked carriages they were converted to Redruth with outposts in Portreath and St. Day'.[17] The Taylors, however, found Redruth and Cornwall 'unbearable' and in 1940 they moved to Clifton, Bristol, where Duncan had secured employment as a schoolteacher.

On 20 January 1940, following Barbara's brother Jürgen's internment, Duncan, along with his mother, Hermione, joined the Left-wing lawyer D.N. Pritt's campaign to secure his release. In early March, Duncan met with Clement Attlee on Jürgen's behalf and wrote a supportive letter to Marguerite on the eve of her move from 36 Upper Park Road (headquarters of the *Kulturbund*) to the Lawn Road Flats. He advised her to encourage Pritt to write to other MPs (especially Cambridge and Hampstead members) and to the radical Liberal MP Wilfrid Roberts.

In the latter's case, however, Duncan wondered whether Pritt's support for the Finnish war had damaged his contacts with Liberals 'who would normally be roused by a matter of principle like this'.[18] For her part, Hermione rallied 'dyed-in-the-wool Tories' behind Pritt's campaign by writing to her Berwick-on-Tweed MP, persuading her brother to write to his MP in North Horsley, Surrey, and her husband to write to his good friend Hugh Macmillan, Baron Macmillan, then chairman of the Political Honours Committee.

In April Hermione visited Marguerite at the Lawn Road Flats and on 7 July 1940 Duncan wrote to Marguerite before their move from Redruth, offering a collection of books from the Left Book Club to the library of the *Kulturbund*. 'Some have lost their interest,' he wrote, but others like 'Hitler the Pawn' would be of interest. In 1940 the Taylors' daughter, Fran, was born.[19]

'A black day,' Barbara wrote to Marguerite on 20 January 1941: 'We cut that out in our family in future. Last year Jürgen was interned, this year Duncan gets his calling up notices. I am off my head but I don't think that will help. He's got to report on 8 Feb. That's all we know. I have decided to go to Oxford with Fran if mother can find accommodation.'[20] She moved to 97 Kingston Road, Oxford, sharing rooms with her sister Ursula and her children, Micha and Janina. Duncan joined the RAF and was stationed at Blackpool, where he trained as a wireless operator before being transferred to RAF Abingdon, just outside Oxford.[21] In March Ursula left Oxford, moving into The Rectory at Glympton, near Woodstock. Barbara returned to London. Her two youngest sisters, Sabine and Renate, now began to play their part in the Kuczynski family network, with Ursula recruiting Renate into the GRU, code name Katie.[22]

Sabine, 'the only one', Ursula opined, 'to inherit her mother's beauty',[23] had joined the *Kulturbund* in 1938 and was a prominent member of its youth section; while Renate, at the age of 18, was on the executive of the students' union at the LSE, apparently a record young age, and played a leading role in the affairs of the Free German Youth.[24] The LSE had been moved to Cambridge during the Blitz along with the offices of the National Union of Students (NUS), and Renate's student union duties included students from both universities. At that time the national organiser of the NUS was Kutty Hookham, a British citizen born in Hampstead in 1915 and a member of the Communist Party. She was on good terms with Sir Stafford Cripps, whom she had met in Moscow in 1936 while travelling in the Soviet Union with her husband, Maurice Hookham.[25] In 1941 Sabine was receiving correspondence at the Hookhams' address, 23 Belsize Park Gardens, NW3, prompting MI5 to write to the Assistant Deputy Commissioner, Special Branch, about the activities of the student body and other youth organisations:

> This is an interesting link up of people who are known to us to be working for different youth organisations and I shall be glad to have any information that comes your way about this association.[26]

Since the beginning of the war, Sabine had been active in a number of 'different youth organisations'. In London she worked with the Save the Children Fund looking after children in air-raid shelters and the Miriam Price Coleman Day Nursery and Sunlight Clinic in Scholefield Road, N19, which was run jointly by the London County Council (LCC) and Islington Borough Council. She joined the Municipal and General Workers Union's campaign to stop the LCC extending the working day without any increase in pay and became a member of the Communist Party West London Teachers' Group. On 7 June 1941 she married Francis Loeffler at Paddington Register Office and soon after joined the British Communist Party. The couple celebrated their wedding with a breakfast in the Lawn Road Flats' Isobar served up by celebrity chef Philip Harben.[27]

MI5 described Francis Loeffler as a stocky, well-built individual, 5ft 7in tall with brown wavy hair and brown eyes, and a sallow complexion.[28] He was born in Oxford on 30 April 1920 to a British mother and German father. He had become a British citizen when his father was naturalised in Canada in 1928. He was educated in Germany, France, Canada, Jersey and Downing College, Cambridge, and had joined the Communist Party while a student at Cambridge in 1937. He was in possession of a Jersey passport issued on 6 June 1939 allowing him to travel to Britain in October that year to complete his third year of study for a law degree at Cambridge. He graduated in June 1940 but owing to the invasion of the Channel Islands he had been unable to finish his studies at Inner Temple, London, and had volunteered for the RAF. However, he was ineligible for the British armed forces as he could not claim two continuous years of residence in the UK.[29] Jürgen, in his somewhat characteristically arrogant manner, assumed the role of patriarch of the family and gave their marriage a less-than-enthusiastic blessing:

> She, with 22, is the older one, he is five months younger. They may have the chance to celebrate their diamond and platinum wedding if they do not separate considerably earlier. I find that they are perfectly matched; both have no money, both have no real job, both are much too young to marry and both are not gifted above the average; what do you want more?![30]

At the time of their marriage, Francis was working for the Youth Relief and Refugee Council (YRRC), founded 'to organise humanitarian assistance and relief by the youth of Britain for victims of war, persecution and civil distress'.[31] In this capacity he worked closely with the Refugee Children's Evacuation Fund (RCEF) and was one of the organisers, along with Johann Fladung[32] and Jürgen's personal secretary Hans Siebert, of an art exhibition entitled 'Children's Art from All Countries', which was shown at the clubhouse of the *Kulturbund* between 16 August and 10 September 1941. The exhibition included drawings, paintings and handcraft work from children of twelve different nationalities and included artwork by interned children as a means of raising awareness of the plight of 'enemy aliens'.[33]

Francis edited the YRRC's journal *The Helping Hand*, later *The Young Refugee*, which was described by the Postal Censorship, Prisoner of War Section as an 'undesirable publication'.[34] Sabine became secretary of the youth hostel run by the YRRC. MI5 monitored the organisation through B8 and the ubiquitous Source Hi, the writer and pacifist Kurt Hiller, who was to become 'a prolific informer on his fellow-refugees'.[35]

Before June 1941 there had been calls to summon a Communist-dominated World Youth Council (WYC) in Moscow to denounce the imperialist war. This all changed quite dramatically in June 1941 following the invasion of the Soviet Union by over 3 million German troops. The November/December 1941 issue of the WYC's journal, *Youth News*, carried an editorial demanding national service in Britain to strengthen the fight against Fascism:

> At last the government have realised that youth has an important task to play in the war effort. Everyone between 16 and 18 is to be registered and given a chance to train for national service.[36]

The new pro-war line was adopted unanimously by the University Labour Federation, which had been expelled from the Labour Party for its opposition to the war in 1940, and the National Union of Students, who now demanded the total mobilisation of Britain and the opening of a second front. Operation Barbarossa, the German code name for the invasion of the Soviet Union, had a profound effect upon world student opinion and international youth organisation, and led to the creation of the Communist-dominated International Youth Rally for Victory (IYRV). The origins of this body can be traced to a visit to the Soviet Embassy by a delegation representing the leaders of British youth on 31 July 1941, with a message of solidarity for the Soviet Union:

> We welcome the youth of the Soviet Union as our brothers-in-arms. We greet the peoples of your country now suffering with us the horrors of war. Your magnificent resistance to the invading Nazis has inspired all freedom-loving people.[37]

This visit was quickly followed by the formation of the Anglo-Soviet Youth Friendship Alliance by Sir Stafford Cripps, who appointed Kutty Hookham as General Secretary.

After the disruption and confusion caused by Hitler's invasion of the Soviet Union, it was several days before the latter resumed wireless contact with its agents in Britain, during which time Ursula did not receive a response to her call sign. When she did get a response, she discovered that the attitude of the Communist Parties towards the war had changed dramatically. Instead of spreading defeatist propaganda and denouncing the war as a conflict between competing imperialisms, the dominant theme was co-operation with the Allied war effort, active help to the USSR, and the liberation of enslaved peoples from Fascism. Churchill promised full support for the Soviet Union with characteristic rhetorical flourish:

> No one has been a more persistent opponent of Communism than I have for the last 25 years. I will unsay no word that I have spoken about it, but all this fades away before the spectacle which is now unfolding ... We have but one aim and one single irrevocable purpose. We are resolved to destroy Hitler and every vestige of the Nazi regime ... Any man or state who fights against Nazism will have our aid ... It follows, therefore, that we shall give whatever help we can to Russia and the Russian people. We shall appeal to all our friends and allies in every part of the world to take the same course. The Russian danger is our danger ... just as the cause of any Russian fighting for his hearth and home is the cause of free men and free people in every quarter of the globe.[38]

In truth Churchill, along with other prominent British Establishment figures, expected the Soviet Union's defeat within three months. It was a sentiment that was not lost on Robert, who made sure that Ursula transmitted the real mood of the British Cabinet to Moscow Centre. 'Father,' she wrote, 'had these views confirmed by Sir Stafford Cripps' who told him privately that the 'German Wehrmacht will slice through

Russia like a hot knife through butter.' She transmitted Cripps's phrase to Centre and received back a telegram of thanks, which she cherished as 'a rare occurrence'.[39] Praise from Centre was rare; but when it came it was always welcome as an object lesson in how to achieve optimum value from spies, and one that Ursula knew how to put to good use. 'Moral support from Centre,' she wrote, 'is important for comrades in dangerous isolated work – however hardened they may be. Respect for their work, acknowledgement of their achievements, and an understanding for personal problems must under no circumstances be neglected.'[40] Her handling of the atomic bomb spies showed the extent to which Ursula had mastered this art.

CHAPTER TEN

Klaus Fuchs, Melita Norwood and Geoffrey Pyke

Shortly after Operation Barbarossa, Klaus Fuchs took his decision to pass atomic bomb secrets to the Russians. He regarded Jürgen as 'the right person to make the contact'.[1] A gifted scientist with degrees in mathematics and physics from the universities of Leipzig and Kiel, Fuchs had been a member of the KPD since 1932. On 28 February 1933, the day following the Reichstag fire, a warrant had been issued for his arrest and he went underground before fleeing to Paris and then to Britain. 'I was lucky,' Fuchs recalled years later, 'because on the morning after the burning of the Reichstag I left my home very early to catch a train to Berlin for a conference of our student organisation (KPD), and that is the only reason why I escaped arrest. I remember clearly when I opened the newspaper in the train I immediately realised the significance and I knew that the underground struggle had started.'

Fuchs was ordered abroad by the KPD, and told to concentrate on his studies in preparation for the new Communist Germany that would follow the collapse of the Hitler regime. 'I was sent out by the Party, they said that I must finish my studies because after the revolution in Germany people would be required with technical knowledge to take part in the building up of the Communist Germany.'

Fuchs arrived in England on 24 September 1933, practically penniless. He was adopted by the physics department at the University of Bristol, who arranged for him to enroll at the university to work on the electron theory of metals. In December 1936 he was awarded the degree of PhD for a thesis on 'The cohesive forces of copper and the elastic constants of monovalent metals'. He then went to the University of Edinburgh, where in 1939 he gained the degree of DSc for his thesis on 'Some problems of condensation, quantum dynamics and the stability of the nuclei'. In May 1941 he was invited to the University of Birmingham by the German scientist Rudolf Peierls to carry out research on the theory of the gaseous diffusion process of separating uranium isotopes. The following month he signed the Official Secrets Act and began working on Britain's Top Secret atomic bomb project, code-named 'Tube Alloys', evaluating the critical size and efficiency of an atomic bomb. He made contact with Jürgen through Johannah Klopstock, a German Communist then working with the KPD's Hans Graf in Glasgow; arrangements were made for him to meet Simon Davidovich Kremer, Secretary to the Soviet Military Attaché at the Soviet Embassy, in London:

> F. [Fuchs] was recruited for intelligence work in England in Aug. 1941 by our operative, former military attaché secretary Cde. Kremer, on a lead from Jürgen Kuczynski (brother of our illegal station chief in England, 'Sonya'). The latter was living in London at the time and was one of the senior workers of the German Comparty in England; Kremer knew him through official connections. F agreed to work on an ideological basis and did not accept payment. F passed us a number of valuable materials containing theoretical calculations for splitting the uranium atom and creating an atomic bomb.[2]

At the time of his introduction to Fuchs, Kremer flitted in and out of the Kuczynski network; along with Boris Dicki, Secretary to the Soviet Air Attaché, who cultivated connections with Barbara Taylor's close friends in the CPGB, Margot and Dorothy Heinemann and Noreen Branson. The Heinemanns' and Branson's flat in Haverstock Hill was used by a courier working for Kremer and Dicki and was kept under observation by MI5.

In April 1941 B4 reported that a woman was seen visiting the Soviet Embassy and later 4 Kensington Palace Gardens, the home of Boris Dicki, before visiting Kremer's address at 27 Palace Court. The woman was then seen returning to Margot Heinemann's address at Flat 35, 99 Haverstock Hill, which she entered with a key. A return of correspondence on this address disclosed that, in addition to Margot, three other women were receiving letters there, one of whom was Noreen Branson.[3] Both Dicki and Kremer had been identified by a source known as 'Thomas' 'as being important Fourth Department (GRU) agents. It therefore seems quite likely,' MI5 concluded, 'that one of the women living at 99 Haverstock Hill is used as a 'runner' for the conveying of information from one Soviet agent to another.' However, MI5's agent was quite adamant 'that neither HEINEMANN nor BRANSON was identical with the woman who visited the Soviet Embassy and the other two addresses'.[4] The woman in question was Hilda Jane Brocklesby Davis, a librarian on the *Daily Worker* staff.[5] MI5 concluded that Mrs H.G. Davis was 'quite likely' the woman who was followed to Flat 35, 99 Haverstock Hill:

Miss DAVIS has a cyst on her cheek and is undoubtedly the woman followed to Flat 35 on the 13 February last, but people who have seen her cannot identify her with the photograph submitted by B.4.c. on the 4 April, 1941. The photograph may be of her when she was younger but the cyst definitely alters her expression and gives an unnatural appearance to the right eye.[6]

At the time MI5 strongly suspected the Heinemann sisters and Branson to be working closely with underground Communist sympathisers inside the Civil Service. On 13 November 1942 at King Street a building trades' activist in the CPGB, Frank Jackson, spoke to a comrade identified only as Robson about 'some man who had been introduced to him by Margot HEINEMAN. This man was in contact with under-cover people, possibly in the Civil Service. ROBSON said. "Oh her! Yes, well, she's one of our ..." (voice dropped away).'[7]

During his spell as Soviet Military Attaché in London, Kremer built up an interesting circle of acquaintances but his excessive caution was not always appreciated. He irritated Fuchs, who was apparently aggravated by his 'insistence on taking long rides in London taxis and regularly doubling back in order to throw off anyone trying to tail them'.[8] Fuchs, however, was prone to lapses of discipline and would summon Kremer to meetings by telephone, to the latter's annoyance.[9] Jürgen discussed the situation with Ursula and following Kremer's recall to the Soviet Union in July 1942 she began receiving material from Fuchs:

On 22 October 'Sonya' informed our worker that her brother J. Kuczynski, had told her that in July 1942, a physicist by the name of F. had lost contact with a representative of the Sov. Emb-ssy's milit-ry department who called himself Johnson. 'Sonya' also reported that at Kuczynski's suggestion, she already established contact with F., received materials from him, and asks us to indicate whether she should continue to maintain contact with him and accept mater-als from him. On our instructions, Sonya continued to maintain contact with F.[10]

At the time Ursula was already receiving intelligence on the behaviour of uranium metal at high temperatures from Melita Norwood. A highly gifted agent, Norwood would become the longest-serving Soviet agent in the UK, outdistancing Philby and more notorious British-Soviet agents by twenty years.[11]

Norwood's information was particularly important on two accounts. Not only did she have access to BN-FMRA documents on Tube Alloys; but she also had access to documents from other leading industrial bodies linked with the Tube Alloys project, including Metro-Vickers and ICI. In the autumn of 1941, when the Tube Alloys project was in its infancy, Metro-Vickers had been given a contract for the design of a twenty-stage machine for isotope separation, and ICI had received a contract for the production of uranium hexafluoride (UF_6). This production was essential to the Tube Alloys project as the separation of the isotope U-235 in any quantity would mean production on a commercial scale.[12] The process adopted by ICI was the one that had been used for the preparation of

3kg of UF_6 for the Ministry of Aircraft Production (MAP) involving the direct reaction between fluorine and metallic uranium.[13] Despite production of U-235 being moved to the United States in July 1943, research being undertaken by BN-FMRA and ICI between 1941 and 1943, particularly the secret reports that Norwood passed to Ursula on the corrosive nature of the fluoride gas on uranium metal, were of immense value to Soviet scientists in their attempts to keep abreast of developments in Britain and the United States:

> 'Tina' – born in 1912, an Englishwoman. Secret member of the CP of England, works as a secretary at the British Non-Ferrous Metals Association. Recruited in 1935 by the OGPU's London station. Works on an ideological basis. Gives valuable materials on metallurgical work pertaining to 'En-s' ['Enormous': Soviet code name for the atomic bomb].[14]

Meetings between Ursula and Fuchs usually took place in the market town of Banbury, midway between Birmingham and Oxford.[15] The first time they met, she later recalled, they 'went for a walk arm-in-arm, according to the old-established principle of illicit meetings' and spent more than half an hour together:

> Two minutes would have been enough but, apart from the pleasure of the meeting, it would arouse less suspicion if we took a little walk rather than parting immediately. Nobody who did not live in such isolation can guess how precious these meetings with another German comrade were. In this respect he was even worse off than I. Our common involvement in trading in danger also added to our feeling of closeness.[16]

Subsequent meetings took place in the woods near the Churchill family seat at Blenheim, the newly acquired wartime home of MI5.[17] Ursula and Fuchs would bicycle there together. 'He would then pass over secrets, which she stuffed under her bicycle seat ... The delivery system was breathtakingly simple, even naïve from an intelligence point of view. There was no dead-letter drop. The secrets were passed hand to hand, which would have been a gift for counterintelligence if it had been watching.'[18]

Meanwhile, Bridget had been taken on as an assistant in the BBC's Listeners' Research Department, writing to Jürgen in December 1941: 'I am busy as usual – and in addition have a full-time job since last week at the BBC which is both interesting and congenial.'[19] She described her employment as '"reserved" and for the "duration!"'[20] The following month the *Kulturbund* held a meeting at the Conway Hall to discuss ways of influencing BBC German propaganda. MI5 reported that over the last two to three months 'a steady flow of *Kulturbund* members' had been 'applying, or thinking of applying, for employment in the BBC'.[21] Such lucrative employment granting key insider access to public opinion provided the Kuczynskis with the ability not simply to discern the morale of the British population in wartime, but also to influence, albeit in a small way, events.

Bridget had managed to secure employment with the BBC before the normal security clearance could be obtained from MI5. On 1 December 1941 MI5 raised their concerns with the BBC that Bridget was 'an active member of the underground organisation of the Communist Party' and advised that she should be excluded from all 'secret or confidential information'.[22] The BBC reassured MI5 that Bridget's Communist views were known to them, but that as her work was 'quite satisfactory' they would not be dismissing her:

> In reply to your letter of 11 December regarding the above [Bridget Lewis], I am informed that the work on which she is engaged cannot be considered confidential. She is doing statistical work for Listener Research. In these circumstances I do not feel that any action is necessary.[23]

MI5 now began to look more closely at Tony Lewis's position as liaison between BIPO and the BBC Listeners' Research Department. BIPO was not a subversive organisation. However, MI5's Captain Lane, responding to an intercepted telephone conversation that had taken place on 9 March 1942 between Lewis and the manager of the Hotel Bristol, requested a note on BIPO from F2a.[24] Lewis had requested a room for a Saturday meeting of BIPO at the hotel between 1.30 and 2.45 and the Bristol Police had been asked to cover the gathering. Captain Lane wanted to know 'how far this covering should go':

> I spoke to Captain Lane on the telephone and told him that the British Institute of Public Opinion was a respectable organisation on the lines of Mass Observation and used by the BBC.[25] It had, however, employed a number of people of left wing views as its observers. I told Captain Lane that we had known that Anthony LEWIS was an employee for some time and that Mrs. Lewis was an employee of the BBC and that her communist activities were well known to us.[26]

At the end of 1942 the BBC, concerned that BIPO had 'left-wing tendencies', severed its connection with the Institute and both Tony Lewis and Bridget were dismissed. Bridget was then five months' pregnant with the child of an RAF corporal, Arthur Long, a Soviet agent and member of the Kuczynski group. Tony and Bridget parted company during the latter part of 1942 and Bridget moved to 60 Belsize Avenue, London, NW3, and began working at Collet's (London) Bookshop, 66 Charing Cross Road, whose owner was Eva Reckitt, a Lawn Road Flats resident and well known to the Kuczynskis. Tony Lewis moved back into 4 Lawn Road Flats and was in touch with other members of the Kuczynski family. He wrote to Jürgen on 27 July 1942, thanking him for his 'kind note' and 'invitation to supper'. He also gave Jürgen his private telephone number, Primrose 2701.[27]

Jürgen was then experiencing family problems of his own. The school attended by his children in the countryside had been forced to close and the Luftwaffe's air raids over London had stopped. Jürgen and Marguerite decided to take the children back home and in September 1941 they moved into bigger accommodation in the highly desirable

Hampstead Garden Suburb, situated just north of Hampstead, west of Highgate and east of Golders Green. Yet trouble quickly followed: 'The oldest, nine years declined my suggestion of writing an autobiography by explaining to me it would be a very short one consisting of one sentence: "living in one stinking school after the other".'[28] In a letter to an old family friend and associate of Otto Katz, Prince Hubertus Löwenstein, Jürgen described his children as 'being rather wild and cannot be left alone when they have come home from school ... one of us has to stay with them. Thus it happens on many days that Marguerite and I see each other only between the doors when the one is coming home and the other leaving it.'[29] Family problems persisted when their son Peter ran away from home and had to be brought back by the police. At the time Jürgen's output was impressive, with the NKVD commenting that between 1942 and 1943 'interesting materials' were being sent by him to their station in New York. His reports covered a wide range of subjects from anti-Soviet intrigues in the Labour Party to the economic situation in India:

> Between 1942 and 1943, for example, the following interesting materials were received from K:
> On anti-Soviet intrigues on the part of the Labour Party's 'left' circles;
> On Conservative policies;
> On the anti-Soviet activities of Eng. Catholics;
> On the activities of pro-Fascist elements;
> On India's econ. situation.[30]

In February 1942 Source 'Kaspar', 'the self-styled Austrian aristocrat Josef Otto von Laemmel',[31] reported to his MI5 handler, William Robson-Scott, that Jürgen was the present head of the illegal Central Committee of the KPD. Along with the emigration Communist Parties in the democratic countries, Kaspar pointed out, Jürgen was continuing to propagate anti-British and anti-American sentiment by praising the military achievements and sacrifices of the Russians. In this way doubts sown by the Nazi–Soviet Pact and the Soviet Union's abrupt volte face following Operation Barbarossa would be dispelled and renegade Communists and fellow-travellers would return to the fold. Jürgen's blind insistence on stressing continuity as opposed to change in Soviet foreign policy was intended to secure Russian dominance in Central and Eastern Europe and pave the way for a Communist takeover of Germany after the war:

> The main work of the emigration Communist Parties in the Democratic countries lies in securing for Russia a certain influence after the war. The ideological and technical conditions necessary for using Communist emigrants for this purpose, exist everywhere. The anti-British and anti-American attitude propagated for two years need not be given up at all. On the contrary, it can easily be strengthened by over-recognition of the achievements of our Russian Ally. The idea of a 'Proletarian World Revolution' under the leadership of the Comintern can at least be propagated again in their own ranks, and secretly, also among others. This will mean that a whole lot of opposition elements can be re-attracted (to the Party).
>
> The efforts of the present head of the illegal Central Committee of the KPD, Jürgen KUCZYNSKY, can be cited as an example of this.[32]

In 1942 Jürgen began to take a keen interest in the 1941 Committee and a similar grass roots organisation of the Labour Left, Forward March, associated with writer and broadcaster J.B. Priestley. The 1941 Committee was set up by a number of Left-leaning politicians, writers and other people of influence in 1940 following the evacuation of British forces from Dunkirk. Their aim was to press for more efficient production through 'stricter planning of the economy and greater use of scientific know-how'. The Committee drew its inspiration from Priestley's seven-minute radio broadcasts *Postscripts*, aired after the Sunday night news bulletin. These talks, listened to by 40 per cent of the British population, called for planning and radical change, and spoke of 'this war as one chapter in a tremendous history, the history of a changing world, the breakdown of one vast system and the building up of another and better one'.[33]   Members and supporters of the Conservative Party were outraged and complained that Priestley was introducing his own political views into his broadcasts. He was taken off the air. Priestley then set about establishing the 1941 Committee with a group of friends and, allied with Forward March, drew up a nine point plan calling for public control of the railways, mines and docks and a national wages policy, works councils and the publication of post-war plans for the provision of full and free education and a civilised standard of living for all. On 3 June the Committee replied to a letter from Jürgen:

> I understand that you are particularly interested in the relationship between the Forward March and The 1941 Committee. I think one can safely say that both organisations are reaching the point when they stand for the same things: both have accepted the Nine Point policy, and both are out to encourage the growth of constituency committees all over the country. Originally there was a difference in construction, that is to say, The 1941 Committee was attempting to build up only a skeleton organisation, whereas the Forward March movement was organised as a mass movement. I think also that there was a slight difference in approach, the Forward March movement having a rather more religious appeal. Within a few weeks now we hope to have reached merging point.[34]

Committee members were responsible for the publication of two anonymous bestselling books: *Guilty Men* by Cato (Driberg, Foot and Wintringham) and *Your MP* by Gracchus (Wintringham), both published by Gollancz, which exposed pro-Fascist sympathies among Conservative politicians.

Jürgen's interest in the 1941 Committee and 'Priestleyism' coincided with his work on Fascist economic strategy and his belief that the United Nations needed to secure the world's future based upon long-term planning. This was in keeping with mainstream Labour Party policy that by carefully managing the economy, weakening Germany after the war, joining hands with Russia, Britain would move away from a society dependent upon 'the survival of the slickest' (Priestley's phrase) towards a fairer society based on social welfarism.[35]

As a patron of the *Kulturbund*, Priestley was very supportive of the German émigré community in Britain and allowed his play *They Came to Britain* to be performed at the *Kulturbund*'s Little Theatre free of royalties. Priestley was also one of a committee of prominent British sponsors; others included D.N. Pritt and Vernon Bartlett MP, who negotiated for an empty shop in Regent Street to be used to house the *Kulturbund*'s very successful exhibition 'Allies Inside Germany' 'in support of anti-Nazi resistance inside Germany'. The exhibition opened in July 1942 before embarking on an acclaimed tour of the provinces.[36]

Jürgen's Priestleyism allowed him to make contact with a broader section of the labour movement than hitherto and he began to reconcile his experience of British-style socialism with support for Soviet Communism. His influential history of Hitler's New Economic Order in Europe, *The Economics of Barbarism*, published in 1942, was reminiscent, in places, of Priestley's radio broadcasts:

> … we must all realise that, while we are fighting for a new and better world, German fascism is already beginning to build a new and more terrible one. Out of the ruins of the old world, they are already trying to build the foundations of a world where freedom and culture are unknown, and where terror and oppression flourish. It is against this 'new' world that we are fighting – against the world they seek to construct out of the worst elements of the old.[37]

Alongside his interest in Priestleyism, Jürgen began to play a more practical role in British trade union affairs; albeit with a view to building up Communist trade unions both in exile and inside Germany in readiness for the Communist takeover of Germany. As chairman of the scientific section of the *Kulturbund*, Jürgen joined the Association of Scientific Workers (AScW) in 1941. The following May he made contact with the International Transport Workers' Federation (ITWF), sending them a copy of *The Economics of Barbarism* and requesting access to their library.[38] He received an unhelpful reply to the effect that following the Nazi invasion of Holland the ITWF had been forced to leave the bulk of its documentary material in Amsterdam: 'It has only been through the collaboration of trade unionists of the various nations that we have been able to maintain publications, which contain some reports about the conditions of workers in Fascist-ruled countries.' They recommended an ITWF pamphlet, published in great numbers, entitled *Fascism* and advised Jürgen that a trip to their library in Bedford would not be productive.[39] There may well have been reasons of a political nature for this rather off-putting reply.

At this time the ITWF was involved in negotiations with the Committee of American Federation of Labour Trade Unionists to Promote Unity of the United Nations Trade Union Movement. The purpose of these negotiations was to exclude Communists from the UN's new international trade union body then in the making. The UN's trade union movement was dominated by the American Federation of Labor (AFL), which rejected the unionisation of scientists internationally outside the UN's jurisdiction. Jürgen, who was in touch with the Communist-led Labor Research Department in the United States, was regarded by the AFL as a dangerous element, particularly as his own union, the AScW, was known to be sympathetic to Communism and was prepared to endorse the creation of an international trade union body of scientists outside UN (and, therefore, AFL) control.[40]

On 4 June 1942 Jürgen wrote again to the ITWF, this time requesting a meeting. On 8 June 1942 the AScW's organising secretary, Mrs Reinet Fremlin,[41] approached the TUC asking for information concerning the organisation of refugees in trade unions. The TUC informed her that a number of national trade union groups had already been formed to correspond with most of the countries then under Nazi occupation. The International Department of the TUC, in agreement with the International Federation of Trade Unions (IFTU), had issued a call to all Continental workers in the UK to belong to a British trade union while at the same time establishing national trade union groups.[42]

This would maintain the structure of free trade unions among foreign workers, encouraging them to rebuild after the liberation of their respective countries.[43] The AScW was advised to make contact with the IFTU as a first step towards creating national groups among scientific workers from the occupied countries. Mrs Fremlin passed the TUC's letter to Jürgen with the memo: 'This letter has not been acknowledged. Please let me have it back with your comments.'[44] Presumably Jürgen did so, although his reply is not in MI5 files. The AScW then agreed to split into two committees – one representing British scientific workers and the other foreign scientists, including a German national group, the Centre of German Trade Unions (CGTU).

The creation of a post-war international trade union movement under Western direction became a major goal of the US with the OSS, forerunner of the CIA, setting up a Labor Branch under a young Jewish attorney, Arthur Goldberg, to work with trade unions in the European underground, including inside Germany. The chief trial examiner of the National Labor Relations Board, established by Roosevelt in 1935 to prevent anti-union practices in collective bargaining, Benedict Wolf, was appointed head of OSS labour activities in London.[45] MI5's B Division undertook surveillance of German trade unionists in Britain, including Marguerite Kuczynski, and on 5 June 1942 B6 reported that contact 'D' (Marguerite) had met with Elsa Sara Cohn (a prominent member of the KPD) in the booking hall at Kingsway Station and that a letter from the 'Trade Union for German Workers in Great Britain' had passed between them.[46]

Jürgen, who had been elected chairman of the Central London Branch of the AScW in April 1942, began addressing union meetings up and down the country, prompting MI5 to step up their interest in the AScW and the CGTU.[47] Their investigation centred upon Jürgen's association with a German Communist, Heinz Kamnitzer,[48] and the inventor Geoffrey Pyke, who was then working with Lord Louis Mountbatten in Combined Operations Headquarters (COHq), the military command responsible for Commando raids on occupied Europe. In November 1941 Kamnitzer had been released from internment in Canada as a result of Pyke's determined intervention on his behalf.[49] To secure his release Pyke had offered Kamnitzer work at his Whitehall office at 19 St James's Square.[50] Kamnitzer, however, had turned down the offer as he had recently been offered employment by Jürgen as a researcher with the AScW:

> Since 16.2.1942 Kamnitzer has been employed as a research worker in the offices of the Association of Scientific Workers, 30 Bedford Row, W.C.1. This organisation is well-known to this office [Metropolitan Police Special Branch] and although its members include professors, scientists and technologists, who are beyond reproach politically, it has attracted a number of communists who are gradually gaining influence in directing its policy on communist lines.[51]

Kamnitzer, a previous editor of the *Kulturbund*'s periodical *Inside Nazi Germany*, had previously worked with Rose Schechter, the librarian to the Soviet Embassy's Press Department and the *ING*'s contact inside the Soviet Embassy. Both Kamnitzer and his wife Helga, who undertook research work for D.N. Pritt, were members of the *Kulturbund* and the Free German Institute of Science and Learning. Between 1936 and May 1940 the Kamnitzers lived at 4 Lawn Road with another German Communist, Hans Hess, and were neighbours of the Kuczynskis and other Soviet agents inside the Lawn Road Flats. In April 1942 MI5's Milicent Bagot began taking a particular interest in Jürgen, the AScW and Kamnitzer:

> KAMNITZER's connection with the Association of Scientific Workers is particularly interesting as Dr Jürgen KUCZYNSKI, the well-known German Communist and a member of the Governing Committee of the Free German League of Culture ... was recently elected chairman of this organisation.[52]

Bagot's interest in Kamnitzer coincided with his appointment as a 'Library Tracer and Reader' to the Ministry of Information (MoI), where he worked under Peter Smollett, formerly Harry Peter Smolka, head of the MoI's Soviet Relations Branch and a Soviet spy. Smollett, Austrian by birth, was suspected by MI5 of exchanging sensitive material with the *Kulturbund* through Kamnitzer.[53] In fact Smollett, who had been recruited as a NKVD agent by Kim Philby, was also passing written reports to Guy Burgess. From 19 October 1942 Kamnitzer increased his value as an agent following his appointment as assistant editor by the Petroleum Press Services, when he began providing intelligence on the economic and commercial aspects of the oil industry. This information was of great interest to the Allies and on 9 November he was issued with a Ministry of Information Press Library Pass 'in order to obtain information on production, consumption, distribution, rationing etc., of oil in Nazi Germany, occupied territories and other axis countries'.[54]

Geoffrey Pyke's association with Jürgen and the AScW was no less interesting. Pyke, one of the most famous of the Second World War's 'back-room boys', was Lord Mountbatten's 'ideas man' in Combined Operations between May 1942 and November 1944. Described by the Conservative MP Leo Amery, 'as a strange creature, Mephistophelian in appearance but with a brilliantly original mind',[55] Pyke 'was responsible for a stream of schemes, feints and military inventions including the idea, known as PLUTO, for an oil pipeline under the English Channel'.[56] He was also a key member of the Kuczynski group. Pyke had initially made contact with Jürgen in Paris in July 1939. The exact nature of this meeting, and why Paris, is unknown but there was certainly a Kuczynski family connection. On the eve of the European war, Pyke, backed by the British Institute of Public Opinion, had arranged for what MI5 then referred to as a group of 'pink' Cambridge undergraduates to visit Germany to conduct a 'Gallup survey' of German political opinion and had approached a member of the KPD's Central Committee in London, Hans Rolf Rünkel, also known as 'Protocol Hans'.[57] Rünkel, in turn, sought Jürgen's advice. Jürgen reported the matter to the KPD's leadership in Paris, who relayed a message back to London instructing Rünkel to assist Pyke. Over the next few weeks Rünkel vetted each of the young Cambridge 'pinks', none of whom was permitted to travel to

Germany until either Rünkel or his superior, Wilhelm Koenen, leader of the KPD in exile, was 'satisfied'.[58]

At that time the Assistant Director of BIPO at Aldwych House was Jürgen's brother-in-law, Tony Lewis. Pyke had also been in contact with Sabine's husband, Francis Loeffler, a propos of engaging translators sympathetic to Communism to work on his projects. Francis was then working for the Youth Relief and Refugee Council (YRRC) in London and often mentioned Pyke as a useful contact in respect of placing translators in potentially interesting positions while the latter was working at COHq. The treasurer of the YRRC at this time was Percy Timberlake, an Oxford University graduate with a degree in politics, philosophy and economics and a member of the CPGB who had worked with Pyke as a translator.[59] While working for the YRRC Timberlake was also employed full-time at the Ministry of Information before being drafted into the RAF as an education officer in October 1941. Shortly after his call-up Timberlake wrote to Francis from his station in Ayr, Scotland, mentioning Pyke's recruitment of translators:

Dear Frankie,

A friend of mine – one Elizabeth MARTINEK – an Austrian girl, is coming up to London for a week on the 14th of this month and will, on my advice, call on you or give you a ring. Could you a) think of any job she could get in London, (she types etc. and speaks French well, English fairly well, and, of course, German).

b) put her in touch with any Austrian or German youth movement or any such body. Politically she's unconscious but she's full of enthusiasm and eager to learn.

Apropos of a) – do you remember Geoffrey? PYKE – the chap I used to do translations and summaries for? He would be useful.[60]

Pyke's collection and translation of material for his 'Gallup survey' of German political opinion would not have been completed without the assistance of the Kuczynski group and the KPD's Hans Rünkel.[61] In March 1940 Pyke had attempted to reopen his investigation into political sentiment inside Germany and had written to the Independent Progressive MP Vernon Bartlett,[62] who had put him in touch with Sir Robert Vansittart.[63] Vansittart was then running his own private department within the Secret Intelligence Service (MI6) – the top secret Z Organisation controlled by the ruthless 'utter shit' Claude Edward Marjoribanks Dansey, 'Colonel Z'.[64] Bartlett also put him in touch with Sir Stafford Cripps, Sir Archibald Sinclair, Clement Attlee and Leo Amery. At this time Pyke was regarded as harmless and was described in MI5 files as a 'well-meaning intellectual along conventional New Statesman lines with a strong sentimental and Pacifist bias for the Germany of GOETHE and BACH'.[65]

The following year Pyke offered Rünkel employment gathering and translating material on the evolution of German public opinion with a view to promoting a clear strand of anti-Fascist opinion in Germany in opposition to Vansittartism, the dominant strand of thinking inside the FO, which identified Fascism as something intrinsic to the German personality. That same year Jürgen's wife, Marguerite, also began working for Pyke as a researcher.[66] On 1 August 1942 Source Kaspar reported to MI5 that, 'Rolf Rünkel was a constant visitor at Pyke's flat and was thought to be his secretary. When Pyke suspended his activities Rünkel's job had appeared to cease, and he was appointed to the leadership of the N-Apparat of the German Communist Party.'[67] Rünkel had first been introduced to Pyke by Wilhelm Koenen, the de facto leader of the KPD in Britain. Pyke, Rünkel and Koenen, therefore, were closely interconnected. Koenen, at this time, was in daily contact with the Kuczynskis. On his release from internment in March 1942 he had moved into 4d Belsize Grove, NW3, the address of Sabine and Francis Loeffler. Other German Communists living at the Loefflers' address included Emmy Damerius, formerly a Communist Deputy of the Reichstag, who was known to have visited the USSR on several occasions on behalf of the German Party. Koenen, who had been a member of the Central Committee of the KPD since 1919, was described by MI5 as 'probably the most important member' of the KPD in Britain.[68] On his release from internment he had taken over the leadership of the party in Britain from Dr E.H. Meyer, and was busy overseeing 'extensive organisational changes' to the KPD from the house he shared with Damerius and the Loefflers. Throughout this period the Loefflers were in constant contact with Ursula, who transmitted information on the KPD in Britain to Moscow Centre. An HOW was taken out on the Loefflers' address, and Milicent Bagot took personal responsibility for monitoring the Loeffler household:

> Other individuals living at 4d Belsize Grove, N. W. 3. include Emmy Damerius ... and Francis Herbert LOEFFLER and his wife, Sabine née KUCZYNSKI both of whom have been associated with Communist-controlled Youth movements. Sabine LOEFFLER is the sister of Jurgen KUCZYNSKI, a German Communist, who is the subject of H.O.W. No. 7215. It is hoped by means of a warrant to obtain information about the organisation of the German Communist movement in this country.[69]

The spy network built around Pyke and the German exiles fitted together in the following way: Kamnitzer and Smollett would work together inside the MoI maintaining contact with Pyke inside Combined Operations HQ. Kamnitzer would be paid by Combined Operations for work undertaken for Pyke while working for the MoI; Smollett would then pass intelligence from Pyke to Burgess.[70] This 'tessellated' network of German and English Communist spies had been put together by Jürgen with the help of the KPD's main intelligence personnel in the UK – Hans Kahle, Professor Alfred Meusel and Hans Rolf Rünkel.[71] Kahle and Pyke were known to be working closely together and were believed to be interested in fomenting anti-British propaganda in America. MI5 investigations in November 1942 into Kahle's activities found that he had suggested to associates 'that a trusted Party member should be sent to America, and as he himself was unable to go ... Pyke should be sent'.[72]

The intelligence gathered from Pyke covered a range of topics and was of paramount importance; it included the joint development with the Americans of a snowmobile, which could easily be adapted to the strategic needs of guerrilla warfare in Norway, code-named 'Plough' – a 'most secret technical invention' coveted by Combined Operations. Pyke called on the Americans to help set up a United Nations snow-warfare board with Norwegians, Canadians, Americans, British and Russians all working together to create an international guerrilla force.[73] In July 1941 the Soviet Union had obtained three Armstead snowmobiles from the United States and Pyke, on a visit to America, told his American military audience that the Russians 'are sure to be at work on them'.[74] The Russians, he reminded them, 'had greater experience of snow warfare and could easily supply logistical support for assaults on Romania and Norway, as well as summer training grounds'.[75]

Pyke was also in a position to give an invaluable insight into scientific and technical (S&T) collaboration between Britain and America during wartime that assisted Soviet efforts to penetrate Anglo-American co-operation on the atomic bomb. On strategic grounds Pyke's knowledge of a planned Allied assault on Norway was of great importance. It not only promised to divert German troops away from France, thereby making possible an Allied landing in occupied Europe and strengthening Russia's insistence on the opening of a second front, but also promised to seriously weaken the Fascist economic order in Europe:

> Norway produced 30,000 tons of aluminium per year from just six plants, each connected to a hydroelectric power (HEP) station. Pyke's scheme would knock out some fifty HEP stations . . . [allowing] the Allies to stunt the growth of Germany's atomic programme ... a tenfold increase in the production of heavy water (deuterium oxide) had been reported at the Vemork HEP station in southern Norway. This was the first step towards building an atomic weapon. Vemork was another of Pyke's targets.[76]

Any information gleaned by Pyke on scientific collaboration between Britain and the US would have been invaluable given the imminent transfer of Britain's atomic bomb project to Los Alamos in New Mexico. Research into nuclear weapons had been developing at a faster pace in the US than in the UK. In 1941 two American scientists, E.M. McMillan and P.H. Abelson, had discovered the new radioactive artificial element 94 by bombarding the isotope U-238 with fast neutrons. They found that 94, which was later named plutonium, was more fissionable than U-235, and offered an alternative route to the bomb without investing heavily in the large-scale separation of isotopes. Co-operation between Britain and the US in this field had always been fraught with difficulty and had reflected concerns over security, both commercial and military. In the early stages of the war Britain had dominated this research and had hoped to maintain her advantage. The formation of the Maud Committee to co-ordinate all aspects of physics and chemistry concerned with the creation of a nuclear weapon in June 1940 had been intended to make Britain's lead in this field permanent. Under the chairmanship of G.P. Thomson, the Maud Committee, working closely with the head of ICI, Lord Melchett, had intended to secure a monopoly of nuclear power production after the war. This scheme had run into difficulties early on in the project when Committee members had accepted that at some stage research would need to be transferred either to the United States or to Canada. The huge amount of capital required, the vast technological resources needed, the danger of enemy bombing, all militated against the building of a nuclear reactor in Britain, although at one point North Wales was seriously considered as a safe location. In October 1941 it was therefore agreed by a majority of the Maud Committee that the world's first nuclear production plant would have to be built in the United States, not the UK. Lord Melchett raised objections that valuable skills would be lost if all nuclear research was allowed to migrate to the US and argued that steps should be taken to safeguard the future interests of the British Empire; but his objections were overruled. A secret agreement relating to atomic energy was signed by Roosevelt and Churchill at Quebec on 19 August 1943. Under the terms of the Quebec Agreement both countries agreed not to 'communicate any information about Tube Alloys to third parties except by mutual consent'.

CHAPTER ELEVEN

The Manhattan Project and Bletchley Park

In December 1943 a decision was taken to transfer Fuchs to the USA.[1] Clandestine arrangements were made for him to contact Soviet agents in the United States and as a precaution the NKVD's New York station 'temporarily suspended' their work with Jürgen 'out of fear that English Counterintelligence might discover his connection ... with [the Soviet] embassy. Moreover, information was received that English Counterintelligence was investigating individuals connected with K [Jürgen] and gathering material on K himself.'[2]

Before Fuchs sailed for America he passed critical information to Ursula on the gaseous diffusion method of separating the uranium isotope U-235 and the mathematical methods then being deployed for evaluating the critical size and efficiency of an atomic bomb. He also reported that similar work was being done in the United States and that there was collaboration between the two countries. She gave him explicit instructions concerning his future handler in New York, who would make himself known to him sometime in February or March 1944. His contact, she told him, would be in the possession of two pairs of gloves; one pair he would be wearing and the second he would be holding in his left hand. Fuchs was told to arrive at the designated meeting place holding a green-covered book in one hand and a tennis ball in the other. Despite these somewhat bizarre recognition signs, the meeting was surprisingly successful, as recorded by his contact:

We were both at the appointed place on time at 4.00 P.M.: he had the green book and tennis ball and I had the four gloves. I greeted him and he accepted my offer of a walk. We strolled a while and talked. He is about 5 ft. 10 in., thin, pale complexioned, and at first was very reserved in manner; this last is good. K. [Klaus] dresses well (tweeds) but not fancily. After a ride on the subway, we took a taxi and went to eat. As I kept talking about myself, he warmed up and began to show evidence of getting down to business. For instance, I would say that I had felt honored at having been told to meet him and he said that he 'could hardly believe it' when he had been told that we would like him to work with us (this was in England, of course).[3]

With the departure of Fuchs to America, Ursula began working with family members and agents inside the armed forces. She had personally recruited Bridget (code name Joyce) and Renate (code name Katie) and she remained an important cog in the Soviet intelligence wheel. Bridget's latest lover, Arthur Long, a corporal stationed at RAF Hawkinge, Folkestone, was relaying important information to the GRU as a member of Ursula's group 'concerning the ordinance carried by British aircraft and the distribution of air squadrons'.[4] Hawkinge was a key RAF base during the Second World War and the closest major fighter base to occupied Europe. During the Dunkirk evacuation in May/June 1940 aircraft based there provided essential air cover for the Allied forces. Hawkinge was also one of the advanced refuelling bases when maximum range was needed for operations over France and was on the front line during the Battle of Britain. Strategically very useful, Hawkinge remained vulnerable to attack. The German commanders planning the invasion of Britain saw the seizure of Hawkinge as vital to their plans to establish a Luftwaffe-controlled airfield in Britain. During the latter part of the war, fighter squadrons from Hawkinge provided aerial support in the run up to the D-Day landings in June 1944. Following the extension of the main runway, Hawkinge acted as an emergency landing ground for returning RAF and USAAF bombers. Throughout this period Jürgen was complaining about the lack of help being given to the Soviets by the British Army and RAF:

According to DR. KUCZYNSKI the heart of the problem of the overthrow of Hitler is the active help of Great Britain for the Soviet Union. In this connection Dr. KUCZYNSKI declared that there had been much tension in the British Army, but above all in the R.A.F. An ever increasing number of men and N.C.O.s were in favour of extensive and active help for Russia, while the officers, particularly R.A.F. officers were more or less Fascist in outlook.[5]

Jürgen also sounded a pessimistic note about the RAF's ability to defeat the German Air Force. He expressed 'grave doubts as to the verity' of Churchill's statement that the British Air Force had achieved parity with its German counterpart. He introduced Ursula to Hans Kahle, 'a fertile source of information', whom she met twice a month at either her parents' or one of her sisters' flats in London. Kahle's input, Ursula later claimed, 'resulted in some useful reports to Centre, who frequently asked follow-up questions which gave us some idea of what was important to them'.[6] By this time Ursula had succeeded in making a number of military contacts and began receiving 'material that could not be sent by radio'. She continued to meet with her Soviet contact, Sergei, who gave her, neatly wrapped in 'a little parcel measuring about eight by six inches', a greatly improved transmitter. She later recalled becoming 'attached to this reliable, handy and technically superior instrument', dismantling her own transmitter, which was six times the size, and hiding the parts for emergency use.[7]

Despite the high level of professional support for Ursula, there were a number of scares throughout her English spying career. From the beginning the behaviour of her husband, Leon Beurton, who at the time of her departure for England had been forced to remain in Switzerland, caused considerable concern. Moscow Centre felt compelled to intervene and instructed Foote in Geneva to tell 'BEURTON to stop sending stupid telegrams to SONIA'. According to Foote, these were telegrams sent by Beurton through normal channels to Ursula in England 'written in plain language code' and containing 'crudely disguised criticism of RADO'. Beurton's behaviour not only threatened Ursula's network in England but also jeopardised Radó's network in Switzerland. These lapses of discipline were only halted by Beurton's return to England in July 1942. Travelling on a newly issued British passport under the name of John William Miller, Beurton had managed to secure Spanish and Portugese transit visas but the French authorities had refused him a visa through Vichy France. The British Consulate in Geneva intervened on his behalf and issued him with a new passport, which he was to surrender on arrival in the UK.[8] On 29 July he re-joined his wife, then living at 134 Oxford Road in Kidlington, and reported for military service as Leon Beurton.

In September 1942 the Beurtons rented Avenue Cottage, a detached house at 50 George Street in the Summertown district of Oxford. Their landlord was Harold Laski's wealthy and influential elder brother Neville, a High Court Judge who conducted legal work for the Home Office and MI5 and had been President of the London Committee of Deputies of British Jews between 1933 and 1939. Neville Laski and his wife Cissie lived in the villa behind Avenue Cottage and became friendly with the Beurtons. Cissie belonged to a fervently Jewish Communist family with Zionist sympathies. Her brother, a lawyer named Jack Gaster, was married to Isaiah Berlin's close friend Marie Lynd. A former member of the Independent Labour Party (ILP), Gaster had been the driving force behind a new faction on the ILP's Left wing, the Revolutionary Policy Committee, which sought independent membership of the Communist International while remaining affiliated to the Labour Party. He worked closely with Hilary and Melita Norwood, who at that time were also members of the ILP. The ILP split over the issue and in 1932 Gaster took a section of its members into the Communist Party, including the Norwoods. Gaster struck up a friendship with the Loefflers soon afterwards and carried out the legal work that allowed Hilary to change his name from Nussbaum to Norwood by deed poll in 1935. Jack Gaster and Cissie Laski's father, Dr Moses Gaster, was the chief rabbi of the Sephardic community in Britain. Cissie Laski and Gaster's connections with the Kuczynskis formed a tenuous link between the German-Jewish Communist emigration and the Zionist movement. Ursula established a good relationship with Cissie and asked her permission to erect an aerial from the roof of her cottage to one of the Laski stables in the adjoining villa. Amateur radio activities had – as in Switzerland – been strictly forbidden for the duration of the war, and the Chief Constable of Oxford, after questioning Cissie Laski, informed MI5 that the Beurtons were in possession of 'rather a large wireless set', and that they had recently erected a special pole for use as an aerial. They had also wanted a telephone installed in the house but the Telephone Exchange Services had been unable to meet their request.[9] About this time Ursula began training a Communist fitter in a car plant, known as Tom, as a wireless operator; she was also cultivating an important contact in the RAF, known only as James, whose wife and child had been evacuated from London to Oxford, who she met once or twice a month:

> James belonged to the technical branch of the Air force and had access to some of the newest developments in aeroplane construction. He got hold of exact data for us, weights and dimensions, load-carrying capacity, special characteristics, and even contrived to let me have blue prints of machines that had not yet flown.[10]

RAF personnel, considering Arthur Long's position at RAF Hawkinge, were a useful source of information for Ursula. Leon Beurton had been accepted by the RAF on 18 March 1943 and would begin training as a wireless operator with the Royal Air Force Volunteer Reserve in November.[11] During the war Barbara's husband, Duncan Taylor, served as an intelligence officer RAF rank F/Lt. A+I.12/USTAAF between 1942 and 1946. In June 1942 he was posted to Cairo as part of 54 Wireless Unit, Middle East. That same month he came to the attention of MI5 as a result of information received 'from a delicate source' that he was 'corresponding with a man called Jürgen KUCZYNSKI'.[12] Further investigation disclosed that MI5, hitherto, had not collected any intelligence on Duncan and instructions were issued to start a PF (Personal File) on his activities. This was a new departure in the investigation of the Kuczynski family and, as an indication of the importance MI5 attached to the Taylor branch of the family, the case was passed to Milicent Bagot. Miss Bagot soon discovered that previous correspondence between Jürgen and the Taylors had taken place, but that MI5 had not been aware of the Taylor surname before now:

There has been correspondence, I know, between Kuczynskis and Duncan B. TAYLOR and his wife, but it is probable that we didn't know the surname before.

As I must now refer TAYLOR to the relevant F.I. section I shd. be grateful if you could trace the previous references and make Duncan B. TAYLOR a file and send that and PF 42628 (current vol.) [Jürgen's PF].[13]

On 3 July 1942, as part of the investigation Brigadier Sir David Petrie (F1b) wrote to the Chief Constable of Oxford, Charles Fox, informing him that as Duncan was in the habit of:

taking some book on economics, lent him by KUCZYNSKI, back to his unit with the intention of spreading the gospel it seems likely that this book on economics would have a bias in favour of Communism. It may be, therefore, that TAYLOR has himself become interested in this doctrine and I should be glad if some quiet enquiries could be made into his antecedents to ascertain whether he is a member of the C.P.G.B. or has come to your notice in the past as active on behalf of any left wing organisation. We do not appear to have any records of TAYLOR in our past records.[14]

The Air Ministry, however, regarded Duncan as a highly competent if somewhat diffident officer. They sent a report to MI5 describing him as being:

of a retiring disposition and though he can at times be obstinate over petty matters he is rarely roused to anger, though he is rather nervous and irritable. He is not of a defeatist nature or a Barrack Room Lawyer and exercises little or no influence good or bad. His manner and bearing is correct. He is not known to hold subversive views and has not indulged in any sort of subversive propaganda in his present unit nor has he been reading objectionable literature. While he holds definite opinions, which are not further particularised, he is not prone to push them down other people's throats and does not air them unless they arise in general conversation. On the whole though he is described as 'peculiar' it is difficult to define this peculiarity. He has not made much show at his work and his progress has been slow.[15]

It was not considered worthwhile continuing the investigation and observation on Duncan in the Middle East was discontinued. His commanding officer was informed of the decision.

While stationed with the RAF in Egypt, Duncan had made the acquaintance of Hilary Godwin Wayment, a Cambridge graduate lecturing in English at King Fuad I University in Cairo. He had taken him under his wing along with Gershon Ellenbogen, a contemporary of Wayment's at Cambridge and a friend of Alan Turing at King's College. Ellenbogen had spent six years in the RAF as a flight lieutenant in the Intelligence Branch, serving alongside Duncan in Cairo in 1943.[16] In 1944 Wayment was back in England and lodging with Duncan and Barbara Taylor, who had been transferred to Bletchley Park. Wayment was treated almost as a mascot by the Taylors and was introduced into their circle of friends. On the 16 February 1944 he telephoned Margot Heinemann but spoke to Noreen Branson:

He would like to come and see Noreen tomorrow morning. He has just finished a journey and is pleased to be back in England. WAYMENT rings again to say he is staying with 'Dunc' TAYLOR and his wife who live only a few minutes away from Noreen. Noreen asks him to come to breakfast at 8–15. Dorothy HEINEMANN then speaks to him, and he tells her he is back on leave as the Priority Board thought he deserved some. Dorothy asks if it is true that he is staying with Duncan and Barbara …[17]

The Taylors', Heinemanns' and Branson's friendship with Wayment may well have been innocent, but it was in casual conversation about him with Margot on 5 September 1944 that Barbara let slip the fact that Duncan was working at Bletchley Park; a fact seized upon by MI5, who marked the relevant passage in their report on the Taylors dated 5 September 1944:

> Margot rang Barbara (slightly foreign) who said that they had come back on Friday. [They had been visiting Hilary in Cambridge].[18] Barbara said that Margot must be free for Hilary (man) one day. Barbara said that she was in bed cutting out educational articles in the 'Times' that he wants! She said that everything is just the same now between herself and her husband after so long as he has been 2½ years in Egypt. He is now in Bletchley …[19] [This last sentence highlighted in the margin of the report with thick pencil lines.]

Supposedly one of the best-kept secrets of the war (discussion of the work at Bletchley Park was not permitted until the mid-1970s), the code-breaking activities of Bletchley Park had been made known to a leading member of the CPGB working at the Party's headquarters in King Street by telephone. Ursula, too, was said at this time to be 'hovering around Bletchley Park', while her brother-in-law, Duncan, was employed there as a highly skilled communications officer.[20] In December 1944 Duncan was recorded as occupying the position of 276 Wing, CMF (Communications Management Force) and was stationed at the Control Commission School (Air), Viceroy Court, Prince Albert Road, Regent's Park.[21] Viceroy Court was one of the blocks of flats requisitioned by the Air Force and lived in by aircrew training at Lord's Cricket Ground during the Second World War. Duncan, however, was billed out at 62a Belsize Park Gardens, the address of Barbara's younger sister Sabine, and later Bridget. Any information he wished to pass to Ursula while billeted in London would have been executed without hindrance despite earlier investigations of Duncan by MI5.

Knowledge in the possession of MI5 that Margot Heinemann and other members of the CPGB knew of Bletchley Park's existence in 1944 should have set alarm bells ringing. Throughout the Second World War, and beyond, the Government Code and Cypher School (GC&CS) at Bletchley Park was analysing not only the diplomatic codes and cyphers of the Axis powers, but also those of the Soviet Union. Of particular interest to the Russians would have been the signals intelligence (SIGINT) organisation in India, then dealing with material from Russian, Iranian and Afghan sources. The official history of British intelligence maintains that, following Operation Barbarossa, Churchill had ordered this activity to stop since the Soviet Union was now an ally.[22] But this has since been shown to be untrue. Work on Soviet material never stopped during the Second World War and coexisted with the development of 'a precarious sigint liaison' between Soviet cryptologists and GC&CS.[23]

For much of this time one of the NKVD's top-secret British agents, John Cairncross, was working at Bletchley Park along with other Soviet experts. These included Helen Lunn, who had been promoted in December 1939 to Senior Assistant, when Dilly Knox had been appointed Chief Assistant to Commander Alistair Denniston following the retirement of John Strachey's brother Oliver from GC&CS.[24] Helen Lunn was the sister of Edith Rothstein, the wife of Andrew Rothstein, TASS correspondent during the Second World War and a leading member of the CPGB and the underground Communist Party in Britain.[25] Andrew Rothstein, who had responsibility for science and technology (S&T), had recruited top Soviet agent Melita Norwood to the NKVD in 1934 and had been working closely with the Soviet Ambassador in London, Ivan Maisky, for a number of years. In July 1934 an MI5 report concerning Soviet physicist Piotr Kapitza commented that Maisky, Rothstein and other members of the Soviet

Embassy staff were 'making mysterious motor-car drives to Cambridge and other neighbouring towns'.[26]

Cairncross had been at Bletchley Park since March 1942, where he worked in Hut 3 on the Luftwaffe order of battle. His main 'moment of triumph' was in early 1943 when he was able to warn the Soviets of the impending German armoured offensive at Kursk, code-named Operation Citadel.

> ... this was the last great German push on the Eastern Front. It proved to be the largest tank battle of the Second World War, and the information provided by Cairncross proved to be important in launching an early attack upon the German tactical air force, much of which was destroyed on the ground.[27]

Long hours of close reading in bad light had left Cairncross with failing eyesight and on 1 June 1943 he was transferred to MI6. However, decrypted material from Bletchley Park continued to find its way to Moscow through a Soviet agent in the War Office, code-named 'Dolly'. For the remainder of the war Dolly supplied the Russians with Japanese diplomatic decrypts as well as German military decrypts, the latter reputedly 'on a vast scale'.[28] The Russians were not short of Enigma material.

Cairncross was not the only one of the Cambridge Five to gain access to Bletchley Park secrets. In late 1942 Anthony Blunt, who had been appointed one of the two MI5 liaison officers to work with Bletchley Park, was monitoring the activities of Communist sympathisers and Soviet secret agents in Britain, providing intelligence that would have been welcomed by King Street and the Kuczynski network. According to his biographer Miranda Carter, in 1942 Blunt was passing to his Soviet controller Boris Kreshin 'wireless intercepts from Bletchley and weekly summaries of them', as well as 'MI5 internal documents' and 'MI5 reports on immigrants'.[29]

Barbara and Renate, both of whom had been recruited to the GRU by Ursula, cultivated a number of fellow-travellers working inside

Bletchley Park.[30] Friendly relations continued long after the war, most notably with Mary Tyler (née Southcombe), Dorothy White (née Gerrish) and the rabbinic scholar, Hyam Maccoby.

Mary Southcombe had joined the Labour Party as a teenager. While studying philosophy at Bedford College she had struck up a friendship with Barbara in London. She moved to Cambridge in September 1939, when Bedford College was transferred during the Blitz. At Cambridge, Mary was befriended by Renate as a result of student protests following the philosopher Ludwig Wittgenstein's refusal to lecture to female students. On graduation she was recruited directly into Bletchley Park, where she 'was told (with a pistol on the desk in front of her), that any mention of the code-breaking could be deemed too important for the courts to be involved'.[31]

Dorothy Gerrish studied at the LSE in Cambridge during the Second World War and joined the same circle of university friends that included Renate and Mary Southcombe. Hyam Maccoby was a 'night translator' at Bletchley Park – someone who actually saw the decrypts.[32]

The fact that Cairncross had left Bletchley Park in 1943 has obscured the fact that there were other Soviet agents, as well as fellow-travellers, accessing its closely guarded secrets. Moreover, by mid-1943 SOE in Cairo began reading Ultra decrypts that were clearly intended for others.[33] James Klugmann, one of the few fully paid-up members of the CPGB serving loyally in SOE's Cairo headquarters, also gained access to this material. A close friend of Margot Heinemann, Klugmann would play a crucial role in persuading Churchill to switch his support in the Balkans from Mihailovich's proto-Fascists to Tito's Communist partisans. In 1944, when Barbara, in casual conversation with Heinemann, informed her that her husband Duncan had been transferred to Bletchley Park this was potentially of great importance, and was unlikely to go unnoticed by the CPGB. Communist access to Bletchley Park, therefore, did not depend solely upon Cairncross; consequently, it is by no means certain that Cairncross's departure had left the Soviets totally ignorant when it came to intercepting and processing non-Morse, encyphered, radio teletype transmissions, as one historian has claimed.[34] The construction of Colossus, the machine designed by Tommy Flowers to crack Hitler's non-Morse cyphered teleprinter, Lorenz, was not a well-kept secret simply because Cairncross's eyesight failed him:

> Cairncross had left Bletchley Park at the end of 1943, well before the Post Office engineers under Tommy Flowers succeeded in re-creating the Lorenz cipher machine without seeing the original. The Kremlin … unknowingly continued using vulnerable ciphered teleprinters well after the war without being alerted to the capacity of Colossus and its successors to break open their transmissions.[35]

The willingness of historians to continue to rely on the Cambridge Five as the only Soviet agents inside British institutions creates a false impression:

> After 1945, when the Russians finally learned the sheer scale of the vast enterprise that GC&CS had established at Bletchley Park, midway between Oxford and Cambridge, and its focus on mechanising decryption, they were completely stunned. An uneasy sense of backwardness reasserted itself with a vengeance.[36]

This assessment may well need to be revised. Undoubtedly, the Soviets lagged woefully behind Britain in cryptology before Black Friday, 29 October 1948, when all Moscow's inadvertent communications with the outside world were effectively severed when they changed their cypher system. But it is by no means certain that they were ignorant of the 'sheer scale' of Bletchley Park before then.[37]

Barbara, too, had been enterprising and in 1943 had applied for employment with the Ministry of Economic Warfare (MEW) through the ministrations of Dorothy Heinemann, who had recently been transferred to the Ministry of Labour and National Service (MLNS). On 31 May 1943 MLNS informed MI5's D.L.R. Osborn that Barbara was 'being considered by the Ministry of Economic

Warfare for appointment as a Research Assistant ... The work on which she will be engaged is not of a highly secret nature and we feel that the circumstances do not warrant our Ministry of Economic Warfare turning down this candidate, who holds somewhat unusual qualifications for the particular post.'[38]

The Ministry of Labour had been trying to place Barbara since early October 1942 and Jürgen was undoubtedly pleased: 'Barbara', he remarked in a letter to Hans Gaffron[39] at the Jones Laboratory, University of Chicago, 'regards herself as a useful part of the government machinery.'[40] The position of the Kuczynskis in Britain had looked assured until April 1943, when the arrest of Ursula's ex-husband Rolf Hamburger by US authorities stoked MI5's smouldering suspicions of the family.

Hamburger's detention in Iran by the Americans was unexpected and triggered something of a crisis in Soviet intelligence circles, leading to his subsequent arrest and incarceration in a Siberian penal settlement for nine years. At the time of his arrest the Allies were not targeting each other's spies and were co-operating on Iranian soil to secure control of the Iranian oil fields and protect Allied supply routes to the USSR. British and Soviet forces had been in occupation of Iran since August 1941 after invading and overthrowing the pro-German government of Reza Shah. Under the agreement, Soviet troops would occupy northern Iran while the British would occupy the south. American troops were stationed in Iran in order to protect its Lend-Lease convoys to the Soviet Union.

Following Hamburger's arrest the Americans informed the British that he had been actively engaged in espionage and sabotage. 'On two occasions', they said, 'he was known to have bought information on railway and military installations – principally British – in Persia.' During his interrogation Hamburger maintained that he was not working against the Allies but was merely collecting information for his 'Group', the particulars of which he resolutely refused to disclose. He admitted to being a Russian agent and explained that his task 'was to collect political information about Allied intentions'. His 'interest in the railway was twofold – to discover if the Allies were really doing their best to send supplies to Russia – and to study its potentialities for post-war supplies, when Russia would be rebuilding her industries'. The Russians were undoubtedly worried by Hamburger's arrest and came forward to claim him as one of their own, demanding that the Americans hand him over to them. He was passed first to the British before being handed back to the Russians.[41]

[Hamburger] was arrested because he was found spying in neutral and British zones, the identity of his employers not being at the time ascertainable. After a week's interrogation he admitted he was working for the Russians. We informed the Soviet Security Officer who told us twenty-four hours later that he could confirm Hamburger's statement, whereupon we refrained from interrogating him further and handed him back to the Russians at dead of night on a lonely road surrounded by all the mystery of the most dramatic spy film.[42]

CHAPTER TWELVE

Jürgen and Vansittartism

In 1944 Jürgen, as we have seen, had been elected to the London area committee of the AScW and was playing a leading role in the creation of a Communist-dominated trade union of scientists in Britain. The union was not only of considerable interest to the intelligence services of Great Britain, but also to those of the United States and the Soviet Union. Jürgen's Communism, in fact, was causing considerable disquiet in trade union circles, particularly among those active in the Centre of German Trade Unions (CGTU), an official trade union organisation founded with the help of the Trades Union Congress and the IFTU. In November 1942 Jürgen's application for membership of the CGTU was rejected, as were all membership applications made by Communists.[1]

As chairman of the AScW's Central London Branch, Jürgen organised classes for scientists on trade union history and wrote an accompanying booklet, *British Trade Unionism. A Short Study Course for Scientific Workers.* It was a straightforward historical account of trade unionism in Britain interesting for its discussion of the role of scientists in production. Patriotic rather than Communistic in content, the booklet's main purpose was to integrate scientists more fully into the Allied war effort. The urgency for such a policy, he argued, had been clearly demonstrated by the 'arrival of some refugee scientists from the Continent with their vivid experience of the fate of unorganised and "unpolitical" science'. Their position in societies torn apart by war, Jürgen continued, called for the formation of a scientists' trade union that would be international – that is to say, acceptable to the United Nations – in character.[2] Given the OSS and the United States government's openly stated interest in organising only non-Communist trade unions on an international basis,

Jürgen sent a copy of his booklet to the United States Ambassador in London. That same year, 1944, the AScW developed plans for a central scientific planning organisation and in September a group of 120 MPs 'put their names to a motion calling for a Central Scientific and Technical Planning Board to organise science for war purposes'.[3]

Jürgen's personal secretary, Hans Siebert, who had been a member of the German Young Communist League in Germany, assisted him in his trade union work.[4] He was described by MI5 as 'an intelligent and clever man who will play a bigger role now that he has become established in this country'; according to Special Branch, he was secretive by nature, calling himself Juan Baptiste Siebert in order 'to cover his true origin when speaking to English persons'.[5] Why he felt this was necessary, Special Branch did not explain.

Siebert was a leading figure in the Free German Institute of Science and Learning and was responsible for the formation of the AScW's Foreign Scientists Committee (FSC). Towards the end of 1942 the FSC had been divided into two Sections: the Allied Scientists and the Free National and Refugee Scientists. A Conference on 'Scientists of the United Nations and the War Effort' was held by both Sections on 5 and 6 December 1942 at Gas Industry House. There were about 100 persons present and Jürgen was among the speakers for the session organised by the Free National and Refugee Scientists. The chair was taken by Professor John Marrack, who had previously been investigated by Special Branch. In fact, six of the speakers at this conference were under Special Branch investigation for Communist activity, including Jürgen.

Marrack was a well-known and well-respected figure in military circles. A Cambridge graduate, he had enjoyed a distinguished First World War career in the Royal Army Medical Corps and had twice been mentioned in despatches. He was appointed Medical Officer on Poison Gas to the British Army and had ended the war in charge of a mobile pathology laboratory specialising in gas warfare. He was awarded the Distinguished Service Order and the Military Cross in 1917, and was highly regarded by the British government. After the war he had returned to Cambridge as a lecturer and had worked as a chemical pathologist before taking up a similar appointment at the London Hospital Medical College. A member of the CPGB, he belonged to a well-known group of Left-wing scientists that included Lancelot Hogben, J.B.S. Haldane, J.D. Bernal and J.G. Crowther. During the Spanish Civil War he was secretary of the Spanish Medical Aid Committee and served with the International Brigade at the siege of Barcelona. He resigned his CPGB membership in 1937 but remained a close friend of Harry Pollitt.

During the depression of the 1930s scientists on the Left, including Marrack, had campaigned for a national food distribution policy to alleviate poverty.[6] Marrack advocated a food and welfare policy at a time when nutrition and food supply were matters of growing interest in scientific and political circles. The Second World War had made state control of food distribution an urgent necessity and in 1942 Marrack published an influential book, *Food and Planning*, with an introduction by John Boyd Orr, the first Director-General of the United Nations Food and Agricultural Organisation (FAO). The book examined the history of food planning, nutrition and dietary requirements during the First World War. It was an important book, setting out a blueprint for social policy in post-war Britain that anticipated the Beveridge Report, published in November 1942. Marrack's book argued for the state control of food production and distribution under a supranational body and also advocated post-war 'planning for plenty'.[7]

During the Second World War Marrack served as an adviser to the Ministry of Food and in 1943 he was appointed Director of the Bureau of Nutrition. Jürgen took a keen interest in Marrack's work, particularly in respect of 'nutrition problems' and labour conditions. Both men followed the negotiations leading up to the creation of the FAO closely and in 1943 Jürgen wrote to Mordechai J.B. Ezekiel, Economic Adviser to the Secretary of Agriculture at the US Department of Agriculture, asking him to send on reports from the recent United Nations Hot Springs conference concerning post-war food planning and distribution published by the Department of Agriculture. They were important documents and Jürgen was anxious that the reports were sent to him openly as he did not want them detained by the British censor:

Dear Mordechai:

Could you do me a very great favour? I am, as you know, always intensely interested in nutrition problems in connection with my studies of labour conditions. I assume that a considerable amount of material has been submitted by various countries to the Hot Springs conference.[8] If any of it is for the public eye could you have it sent to me to my above address. It does not matter how bulky it is: I am interested in everything I can get. Would you, if there is such material, have it sent to me from the Department of Agriculture so that the Censor sees at once that it is O.K. and does not need to make enquiries whether the material may be sent to me.[9]

Jürgen's interest in the Hot Springs conference, Marrack's *Food and Planning*, his earlier involvement with the 1941 Committee's campaign for a better future and the Beveridge Report came together to form an intrinsic part of his trade union work. As a result, the AScW increasingly addressed a number of social as well as scientific and economic questions that had a direct bearing on the Allied war effort. The AScW was gaining members in a number of important government establishments, including the Admiralty Signal Establishment (ASE) at Witley, where in February 1944 Jürgen addressed seventy members on the subject of 'Trade Unionism and the Scientist'. The meeting was to be open to all scientists working at the ASE with the specific aim to 'stimulate recruiting and to educate our present members'.

In December 1942 Jürgen had received a letter from the union's Executive Committee asking him to prepare a policy document for the AScW on the Beveridge Report.[10] On 9 April 1943 the German writer and journalist Alexander Abusch,[11] a founder member of the KPD, wrote to Jürgen from Mexico requesting an article on the Beveridge Report for publication in the Communist newspaper *Freies Deutschland*.[12] The Beveridge Report applied to Germany offered a blueprint for the reconstruction of an undivided Germany, purged of all remnants of Nazism and militarism, built upon a social welfare model that rejected the Soviet economic model of 'full employment'.

The establishment of the Free Germany Movement to create non-partisan unity among all German opposition groups to Hitler, including the exiled German trade union movement, followed *Freies Deutschland's* publication in early 1942. On 12/13 July 1943 Stalin and the Politburo of the CPSU devised a counter-strategy and moved to strengthen their grip over the KPD by overseeing the creation of the *Nationalkomitee Freies Deutschland* (NKFD, National Committee for a Free Germany) at Krasnogorsk near Moscow. The Committee consisted initially of thirty-eight members, elected at meetings of prisoner-of-war camps, twenty-five of whom were soldiers and officers up to the rank of major, while thirteen were Communist émigrés. The NKFD was inaugurated with the ratification of a manifesto for the Committee written by two German Communists, Alfred Kunella and Rudolf Hernstadt, at the beginning of June praising a number of historical Prussian liberal heroes who had allied with imperial Russia against Napoleon in 1813.[13]

The stated goal of the NKFD was a return to the borders of 1937, the opening of negotiations for peace, and the deposing and punishment of the Nazi leadership; its programme was not meant to include total defeat of Germany, let alone the 'unconditional surrender' announced by President Roosevelt on behalf of the US and Britain at the Casablanca conference in January 1943. The manifesto adopted by the National Committee was designed to attract the broadest possible support and made no mention of socialism, explicitly guaranteeing free enterprise in trade and industry:

The goal is a Free Germany.

That means:

Freedom of the economy, trade, and industry. Securing the right to work and to legitimately acquire property; returning those possessions plundered by the National Socialist ruling powers to their owners; confiscation of the assets of war-criminals and war-profiteers; the exchange of goods with other countries as the healthy foundation for a secure national prosperity.[14]

An 'Initiative Committee for the Formation of a Free German Movement' in Britain was set up by the KPD and SPD at the end of July 1943 and Robert Kuczynski was elected as president.[15] In December he was offered the position of Demographic Adviser to the Colonial Office in Downing Street and his application vetted by Milicent Bagot at MI5, who did not raise any objections to his employment on the understanding that he would not to be given access to confidential information:

> As spoken. Professor Robert Rene KUCZYNSKI, although not known definitely to be a member of the Communist Party is a leading member of the Free German League of Culture, which is under Communist control, and of the Executive of its recent offshoot, the Free German Movement. Moreover his son, Jurgen, is a prominent member of the German Communist Party in this country.
>
> I do not wish, however, to raise any objection to Professor Robert Rene KUCZYNSKI's proposed employment as I understand from you that it will not give him access to confidential material.[16]

However, on 13 January 1944 Miss Bagot, on learning that Robert would be granted office space in the Colonial Office, had second thoughts and advised MI5 'to put up a case against his appointment'. 'All his children', she pointed out, 'have come to notice in a Communist connection.'[17] She was supported by Roger Hollis in F Division (Countersubversion), who sent her the following handwritten memo:

> With reference to Min 331 you should tell the Colonial Office that Kuczynski is an associate of Communists, that his children have come to notice in a Communist connection, and that there is a

distinct risk that information he gets will be given to the Communist Party. The Colonial Office must assess the danger of employing him in the light of this.[18]

Hugh Shilito, the head of F2(b) and F2(c), respectively Comintern and Soviet intelligence sections within F division, shared Hollis's opinion: 'We spoke about this case to-day ... I think it would meet the case if you would reply to the Colonial Office on the lines suggested by Hollis at [Minute] 332.'[19] The Colonial Office, however, was not impressed and overruled their objections.

At this time Robert and Jürgen were campaigning against Vansittartism – the belief that Germany was inherently militaristic and Fascist in outlook – among the German exile community and sympathetic elements in the British labour movement. On 3 August 1943 at a joint meeting of the Birmingham Co-operative Society and the *Kulturbund*, Jürgen had spoken out on the 'Situation Inside Germany', the subject of an article he had published in the June edition of the *Left News*. Its significance lay in the distinction Jürgen drew between good and bad Germans, which in the climate of anti-German prejudice then prevailing in Britain was directed against the views of the Foreign Office and anti-German sentiment in the labour movement.

Vansittart, by attacking German traditions and culture, had given his name to an anti-German racialism that regarded all Germans as inherently aggressive and made no distinction between Nazism and the German people. Jürgen believed that if Vansittartism became the dominant 'ideology' in the Foreign Office then opposition to Nazism inside Germany would become increasingly difficult. An MI5 informant, who met with Jürgen socially after the Birmingham meeting, reported that Jürgen was profoundly distressed about the tendency to support Vansittartism in the Labour Party – 'this', he complained, 'boded ill for the German workers getting much backing officially from the British Labour Party if they attempted to take over German Industry.'[20]

Jürgen's lecture and article in the *Left News* reiterated the Communist line that it was actually the strength of the opposition to Hitler inside Germany in 1939 that 'induced Hitler to start war in September 1939'.[21] There was some truth in this. Ever since 1938 economic discontent had been growing in Germany, where a shortage of consumer goods coupled with measures for the conscription and direction of labour had sparked widespread labour unrest, culminating in the autumn crisis of 1939. This crisis had forced the Nazi government to back-pedal in the economic sphere while at the same time forcing them to adopt desperate plans to extend the war.[22] 'The opposition', Jürgen argued, 'had thrown down a challenge to the Nazi Government but had simply been too weak to stop Fascism and overthrow it.'[23] Hitler's barbaric campaigns, he maintained, owed more to the pernicious nature of Fascist ideology and its ability to destroy a whole people than it did to any inherent aggressive inclinations in the German people. It was a dangerous error for Vansittartism to simply dismiss Fascism as something peculiar to the German people. To do so not only ignored the ideology's ability to survive and adapt to its environment, but also downplayed the danger that it could easily re-emerge in a more acceptable form:

You all know how German troops – not only the officers, not only special Fascist formations – behave in the conquered countries, and especially in the Soviet Union. It is not necessary to emphasize this here. But what must be emphasized here is that all this shows what Fascism can do to a people. Some say that it is in the character of the German people to have soldiers committing such crimes. These people insist that it is only natural for Fascism to have grown in Germany, a country predestined to such a regime. For them Fascism is only the expression of the German character. I think that such people underestimate the danger of Fascism; they do not understand the true character of Fascism. It is not the character of the German people which makes them willing tools of German Fascism, such as the German soldiers are to-day. No, it is the character of Fascism which enables it under certain circumstances to turn any people, the

German people as well as other people, into hordes of barbarians. Once Fascism has come to power – in any country – the task of overthrowing it is a terribly hard one, and is of the utmost urgency in order to stop it from poisoning a whole people.[24]

Jürgen, however, often strayed dangerously close to Vansittartism. There was a real fear, he concluded, that if the German people failed to accept shared guilt for the atrocities committed against other peoples, then nationalist thought would continue to disrupt Germany and rob the nation of its people:

That is the historic guilt of the German people, and that is also the personal guilt of the common people of Germany. Never in the history of mankind have a people borne so heavy a historic guilt, and never have a people counted among their sons and daughters so many criminals. That is the appalling evil which Fascism has brought to the German people, and that is the reason why we German anti-Fascists, who have grown up as sons and daughters of this people, feel a special hatred for Fascism. For Fascism has done something to us which it has not done to anyone else: it has robbed us of our people.[25]

Gollancz, the publisher of *Left News*, printed Jürgen's article without editorial comment in the column headed 'basis of discussion', which was unusual. He would only comment, he told Jürgen, when he 'specifically' disagreed 'with a good deal of what is said. I agree <u>broadly</u> with your lecture though I think there is just a tendency in it to slip near to the border of Vansittartism. I know, however, that you would never actually slip on to the border or over it!'[26] To counter such criticism, Jürgen drew attention to the shift in Communist politics towards 'National Bolshevism', a position that had first appeared in Germany in 1919 and had reappeared in the manifesto for the National Committee for a Free Germany to the Wehrmacht and to the German people issued in Moscow. National Bolshevism and German patriotism had found common expression in the concept of the Soviet regime as the culmination of a thousand-year, popular patriotic struggle to maintain Russia's independence in the face of foreign threats, which recalled the creation of the Russo-German Legion in 1812 enabling Prussians to fight in the Tsar's armies.

During the course of the Second World War Soviet Communism had redefined itself as being more of a patriotic political movement than a revolutionary and socialist one. This did not mean that the Communist Party of the Soviet Union had abandoned Marxist ideology or reneged on its commitments to international revolutionary goals but it did mark 'a sea change in Soviet ideology': an acceptance of the 'superiority of populist, nativist, and even nationalist rallying calls' over 'utopian idealism'.[27] Jürgen drew heavily upon the National Bolshevism of Dr Heinrich Laufenberg and Fritz Wolffheim, writing enthusiastically about those historical Prussian figures that had featured so prominently in Kunella and Hernstadt's NKFD manifesto. On 28 August 1943 he wrote to Paul Merker in Mexico[28] suggesting a pamphlet criticising the Western Alliance's failure to open a second front in Europe by comparing the current war situation to that of 1812 when, with Napoleon's forces laying waste to Moscow, an anticipated British–Swedish landing on the Continent had failed to materialise because of fears of 'Jacobinisation':

> I have just prepared a lecture on Free Germans in Russia in 1812 and in 1943. It is absolutely incredible, how many problems were solved in a similar way. To read about the work of Stein's friends among the prisoners of war in Russia, or their expectations of a British–Swedish diversion by landing on the Continent, or Stein's warning against a 'Jacobinisation' of the freed territories while emphasising at the same time the need for united action in which everybody from the decent prince to the peasant must take part – all this and much more in 1812![29]

The campaign against Vansittartism and in support of a second front was seen by Jürgen as much in patriotic as revolutionary socialist terms and was, therefore, compatible with Stalinism. It was both a continuation of the fight against Fascism and a vehicle for support of the Soviet Union in anticipation of a post-war settlement favourable to Communism. It fed directly into the formation of the Free German Movement (FGM) in the UK on 28 September 1943 at Trinity Church Hall, Finchley Road, NW3.

At the foundation meeting two distinct tactics could be discerned: support for the stated goals of the NKFD in Moscow and action against anti-German racialism in Britain centred upon Vansittartism. The first plenary session of the FGM took place on 17 November 1943 at the premises of the *Kulturbund*, where Robert gave a short address on the immediate aims of the FGM, which he listed as:

To influence the British public in favour of the Free German Movement's activities.
To exert an influence on propaganda to Germany and especially on the B.B.C.'s German transmissions.[30]

The FGM, Robert concluded, 'also had the task of preparing a constitution for post-war Germany and shaping its political and economic form'.[31] While strongly anti-Fascist, however, at heart he remained a German patriot opposed to the partition of Germany. At a meeting of the FGM's organisation committee on 11 January 1944, called to discuss recent statements by the Russian and Polish governments on their plans for a post-war Germany, he forcefully attacked both governments for their anti-German position and strongly condemned their decision to partition Germany:

If Germans were to be put under the Poles he could only advise them to stick to the Nazis, for their lot would be far worse with the Poles than with the Nazis. The intentions of Russia and Poland were the greatest cultural outrage of the 20th century. There was not an atom of justice in them.[32]

After the German defeat at Stalingrad in the winter of 1942–43 and the great tank battle in the Kursk salient in July 1943, German refugees of all political persuasions began to discuss what a post-war Germany would look like. This opened up divisions within the German refugee community and violent differences of opinion within the KPD. These divisions practically paralysed the British and Mexican Free German Movements. In Britain, zealous supporters of the Moscow line opposed the more appeasing policies of Wilhelm Koenen. Although Moscow had outlined its plans for post-war reconstruction in Germany by identifying a number of specific goals, Koenen had wanted to learn more about Allied plans before endorsing the Moscow line. However, the reluctance of the Allies to discuss their plans openly, particularly with the Communist opposition to Hitler, weakened Koenen's position. Jürgen, as a member of the editorial committee of the London-based FGM's monthly periodical *Freie Tribüne,* was drawn into the dispute and made good use of his contacts inside the CPGB. On 4 April 1944 he addressed the Commercial Group of the CPGB, deploring 'the lack of official Policy on the intended Allied occupation and re-education of Germany', insisting 'that the progressive forces, and especially the Communists, would play a leading part in the post war Reconstruction'.[33]

Jürgen now published two articles in the *Left News,* July and August 1944, setting out the case for the preservation of the trusts and large-scale economic enterprises in Germany after Hitler's defeat. This was regarded by the KPD in Britain as heresy and Jürgen was accused of taking a reactionary stand and of deviating from the Party line. He was forbidden to speak in public and his talk to the *Kulturbund* scheduled for 15 September on 'Germans and Poles' was cancelled. Over the following month the breach between Jürgen and the KPD widened following the publication of his pamphlet *Ueber die Unpraktischkeit des deutschen Intellektuellen* (*On the unpractical nature of German intellectuals*). The KPD in Britain took 'severe measures' against him as a result and, despite an impeccable Party record, he was threatened with expulsion. Stern criticism of Jürgen's pamphlet came from the

Czech-German-Jewish Communist Paul Reimann, who described it 'as a false interpretation of new and right ideas, as a reactionary distortion of history and as containing a description of Hitler's war against which no German imperialist would protest'.[34] However, *Ueber die Unpraktischkeit des deutschen Intellektuellen* had been issued by the Communist-controlled *Kulturbund*, which meant that the Central Committee of the KPD in Britain had been familiar with the manuscript before it was published. Since the Central Committee had approved its publication before sharply criticising and vehemently rejecting its argument, MI5 believed that the KPD's attack on Jürgen was 'a put up job'. The KPD, they concluded, 'wishe[d] to use KUCZYNSKI for some purpose whereby he must appear not as a member of the Communist Party but as a renegade and a reactionary'.[35]

MI5 were, in fact, working along the right lines. The Economic Warfare Division of the American Embassy had first approached Jürgen with a request for detailed information on economic conditions inside Germany in October 1944. Subsequently, the US Bombing Research Mission (USBRM) had asked for Jürgen to be vetted by MI5 as they wanted to send him to France as a statistician with the US Army Air Force Survey team.[36] Jürgen's technical qualifications made him eminently suitable for the job and the security service raised no objections other than to warn the Americans that he was a leading member of the KPD. He 'should be employed in such a way', they warned, 'that his political bias would be prevented from coming into play and influencing his conclusions'.[37] This latter request proved impossible to implement, and MI5's decision to give Jürgen full security clearance had disastrous consequences. As an intelligence analyst in the economic field he was granted access to key ministerial and municipal records relating to Germany's war economy as well as the political and morale effects of bombing on the German population. Employed at the headquarters of the Air Service Command of the United States Strategic Air Forces in Europe at 40 Berkeley Square, Jürgen was no longer under British jurisdiction, and was only answerable to the American authorities. He was given the rank of lieutenant colonel in the US Army and worked closely with two OSS officers, Richard Ruggles and a Norwegian called Ohlin. Between them they worked out a system accessing 'statistics of production' relating to armaments production and oil consumption. This was Top Secret material sent direct to Roosevelt, Churchill and their General Staff. Jürgen, with the assistance of Ursula, made sure that Stalin and his General Staff were also added to the list of recipients.[38] At the same time, Jürgen's LBC associate, John Strachey, became secretary of the Anglo-American Strategic Targeting Committee with responsibility for deciding what should be bombed. Strachey now began a series of broadcast talks, 'air commentaries', that made him as popular a radio personality as J.B. Priestley had been in 1941. The inspiration behind these talks was 'the ubiquitous Guy Burgess, who was then at the Ministry of Information'.[39] According to the Labour MP Richard Crossman, these talks were 'a vital factor in quelling public protest against Bomber Harris's total destruction of German cities'.[40] The British intelligence agent given the responsibility of monitoring Jürgen's activities for the US Bombing Research Mission was Kim Philby.

In the autumn of 1944 Jürgen had been offered the position with Air Service Command of the United States Strategic Air Forces in Europe because of his knowledge of economic conditions in Germany. Before Jürgen accepted this employment, Ursula had contacted Moscow Centre seeking their approval for his employment by the American intelligence service, the OSS, forerunner of the CIA. Moscow Centre did not waste any time: according to Ursula their 'reply came quickly. They were very interested. Now I regularly obtained useful reports from Jürgen.'[41]

At the beginning of 1945 Jürgen spent three weeks in Paris on a confidential mission for the OSS. According to his account, the Americans provided him with 'a special plane to take him over', and put a car at his disposal. While there he met with a number of German Communists including Thea Saefkow, widow of the leader of the German Communist resistance in Berlin, Anton Saefkow. Before his arrest in June 1944 and execution at Brandenburg-Görden Prison in

September, Saefkow had been the architect of a very effective anti-Nazi organisation in Germany, which involved a number of factory groups in the main Berlin armament works. These groups were organised on a clandestine three-member cell system and were engaged in anti-war propaganda and industrial sabotage.[42] Jürgen's 'confidential mission' was to try and establish contact with the remnants of these groups through exiled German Communists in Paris. During his stay in Paris he was approached by a high-ranking American intelligence officer, who informed Jürgen that he was 'furnished' with the 'most precise information about his past', that he knew 'all about his Communist activities in England and also his relations with Moscow'.[43] He offered Jürgen 'a special mission to Germany after the war', an offer he accepted without hesitation.[44]

On 7 May 1945 Special Branch reported that Jürgen had 'been arranging for members of the German Communist Party to be dropped into unoccupied parts of Germany through the American Air Force in this country'.[45] Joseph Gould, an OSS lieutenant who had been assigned the task of recruiting German refugees for espionage missions inside Germany, had made the approach to Jürgen asking for assistance in selecting suitable recruits. Jürgen, the report warned, appeared to be making use of the Americans to establish 'a nucleus' for the KPD inside Germany. Ursula passed details of the plans to Moscow Centre, who gave her instructions to work with Gould but to exercise extreme caution. Jürgen, who had planned to follow the US Army into liberated Germany and to take charge of a re-established Communist Party on German soil, was stood down. Jürgen had nothing more to do with the affair, and Ursula took over, never meeting Gould directly. 'The comrade who was chosen as go-between was Erich Henschke, a member of the London branch of the German Communist Party.'[46]

Working with Hans Kahle and Wilhelm Koenen, Henschke drew up a list of suitable German Communists living in Britain and Ursula relayed their details to Moscow for approval. They then 'underwent two months' of intensive training, which included parachute jumping and how to operate a 'walkie-talkie', a sensational invention that the

GRU later claimed had been developed especially for the parachutists.[47] Invisible ink, poison capsules and food concentrates were all part of their equipment. They also had to learn a numerical code system by heart; their passports, clothing and life stories were prepared with great care. Ursula reported all the details to Moscow Centre, despatching photographs and biographical information on the seven parachutists labelling them 'Denis 1' to 'Denis 7'. Ursula also sent Moscow Centre a description of the walkie-talkie (code-named 'Rabbit') and the cypher code to be used by the parachutists when making contact between the ground and aircraft overhead:

> Each of the comrades was to be parachuted into Germany on a predetermined day, at a specific time and place. Immediately after landing they were to hold their walkie-talkies in readiness so that a US plane circling the area could establish contact with them.[48]

Of the seven parachutists, five were known to have survived. One 'almost certainly lost his life', while the fate of the parachutist known as Kurt Gruber remains unknown, though Special Branch concluded that it was 'highly probable' he had been killed. Either his plane crashed on take-off, as Ursula claimed, or he was successfully dropped into the Ruhr by the American Air Force and soon disappeared. It was also possible that he had gone 'underground' as a Communist organiser and that he had simply not made himself known to the Allied Forces of Occupation.[49]

Jürgen returned to Germany in November 1945, residing at Berlin-Zehlendorf, Klopstockstrasse 34 in the American Sector until 31 December 1947. Between 17 November 1945 and 30 April 1946 he was employed by an American Air Force Unit in Berlin-Dahlem as a civilian 'adviser and statistician' as part of the US Office of Military Government for Germany (OMGUS). He then lost contact with the Americans, while the Soviets made enquiries as to his whereabouts.

A 'Report on Jürgen Kuczynski aka "Karo"' prepared by a Russian NKGB agent in 1946 working in the United States,[50] claimed that about this time the American station took steps to renew contact with Jürgen after first checking out his position. The NKGB's Berlin station also made an approach in December 1945 in an attempt to renew their own ties. However, according to the report on 'Karo', he 'categorically refused the offer to work with our organs for a long time, saying that this would be a burden on him, that as a German Communist, he supposedly wanted to work only for Germany, not for the Allied occupying forces, and so forth'.[51]

As a consequence of Jürgen's reticence to work with the NKGB, the Soviet intelligence organs in Berlin remained highly suspicious and dismissed him as a 'double-dealer' and of little operational value. His earlier confrontation with the KPD leadership in London over the decision of the Big Three[52] to pursue the destruction of Germany's military and industrial potential taken at Tehran was brought up and used against him. Far from being the put-up job MI5 had suspected, Jürgen's 'reactionary' views on Tehran had undermined his position with the NKGB and the London and Moscow factions of the KPD. As far as they were concerned, he could no longer be trusted even after he had agreed to co-operate:

> He agreed to co-operate in the future only under strong pressure, but in all this time he has not given any valuable material, getting away with reports of low value. At the same time he made a great effort to find out from us which of the Germans trusted by Soviet occupying forces we would like to install among the leading personnel of the future German central departments, saying that he has the necessary connections in the circles of the Amer. Military administration to potentially advance the necessary individuals to these positions. Considering K's blatantly suspicious behaviour, we did not give him these individual's names. K subsequently continued to insist on being excused from working with us and submitted several written statements to this effect. Around the same time, we received a copy of the resolution of the London organisation of the KPD for 1944 through the CC KPD apparatus, in which K is described as someone

with reactionary views who does not agree with the decision of the Tehran Conference of the Big Three regarding the need to disarm G[ermany] and destroy its military and industrial potential created by the Nazi regime.

Given the suspicions about K as a double-dealer, as well as his unequivocal declaration that he does not wish to work with us and his low operational value, it was decided to sever future ties with him as an agent, and since 6.8.46, the Berlin station has stopped being in contact with him.[53]

Jürgen had, in fact, resigned from OMGUS in 1946 in order to take up a chair in economic history at Humbolt University, East Berlin, on 1 September and the Soviets, if not exactly hostile, had continued to regard him with suspicion.

CHAPTER THIRTEEN

Bridget, Arthur Long and Paul Jacot-Descombes

In May 1945 Ursula moved to a farmhouse in the picturesque Cotswold village of Great Rollright. Micha was at boarding school and her husband was serving with the RAF in Germany, but she took with her Janina and Peter, her two youngest children.[1] Two months later, new evidence came to light linking Ursula with Radó and the *Rote Drei*. The FBI had obtained an address book belonging to Rolf Hamburger's father from a highly confidential source. Inside they found a note saying that his son could be contacted through the address 129 Rue de Lausanne, Geneva. This was the former address of Ursula and Leon Beurton and within striking distance of Sandor Radó's residence at No. 113. The FBI now approached MI5, asking for Ursula to be interviewed about the present whereabouts of Hamburger; MI5's J.H. Marriott, however, advised against this. If Ursula was questioned she would simply warn the group that they were being investigated. Marriott wrote instead to Philby, asking him to make enquiries in Switzerland about the Rue de Lausanne addresses:

> The F.B.I. have now asked us to question Ursula BEURTON ... For a variety of reasons I do not feel able to comply with this request, but I observe that when Ursula BEURTON arrived in this country in February 1941 she gave as her 'last address outside the U.K.' 129 Rue de Lausanne, Geneva, and furthermore stated that to the best of her knowledge Leon BEURTON was still residing there. I am wondering whether you could make enquiries in Switzerland as to this address, and also whether you could let me have any information as to the present whereabouts of Rudolf HAMBURGER.[2]

144

Philby's enquiries revealed very little other than that the concierge at 129 Rue de Lausanne knew nobody by the name of Rudolf Hamburger and that there was no nameplate on or inside the building containing the initial R. 'There were some 24 tenants living there (an apartment house), the majority of whom were, according to the concierge, Swiss businessmen.'[3] Further checks were to be made to ascertain whether or not Beurton was still in residence. Beurton, at this time, was serving as a Guardsman with the 1st Battalion of the Coldstream Guards, British Army On The Rhine (BAOR).

The American station of the NKGB learnt of these investigations and, as a result, in January 1946 Ursula was made 'inactive'. A memo to the NKGB from the GRU stated that 'no personal contact with her is maintained'.[4] A special arrangement, however, setting up a 'dead drop' was agreed to help Ursula overcome the psychological and financial consequences of loss of contact:

> A few miles from Great Rollright, the Oxford to Banbury road passed under the railway; beyond the first crossroad after the underpass a message would be found under a hollow root of the fourth tree on the left. A monthly date for collecting had also been fixed.[5]

Ursula cycled to the 'dead drop' every month but on each occasion there was nothing there. It was a frustrating period; having been active for so many years, she missed the excitement and found it difficult to fill her empty days. Although she had recently joined the CPGB, together with Beurton, her local branch in Banbury was too far away for her to make any meaningful contribution. The situation changed dramatically in July 1947 following Alexander Foote's defection to the British with specific information that he had worked with Ursula in Switzerland. He told his MI5 interrogators that in all probability she had remained a Russian spy. On or around 18 August 1947 he informed his interrogators that both Bridget Lewis and Robert Kuczynski had also known the true nature of Ursula's activities at the time of his recruitment. Bridget now resurfaced as a person of immediate interest.

Foote also told his captors that both he and Leon Beurton had been recruited to the Russian intelligence service by Bridget at the Lawn Road Flats in 1938. He also alleged that Tony Lewis, who was still living in the Lawn Road Flats, had been a member of the CPGB since 1940. In a minute written by MI5's J.H. Marriott it was made clear that while there was no significant evidence linking Tony Lewis with his wife's espionage activities, suspicions remained.

Marriott pointed out that Lewis was known to be in touch with Jürgen and it was therefore 'likely' that he was fully aware of the nature and extent of the Kuczynski family's spying activities.[6] A decision was taken to apply for an HOW on 'Any Name' 4 Lawn Road Flats, NW3 and for a telephone check on Primrose 2701, the telephone installed at this address. 'This check,' it was stated, 'is likely to provide useful information not only about their [Tony and Bridget's] own activities, but also about those of the other members of the KUCZYNSKI family.'[7] It was also decided to inform the BBC that while the security service had 'no direct evidence as to the political sympathies of LEWIS himself, his wife is well known to us as an active member of the underground organisation of the Communist Party, and continues to come to our notice in that connection'. Owing to the fact that 'LEWIS may have come under his wife's influence he should not be employed in any position where he may have access to secret or confidential information'.[8]

Consequently, in 1947, prior to his appointment as Assistant in Charge of Overseas Audience Research with the BBC, Lewis came up 'for urgent vetting'. At this time Anglo-American intelligence was scooping up all the ordinary radio programmes being broadcast round the world and analysing them for 'Communist propaganda' or 'political significance'.[9] Lewis followed developments in this field closely. The formation of the Information Research Department (IRD) by the Labour MP Christopher Mayhew in 1948 to counter Soviet propaganda in the British labour movement had put in place a 'set of Anglo-US arrangements' for this purpose. The BBC monitored its share of international programmes for the CIA from its station at Caversham, just outside Reading, while in the United States the

Foreign Broadcast Information Service undertook the same job. The CIA kept a liaison officer at Caversham to dictate requirements, and the Foreign Office paid the BBC's bills.[10] Nevertheless, despite working closely with MI6 and MI5, Mayhew's IRD was almost immediately betrayed to the Russians by his personal assistant, Guy Burgess.

Bridget, who had recently fallen upon hard times, now began to show an interest in her ex-husband's work. Following their separation she had moved to 62a Belsize Park Gardens, NW3, in January 1946 and had changed her name by deed poll to Long on 26 February.[11] Her partner, Arthur Long, the one-time RAF corporal who had been based at Hawkinge and a GRU agent, had been demobilised on 1 January 1946 and their second child, Laura, had been born four months later on 31 May.[12] Exactly a year later Long moved to Glasgow to work with the *Daily Worker*'s Scottish correspondent, Harry McShane, and his relationship with Bridget ended. On his return to London he married Pauline Miller, née Ornadel, and Bridget was left without financial support. In July 1947 Long signed an application for a passport for his two children, describing himself as their father, but then had very little to do with them.[13]

Bridget now relied on the Communist Party for support. MI5's listeners monitoring Bridget's telephone calls reported that she was very well known in the offices of the paper and appeared to have a good relationship with the chief sub-editor, Allen Hutt. She began writing the *Daily Worker*'s 'Radio Recommend', dictating over the telephone her selection of radio programmes for the following day. On 28 August 1947 she rang Tony Lewis to ask him what he knew about forthcoming discussions concerning the setting up of a UNO radio station scheduled for a UNESCO conference to be held in Paris the following week. Bridget was writing an article for the *Daily Worker* on the subject: 'You see,' she informed Lewis; 'the whole thing is meant to be an article on radio, and not necessarily on programmes only.'[14]

Despite Bridget's long association with the CPGB and Foote's recent testimony against her, MI5 decided not to interrogate her for the following reasons:

the amount of information we had regarding her role in the [Beurton] affair was insufficient to act as a basis for an interrogation; because she was an active Communist whose attitude was not likely to be helpful to us.[15]

It was a foolish decision. Bridget, at this point, had begun taking in lodgers associated with the Egyptian Communist Party, among them the Swiss journalist Paul Jacot-Descombes. An important figure on the French and Egyptian left, Jacot-Descombes had been the inspiration behind the creation of the *Ligue Pacifiste* in Egypt in 1935 and its affiliation to the *Rassemblement Universel pour la Paix* (Universal Peace League), a pre-Popular Front organisation in France. In Egypt the *Ligue Pacifiste* had been exclusively made up of foreigners, most of them Greek or Jewish, and had worked closely with the Egyptian Women's Movement and Leftist circles within the Wafd Party.[16] During the Second World War the threat emanating from the Fascist axis and the growing influence of the Soviet Union had encouraged the formation of a number of Marxist study groups in Cairo by both foreign and Egyptian intellectuals including the *Groupe d'Études*, which was founded by Jacot-Descombes in 1939 to succeed the *Ligue Pacifiste*. The *Groupe d'Études* included among its twenty to thirty members virtually all the Jewish activists who were to go on to direct the Communist movement in Egypt in the 1940s, among them the Soviet agent George Blake's influential cousins, Henri and Raoul Curiel.[17]

On 18 July 1947 MI5 intercepted a letter from Bridget to Ursula inviting her to visit and letting her know that Jacot-Descombes had agreed to prolong his stay: 'Paul is going to stay after all, he'll move into the little room ... Let me know when you come here – better announce yourself.'[18]

Jacot-Descombes's Swiss connection alone, given Foote's recent denunciation of Bridget and Ursula's work in Switzerland, should have been reason enough for MI5 to question Bridget. Nevertheless, they persisted in their hands-off approach.

Also among Bridget's lodgers in 1947 were Barbara and Duncan's acquaintance from Cairo and Cambridge, Hilary Wayment, now working for the British Council, and Alan Whittleton, a leading member of the Egyptian Communist Party (ECP). Whittleton and Jacot-Descombes worked together closely in the offices of the *Daily Worker* producing the CPGB's influential *Egyptian Newsletter*, until it folded in mid-1952. Bridget's ex-lover, Michael Carritt, along with Allen Hutt, also worked on the production of the *Newsletter*.[19]

Whittleton, alias Alan Nicholson, a Cambridge graduate and a teacher in Egyptian schools for nearly twenty years, had been secretary of Gollancz's Left Wing Book Club in Moharren Bay, Alexandria, Egypt. He had been active in the peace movement in Egypt and had organised the ECP's education study groups in Alexandria and Cairo. Fluent in Arabic, he was also a member of the Middle East Committee of the CPGB along with his wife Serena. Other members of the Committee included R. Page Arnot, (chairman), the historian George Rudé (vice-chairman) and the Jewish scholar Chimen Abramsky (secretary).[20]

Bridget worked with the Egyptian Communist Party and fully supported the 1947 UN plan for the partition of Palestine, which saw the immediate task as the liberation of Palestine from British imperialism. She was not drawn towards Zionism and neither Jacot-Descombes nor Whittleton were Jewish. All three supported Arab independence movements and accepted the Soviet line in the Middle East. In May 1947, however, the Moscow line changed dramatically. The Kuczynski family had contacts on both sides of the Arab–Jewish conflict and the fault lines between Arab and Jew were often thrown into sharp relief by the outgoing telephone calls of Jacot-Descombes from Bridget's flat in Belsize Park. These calls, monitored by MI5, gave evidence of confused loyalties among opponents of the British Mandate for Palestine. On one occasion Jacot-Descombes criticised D.N. Pritt, a close Kuczynski family friend, for his support of the Jewish Agency's illegal immigration policy and response to the '*Exodus* 1947' incident.

The SS *Exodus* carrying 4,515 Jewish immigrants from France to British Mandatory Palestine had been boarded by the British Navy in international waters and returned to France and the British-controlled zone of post-war Germany. Pritt, acting as counsel for the Jewish Agency, had served a writ of habeus corpus on the Colonial Secretary Creech-Jones and Foreign Secretary Ernest Bevin, designed to prevent the return to Germany of the *Exodus* refugees, many of whom had no legal immigration certificates for Palestine and were Holocaust survivors. Jacot-Descombes sympathised with the British Labour government's view that immigration into Palestine from Europe was illegal and that the Jewish problem could not be solved in Palestine alone. The Egyptian Communist Party favoured Jewish–Arab co-operation under the aegis of the Soviet Union leading to a two-state solution, but both of these positions were rejected by Zionists as dangerous and subversive:

Paul (Jacot-Descombes): ... Pritt is briefed by the Jewish Agency. I don't think he is permanently with them though. I know that when he was in Egypt he met some of our friends there and they discussed the situation in Palestine and so on, and he was very astonished to hear that they were against immigration.

I read just by chance in a Swiss paper that the International Red Cross had appointed three doctors from Switzerland, in agreement with the British Government, to examine these refugees – the whole point is that the British obviously knew about the whole thing before those Jews ever left on their first trip to Palestine. Of course it is simply outrageous what the British are doing to these Jews – to keep them at sea all this time.

Unknown: The Daily Worker articles simply do not meet the case at all. And I gather they have turned down your article.

Paul: No, they didn't turn it down.

Unknown: Because I heard Michael Carritt say ...

Paul: No, it was a question of Arab Jew clashes – they agreed that if and when serious outbreaks occurred, they would use my article, and have a leader on the subject, but so far no more serious clashes have occurred … But I think I will ring them up tomorrow about this Jewish ship business, or perhaps I will ring up somebody on the Jewish Committee.[21]

In fact, Jacot-Descombes took a highly critical of the position taken up by the *Jewish Clarion*,[22] the newspaper of the Jewish Communists in Britain, for its attacks on the Arab Liberation League and for its stance on Jewish immigration to Palestine:

> Paul: I want to add something more on the attitude of the Communists as regards the bourgeois movement and so on. Have you seen the Jewish Clarion? The last issue?
> ? No. I will get it.
> Paul: I am going to raise the question of this article by Abramsky in which he condemns the fact that the Arab Liberation League has not given evidence before the Commission. I am going to raise the question as a matter of principle, because I hear from Michael Carritt that the Political Committee has discussed the Liberation League in that way and that they think that the League is entirely justified … I think that the Jewish Clarion has no right whatever to write something contrary to that. In any case it is not the business of the Jewish Clarion to criticise the movements of the Arab Liberation League. It is really very serious, as the Jewish Clarion is issued in the name of the Jewish Communist Party.[23]

The next day Jacot-Descombes rang Abramsky and discussed with him the Jewish refugee ships and immigration at some length, 'putting in an occasional "yes" and "no"'.[24] The issue was complicated by the position taken up by the Soviet Union, who were seeking to unite Jewish and Arab Communists in opposition to British Mandatory Palestine. The Zionist terror campaign against the British relied upon support from the Soviet Union and its wartime Jewish intelligence operatives:

The last major terrorist effort directly mounted by the Soviets against a Western European state was the supply in 1946–7 of base facilities, arms and explosives for Jewish groups to operate against British targets – an operation carried out on Stalin's personal instructions by the Deputy Minister of Defence, Marshal Vasilevsky.[25]

The Kuczynskis were first and foremost Communists and as such played their part in the Communist opposition to Fascism. They were not part of the Jewish opposition to Nazism and were not attracted to Zionism. Nevertheless, as Jews, they encountered anti-Semitism in both Germany and in Great Britain. In August 1947, Barbara was accosted by an angry stall holder while shopping in Camden's King's Crescent market, who called her 'a Foreign bastard and a bloody Jew, and this and that … There were 20 to 30 other people listening to all this,' she told her brother-in-law, Francis Loeffler, 'but nobody stopped her … Nobody came forward, so I felt no-one would be a witness for me, otherwise they would have told her to shut up.'[26] An experience which separated her from her husband's simmering sense of British patriotism, which he tried unsuccessfully to reconcile with his Communist beliefs.

CHAPTER FOURTEEN

William Skardon's
Interrogation of Ursula

On 30 July 1946 Robert and Berta Kuczynski became naturalised British subjects.[1] One year later MI5 took a renewed interest in Robert following Alexander Foote's claims that he had known of the true nature of Ursula's activities since 1938. However, as the war drew to a close, Robert's skills as a demographer were in demand. The Colonial Office, reluctant to lose his expertise, chose to ignore MI5's warnings that he was a security risk. Between 1943 and 1946 Robert sat on the Colonial Office's Colonial Demography Committee, in which capacity he visited the West Indies for several months in 1945.[2]

Ever since the suppression of the West India Royal Commission into the labour unrest in Trinidad and Jamaica in 1939, the Colonial Office had been planning a more salutary review of Britain's Caribbean territories.[3] The earlier commission had been suppressed on the grounds that conditions in the colonies were so appalling that adverse reporting would have seriously damaged the Allied cause. As with the threat from Communism in the Middle East, there were concerns that militant trade unionism in the West Indies could threaten British rule if common cause was made with political movements for independence. Robert's work was intended to assist the Colonial Office in preparing plans for a future colonial census as part of the Colonial Social Studies Research programme under the Colonial Development Schemes. He was not, however, made a member of the Colonial Office staff, although he received his salary from the Colonial Development Vote.[4]

Before Foote's damning testimony against him in 1947, Robert was widely accepted in professional circles as an associate of the Colonial

Office. He was now 70 years old and Berta 67. The following June, while visiting Ursula at Great Rollright, Berta suffered a fatal heart attack and 'was buried in the beautiful old village graveyard. Her name,' Ursula recalled, was 'carved on the gravestone above the names of those who mourned her – father and her six children.'[5] Robert remained at Great Rollright until the last week of September, while Barbara and Duncan made their arrangements to move into the flat at 12 Lawn Road. There they would care for Robert until his death in November 1947.[6]

Robert was staying with Ursula at Great Rollright when MI5's William Skardon, regarded as 'the most foremost exponent in the country' of the interrogation of suspected spies, arrived to question Ursula on 13 September 1947 about her activities in Switzerland.[7] As Foote was due to be released on or around that date it had been decided that the Beurtons should be interrogated as soon as possible, preferably before the Russians could warn Ursula of Foote's defection:

> As we entered the house – a squarish stone farmhouse abutting directly on to the road with double gates at the side giving on to a large farmyard with barn outhouses – we noticed Professor KUCZYNSKI sitting in the lounge reading a periodical. The door was answered by Mrs. BEURTON who is a somewhat unimpressive type with frowsy unkempt black hair perceptibly greying, and of rather untidy appearance. She acknowledged her identity and we were shown into the lounge. The Professor bowing his way gracefully out.[8]

From the start of the interview, Skardon reported, Ursula made it quite clear:

> that she did not 'think she could cooperate', stating that she did not intend to tell lies and therefore preferred not to answer questions. It is fair to say right away that by the stand she took up she tacitly admitted that she had worked for the Soviet Intelligence Service. The manner in which she did so was a credit to her earlier training. Every

possible piece of cajolery, artifice and guile that could be used by Skardon was employed – without any success whatsoever. She made no denial, sheltering always behind the rock of 'non-cooperation' … As a result of this interrogation, we regard ourselves as confirmed in our beliefs, and take FOOTE's story to be substantially true.[9]

She remained indifferent to Skardon's warnings that she might be placing family members in jeopardy:

> It was urged upon Mrs. BEURTON that her refusal to talk might well be a positive disadvantage to some of her connections. They might be, it was said, under some suspicion which could be removed were she frank. By inference it was implied that these suspicions might be directed against those near and dear to her, but she preserved a Slav-like indifference to this line of argument.[10]

Nevertheless, two days later, MI5 decided to suspend HOWs endorsing letter checks at Ursula's Great Rollright address and at 12 Lawn Road. Robert had recently been diagnosed with cancer and had returned to Lawn Road. Letter checks for Bridget's flat at 62a Belsize Park Gardens and at her former address at the Lawn Road Flats were also stopped. Telephone intercepts, however, continued.

On 17 September Bridget rang her former lover, Arthur Long. The conversation was not about money and appeared to be about past activities that could not be discussed over the phone or put in writing. Bridget was undoubtedly anxious:

B: I must see you.
A: I'm afraid there is no possibility of that.
B: But it's urgent. I don't want to talk on the telephone, but I absolutely must see you, tonight if possible, or tomorrow morning.
A: Look Bridget, I must know what it is, because if it is the usual subject I don't want any of it.
B: No, it isn't. You will understand if you see me.

A: Then you could write to me.

B: No, no I can't write it either.

A: It simply means, I suppose, that you want to have the usual acrimonious discussion …

B: No, it is nothing about our personal affairs. Won't you understand? It is something quite different and very important.

A: (who seems impressed) Well, I'm engaged up to 11 o'clock tonight.

B: That's all right. Come at 11.

A: Look frankly I don't like this. Why can't you give me an idea on the telephone.

B: You will understand I can't talk on the phone. You must come.

A: All right I'll drop in at 11 tonight.[11]

Bridget had obviously been informed of Skardon's interrogation of Ursula and had decided to warn her former partner, a one-time member of Ursula's group. B1b's J.H. Marriott flagged the conversation as 'interesting' and gave notice to colleagues that he had decided to delve further into the activities of Long and his partner, Pauline Miller.[12]

On 30 September Barbara received a telephone call from Sabine. Francis had just returned from visiting Ursula at Great Rollright and wanted to speak to Barbara urgently. It was agreed that Francis would call round later that evening:

30.9.47 i/c [incoming call] from BINA [Sabine] to BARBARA to say that FRANCIS would like to come and see her that evening about one or two things. BARBARA wants to know what about, but BINA repeats rather pointedly 'one or two things' and that he particularly wants her to be in. BARBARA says she has several arrangements for that evening – … It is finally decided that Francis will come round to see her at 7.15 p.m. that evening, BINA stating that he is first going to see BRIDGET before BARBARA. He should be at BRIDGET's about 6.30 p.m.[13]

At some point MI5's 'ferrets' had installed telephone receivers on the Kuczynskis' home telephones that had been modified so as to be always switched on, allowing them to listen to their ambient conversations.[14] The practice, known as Source 'TABLE', permitted MI5 to listen in to most of the conversation held between Francis, Barbara and Duncan that evening. Francis said that the investigation into Ursula's past 'had come rather at an awkward time, one way and another'.[15] He went on:

> Well you know my theory in all this business is that, I don't know how the Internationalists work, it always seems to me, that you always know who the other chap's spies are, all the time … just keep your watch on her, and as long as … you let them carry on, I don't know, it was so in War time … Once they start asking questions, they know things and you don't know what they know, that's the point … Now what would be the point of going there, it would have been much better to have caught her red-handed, and actually searched the house and they would have found something that they wanted to find, whereas, now they could search the house till they were blue in the face and they would not find anything.[16]

Source TABLE had made it quite clear that both the Loefflers and the Taylors had been made fully aware of the full extent of Ursula's espionage activities and that incriminating documents had been destroyed as a result of Skardon's visit to Great Rollright:

> Source TABLE of 30.9.47 showed that the reason Francis LOEFFLER particularly wished to see Barbara TAYLOR was that he had obviously been told by Ursula BEURTON of her interrogation which took place on the 13th and 14th September 1947. TABLE showed quite clearly that LOEFFLER and Duncan and Barbara TAYLOR knew of Ursula BEURTON's espionage activities. It also appeared that Ursula BEURTON had, in fact, incriminating documents in the house at the time of her interrogation, and LOEFFLER implied that they were disposed of the next day.[17]

MI5, fully aware that the Kuczynskis had engaged in a number of undercover activities, appeared reluctant to bring this family to book. About this time Sabine and Francis moved into Francis's mother's house at 57 Aberdare Gardens, NW6, which was also being used as a postbox for the Swiss-Egyptian Communist Paul Jacot-Descombes, then lodging with Bridget at the Loefflers' previous address, 62a Belsize Park Gardens. Letters for Jacot-Descombes were addressed to Francis, who would then place them into fresh envelopes before sending them on to Jacot-Descombes at Bridget's address. At this time Francis was working in a legal capacity for the Left-wing lawyer John Platt Mills. This, of course, may well have been legitimate political activity in support of the Egyptian Communist Party but if MI5 wanted to push home their advantage this would have been an optimum time as family relations, as they well knew, were becoming increasingly fractious. Since the death of Berta, Skardon's interview with Ursula and Robert's cancer diagnosis the family began experiencing high levels of stress. A dispute between Barbara and Jürgen over the ownership of Kuczynski property in Berlin strained relations even further.

On 24 October 1947 Ursula rang Bridget, inviting her to Great Rollright for the weekend. 'Nothing is to be said to BARBARA,' Ursula told her over the phone, as Barbara had already asked to visit that weekend. She had been told there wasn't room; a serious breach of family etiquette as Ursula had spent the previous week with Barbara at 12 Lawn Road visiting her seriously ill father. It was customary for family visits to be repaid and for Ursula to refuse Barbara hospitality while welcoming Bridget was an indication of a serious rift in the family.[18]

Bridget accepted Ursula's invitation and readily agreed to her conditions. However, she immediately telephoned Sabine to complain about Barbara's behaviour, Sabine agreeing with Bridget that Barbara was 'very mercenary about money matters'.[19]

The cause of this family feud was a parcel of land in Germany (*Grundstück*) that Berta had bequeathed to Barbara in her last will and testament. Jürgen believed that as he was the eldest son this land was rightfully his. The elder Kuczynski sisters, presumably sharing his views on male primogeniture, turned Jürgen's spat with Barbara into a family dispute. Family sensibilities were further strained by Barbara's insistence that Jürgen should pay rent for the house he occupied on her land. Ursula was particularly incensed and was said to be 'very shocked' that Barbara really thought that 'the land was rightfully hers'.[20] Later that evening she wired Jürgen in Berlin telling him that their father was seriously ill.[21] Jürgen replied on 4 November and was really rather scathing about Barbara:

Dearest Ursula:

Your letter arrived together with one from Barbara … It seems now only a matter of weeks, perhaps days with father.

Under these circumstances I think I want to discuss some of the questions raised in your letter. As to Barbara's attitude we do not need to discuss it. The house was officially rated as 100 per cent destroyed and the rebuilding cost much more than the house originally; the only thing I urge you and the sisters to do, is to see that she does not sell the estate to somebody else. Otherwise I agree to everything you propose, that is, please regard me as voting, if such disgusting thing comes up, in every way with you. The more I write, the more furious I get about the whole situation especially with father still alive. It is really incredible that we have somebody like B. in the family. I would like to have, if nobody objects, father's personal papers, such as letters, etc., manuscripts, and so on.[22]

His father died in Oxford on 27 November 1947, six months after his wife Berta. Ursula wrote to Jürgen in Berlin:

Father was marvellous right to the end. In some ways unexpectedly wonderful. He had, after all, never been seriously ill before and he proved himself to be courageous and patient, he never had any complaints, was touchingly grateful for every one of our visits and even during the last days he smiled whenever one of us came …

Monday evening he was still talking about everything under the sun. Tuesday he slept and only woke up once, between six and eight in the evening. Then he went to sleep and did not wake again. Of course we had known what to expect for some time, and during the last two weeks we could only wish for the end. All the same his death has been a great shock.[23]

Over the next four months family relations deteriorated further, with Jürgen sending Ursula a letter he had received from Duncan together with a copy of his reply. Duncan's letter was extremely angry, accusing the Kuczynski family of trying to get Barbara to renounce her claim to the property in Germany. He told Jürgen off for not writing to Barbara on the matter and for communicating only with Sabine and Francis:

Dear Jurgen,

I got involved in the … row tonight. B. had not told me before that there was a row, but tonight Francis rang up and read some letter he'd had from you and B. cried and said why did you always write to Francis and never wrote a nice (B. says delete 'nice', write 'any bloody letter, but to <u>her</u> not to Francis or Ursel') letter and after all she is filling in a hell of a lot of forms for the books and sending off parcels and one thing and another.

B. is overwrought at the moment. We've just been forced to buy the house, which puts us in debt for many years. She is due in about 3 months. She is nearest of all of you to your father's death because of being in his flat, with his things still around.

I asked Francis what the trouble was. I gather B. has been left the Grundstuck and you want her to renounce her claim. Also that you want a family conference to force B. to do this. Perhaps this is all wrong, but it's what I got amid tears and from F. [Francis] over the phone. It seems that the trouble about the Grundstuck is simply that there's been an attempt to coerce B. instead of her being allowed to act on her own. Anyway, asked for my advice I said For God's sake ask J. to write a civilised letter and incidentally ask Madeline not to write uncivilised letters and <u>please</u> acknowledge parcels by number. We never know which arrive.

No further discussions of Grundstuck. The last family meeting was in this flat. Bedlam. B. must be left alone to have her child. If we'd been willing to have a row we wouldn't have bought the damned house.

Yours Duncan.

Jürgen's reply, dated 18 February, did little to calm things down, merely pointing out that as Francis was joint executor with himself, it was only proper that he should write direct to him and not to Barbara:

Dear Duncan,

I am sorry that you got involved in the matter of the Grundstuck. I cannot quite understand why you did not explain to Barbara that this is a matter which does not concern herself and myself, but all of us, and that it was therefore only proper to discuss the matter between Francis and myself as executors; if I kept Ursula informed this again is easily explained as she is the oldest of us present in England.

In my letter to Francis I explained that I did not intend to discuss the matter any further after the sisters had come to a decision, whatever the decision. So there is no need to pursue the matter in a letter to Barbara, civilised or otherwise, (though I do not remember having written her an uncivilised letter).

The unpleasantness continued for a number of years until October 1954, when the house and the land were eventually sold. Francis handled the legal aspects of the affair while Renate did her best to bring the Kuczynski family together and paper over any remaining difficulties. Jürgen would not be mollified. In a letter to Jürgen, Renate said that she thought Francis had handled the affair with some skill and that he deserved to be rewarded for his trouble: 'I suggest £40, that is £10 from each of us, or if you think that too much, then half that, but not less. Please let me know soon what you think of this?'[24]

Jürgen thought very little of it and wrote a letter to Renate taking issue with her defence of both Barbara and Francis. 'I do not agree at all,' he wrote,

> to your suggestion with regard to FRANCIS. Everything has been frittered away and nothing has been accomplished. Nor has the situation with BARBARA been clarified, the money has not been handed over to you yet. I have several times suggested that he [Francis] should come here and get things cleared up; and he has not done so. Until you have received the money I oppose anything being done.[25]

Francis settled the money question in November, with Jürgen finally thanking Renate for her efforts: 'You of course', he wrote, 'handled the matter correctly under the circumstances.'[26]

1. Robert Kuczynski in his student days.

2. As a politician Robert was, according to his associate Otto Lehmann-Ruessbueldt, 'a popular
radical, courageous and soft to the point of demagogy, officially divided from the Communists …
He belonged to the circle of "bourgeois sympathisers" so painstakingly cultivated by the KPD.'

3. Robert and Berta with their son, Jürgen, in Berlin.

4. Jürgen, while a student of economics at the Brookings Institution in Washington, DC.

5. Marguerite Steinfeld was born in Strasbourg and had been living in the US for seven years before her marriage to Jürgen.

6. Ursula Kuczynski, a 'Red' Sally Bowles in a fading Weimar Republic: 'There are those who say I kissed 20 boys, but without counting Rolf it can't have been more than 19.' Rudolph 'Rolf' Hamburger, her childhood sweetheart, became her first husband in 1929. Three years later the Soviet agent Richard Sorge arranged for Ursula to undertake professional training in Moscow, when she was given the code name Sonya.

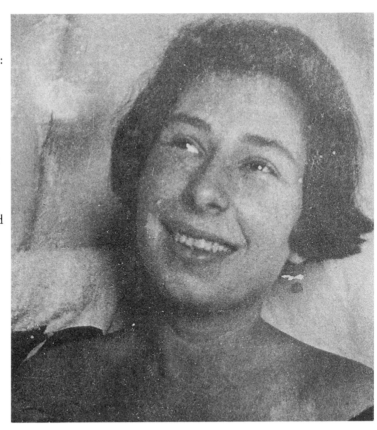

7. On 9 September 1934, Jürgen's associate and fellow-traveller John Strachey organised a huge demonstration in London's Hyde Park against Oswald Mosley's Blackshirts.

8. Lawn Road Flats, Hampstead. No fewer than seven secret agents for Stalin's Russia lived here in the 1930s and '40s. Brigitte Kuczynski moved in on 4 July 1936 and recruited Alexander Foote and Leon Beurton, who were sent to Switzerland to work with Ursula.

9. Ursula in Switzerland in 1938.

10. Ursula fell in love with Leon Beurton at first sight: 'He was lean and athletic, strong and muscular. Half shy, half-aggressive, he gave the impression of boyish immaturity.' They married in 1940.

1. And 12. As Agent Sonya, Ursula controlled two of Britain's most important spies in the field of science and technology: the demure, self-effacing secretary Melita Norwood and the German-born physicist Klaus Fuchs.

MITGLIEDSKARTE Nr.: 250. **Sektion:** _Sch._

FREIER DEUTSCHER KULTURBUND IN ENGLAND
FREE GERMAN LEAGUE OF CULTURE
6, Holly Mount, London, N.W.3. Phone: Hampstead 6214

Jürgen Kuczynski

36, Upper Park Road

_N.W.3._

Nicht übertragbar. Not transferable. Eintritt: _1 . 3 . 39_.
Diese Karte muss auf allen Veranstaltungen des F.D.K.B.
vorgezeigt werden.

13. Jürgen's membership card for the Free German League of Culture in England, issued 1 March 1939.

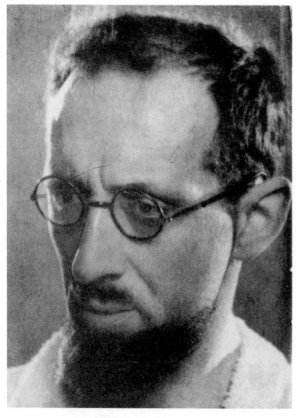

14. Geoffrey Pyke was Lord Mountbatten's 'ideas man' and is now one of the most famous of the Second World War's 'back-room boys'. In the assessment of one Conservative MP he was 'a strange creature, Mephistophelian in appearance but with a brilliantly original mind'.

15. A portrait of Robert by Berta in 1942. Early in the war, the couple were subject to restrictions as enemy aliens. These were subsequently removed to enable Robert to carry out his work for the London School of Economics.

16. William Skardon, the nation's foremost exponent for the interrogation of suspected spies.

17. Jürgen in American uniform in March 1945, two months before Special Branch reported that he had 'been arranging for members of the German Communist Party to be dropped into unoccupied parts of Germany through the American Air Force'. Jürgen, the report warned, appeared to be making use of the Americans to establish 'a nucleus' for the party.

Certificate of Appreciation

awarded to

Jurgen Kuczynski

In grateful recognition of
his conscientious performance of duty to the nation
through his service with

THE UNITED STATES STRATEGIC BOMBING SURVEY

in the
European Theatre of Operations

August 1945

Franklin D'Olier
Chairman

8. The certificate awarded to Jürgen by the United States Strategic Bombing Survey in August 1945.

9. In Jimmy Friell's cartoon for the *Daily Worker*, Labour Foreign Secretary Ernest Bevin and Leader of the Opposition Winston Churchill see no reason why the elections in Greece should not be postponed despite Royalist terrorism preventing a free and fair vote. Sabine's husband, Francis Loeffler, covered events in Greece for the Haldane Society of Socialist Lawyers while MI5 increased their surveillance of the Kuczynski family.

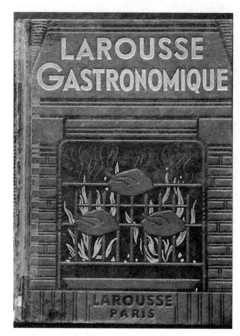

20. Barbara Kuczynski was an extremely good cook who mixed politics and food splendidly: 'I will never eat inferior food unless I have a professional reason to do so.' She was one of four translators of the *Larousse Gastronomique*.

Herausgeber: Parteivorstand der DKP, Abt. Frauenpolitik

To Letty
"Sonya" salutes you and
"Reni" sends her love.
Enjoy the pictures and
captions and lend it to
your family – ask them
to give you a summary !!

21. and 22. The card that Renate sent to Melia Norwood with a copy of Sonya's memoirs.

CHAPTER FIFTEEN

Ursula's Flight

The defection of the cypher clerk Igor Gouzenko from the Soviet Embassy in Ottawa, Canada, on 5 September 1945, three days after the end of the Second World War, with 109 documents on the Soviet Union's espionage activities in the West exposed several spies and raised serious questions about the loyalty of a number of leading nuclear scientists, including Klaus Fuchs. This, along with Sandor Radó's attempt to defect to the West in the same year, alerted Moscow Centre to the fact that Ursula's security in Britain had been compromised. A number of important spies were at risk, among them Melita Norwood, who was continuing to supply documentary material on Britain's atomic bomb programme. Only recently Centre had presented Norwood with a specially cut set of keys allowing her to gain access to the safe at BN-FMRA where Top Secret documents on Britain's atomic bomb project were deposited for safekeeping:

London – C [Centre] dated 22.6.1945.
Igor reported on the second removal of documents via 'Tina.' [Norwood] 20 new reports were obtained, as well as a scientific correspondence among specialists working on these questions at the institute. As a result, all the materials on E. ['Enormous', Soviet code name for the atomic bomb] that were in 'Tina's' office – over 35 reports and a scientific correspondence have been obtained. In the fall, we intend to organise a new removal, using specifically prepared keys to the safe where materials are kept. By that time, new materials and reports will have accumulated.[1]

Ursula's contact with her Soviet controller appears to have been lost at this time and was only re-established through her youngest sister, Renate, who acted as a reliable go-between when all other means of communication had been lost:

> Since January 1946 S. [Sonya] has been inactive, and no personal contact with her is maintained. However, from time to time she keeps us informed about her situation using pre-arranged signals, which we passed on to her through her sister, Renata [sic] Simpson, in 1948 … We provide S. with mater. [material] assistance without personal contact through a dead drop (the money is paid twice a year).[2]

How serious the threat was to the Kuczynski family as a whole became apparent at the beginning of 1948 when Foote came across Bridget by accident in St John's Wood. According to Foote, she had been very surprised to see him as she thought that he was still living in Switzerland. Unaware that Foote was now talking to British intelligence, she warned him that Ursula had recently been visited by two policemen and that she had been 'so upset by this … and was so scared that she had been obliged to break off and not go to a most important rendezvous which she was due to attend the next day'.[3] In fact, Ursula had been so worried by her encounter with Skardon that she requested permission from the GRU to return to Berlin. For some unexplained reason, in August 1949 Ursula did not remove the money from the dead drop 'in the agreed period of time', and the GRU 'took the money back'.[4] The following month she left a signal to indicate that 'all is well', and in January 1950 she retrieved a message agreeing to her return to Berlin.

Ursula wasted no time in arranging her flight, burying her transmitter and her Party card before buying four US Army waterproof canvas kitbags with zip fasteners, the sort GIs used to transport all their belongings. She tried to persuade Beurton, who had recently broken his leg in a motorcycle accident, to move in with one of her sisters.

They had all, apparently, offered to take him in, including Barbara but he refused to leave Great Rollright. Micha, now 18 years old, also remained in England. Janina and Peter, aged 13 and 6 respectively, were both minors and could travel on Ursula's passport.

Fuchs, who had returned to England in June 1946 to work on the British bomb at Harwell, was arrested at the end of January 1950 and charged with violating the Official Secrets Act. Fuchs made a complete confession to Skardon and following a press announcement that he had been meeting a foreign woman with black hair in Banbury, Ursula's arrest was expected any day.[5] Fuchs's trial was set for March and Ursula fled England on 27 February, two days before the trial commenced. MI5, she claimed later, had either demonstrated 'complete stupidity' in not connecting her with Fuchs or they had let her get away with it to save 'their disgrace'. She also hinted darkly at the possible existence of a mole inside MI5:

The American FBI were furious about the indolent attitude and naivety of MI5. The US had put their development in Klaus's [Fuchs] field of work at England's disposal, and he had passed all of this on to the Soviet Union. The British were not anxious to reveal their ignorance any further … Or was it possible that there was someone at MI5 who was, at the same time, working for the Soviet Union and had protected us?[6]

Ursula flew from London with her two children to West Berlin via Hamburg in a depressed state. She believed that she was unwell, possibly with a terminal illness, and before leaving the UK she visited the Kuczynski family doctor, Dr Manasse, who found nothing wrong.[7] On arrival at Berlin's Friedrichstraße station, she immediately telephoned Jürgen, who was then living in Schlachtensee, in the south-west of Berlin. She spoke with Marguerite, who told her 'that they had just moved and that Jürgen was staying with friends'.[8] Without accommodation they went from one hotel to another looking for a place to stay and ended up in very dingy surroundings.

The children slept together in one cold, damp bed, I in the other. It was early March. The room was only heated one day in three, with three or four pieces of coal. The ravages of war were still very evident in that part of town. Lots of pubs, lots of drunks and many bombed-out houses. Peter was the only one who found the room wonderful because he could spit from the fourth-floor window on to the street.[9]

An agent visited her from Moscow and listened to her recount her last stressful years in England when all personal contact with Centre had been lost:

He explained … that Centre had reason to interrupt contact for a prolonged period, but they had put money and news … under the fourth tree after the railway underpass and not after the crossroads beyond the underpass … Either they or I had made a mistake.[10]

The agent from Moscow agreed that it had been dangerous for her to remain in England and reported back to Centre advising immediate assistance:

'Sonya' flew into Berlin on 28.02.50. It is dangerous to stay in England. Together with her – daughter age 12 and son age 5. She was able to get a small room in the Sov[iet] Sector of Berlin. She needs help. Her husband stayed in England b/c he is in the hospital with a fractured leg.[11]

Back in England, scapegoats were sought. On 1 March, after a trial lasting less than ninety minutes, Fuchs was sentenced to fourteen years' imprisonment. He had expected the death penalty. The following day the *Evening Standard* published a banner headline linking him with John Strachey, who earlier in the year had been appointed Minister of War:

FUCHS AND STRACHEY; A GREAT NEW CRISIS. War Minister has never disavowed Communism. NOW INVOLVED IN M.I.5 EFFICIENCY PROBE.[12]

It was not the first time, nor would it be the last, that the press would link a leading member of the Labour Party with Soviet espionage. The accusation was taken up by the Beaverbrook press, the *Daily* and *Sunday Express*, and it was left to future Labour Party leader Michael Foot to defend Strachey in the *Tribune*,[13] while the Soviets professed bewilderment as to the true aims of the Fuchs trial and 'the related propaganda in the press'.[14] Moscow made a public disavowal of any involvement in atomic espionage, authorising the Soviet news agency TASS on 8 March to report that 'F. [Fuchs] is unknown to the Sov. Gov't and no Sov. Gov't agents have had anything to do with F-s.'[15]

On the 18th, Ursula was interviewed by Soviet agents in Berlin about her work with Fuchs. She was adamant that his political education had been neglected and that if more attention had been paid to his 'educational work' he would not have divulged so much information to his interrogators:

'Sonya's' opinion of Ch. [abbrev. of Fuchs's code name Charles] can be summed up as follows: Politically speaking, he turned out to be weak; evidently he did not give anyone's name for humanitarian reasons. His entire confession stemmed not from malicious intent, but from polit[ical] short-sightedness.

In her opinion, our educational work with agents is kept to a minimum, and in many ways this has been a reason for a number of serious consequences. She knows of a number of examples where people were not given proper attention. S.[Sonya] felt the same thing with regard to herself, but with her this could not have had a negative effect. She told us this so that we could change this 'faulty' system in our work.

S. thinks that if Ch. had been handled by her, she would have found time for his polit. education, and this affair would not have ended so regrettably.[16]

On Thursday, 13 July 1950, all Ursula's household effects were sold by public auction, with Renate supervising the affairs of the sale. Beurton had left to join Ursula in Berlin earlier in the year.[17]

On 1 December 1950, with Ursula safely in Berlin, Fuchs was able to identify her to Skardon as his controller in the UK. In his report Skardon sounded more than a little exasperated, and must have wondered why he had not pressed the matter harder during his interview with Ursula in September 1947:

In placing this photograph of Ursula Beurton before Fuchs I said to him: 'This is a photograph which I have already shown to you earlier' and he immediately said, 'That is the woman at Banbury'. I went into the matter very carefully with him since I did not want him to be identifying merely a photograph which he had seen before, but his identification was quite positive though he would have expected to find the woman rather more disheveled than this photograph portrays. In this connection I entirely agree with him, for Beurton had a very untidy mop of hair.[18]

CHAPTER SIXTEEN

Skardon on the Kuczynski Network

Following the arrest and trial of Karl Fuchs, MI5's attention turned to the remaining members of the Kuczynski family in Britain. Between 1947 and 1951 MI5 intercepted several phone calls between Patience Gray and Barbara in which they discussed things like going to the opera, 'matrimony' and Patience's 'latest boyfriends'.[1] There was also an oblique reference in MI5 files to correspondence between Patience and Otto, Rudolf Hamburger's brother, conducted through Barbara, although Patience had never met Otto.[2] MI5 surmised that while Patience was in correspondence with Otto she was not aware of his surname or Russian intelligence connections:

> From the conversation it appears that a number of people write to HAMBURGER at the TAYLORs' address, including a woman named 'Patience', who is apparently unaware of his surname and merely addresses the letters 'Otto'.[3]

On 6 February 1951 a telephone check was raised on HAMpstead 8255, the Taylors' phone installed at their new London address in Hampstead Garden Suburb. MI5 now felt that if the telephone check showed that they were not Communists then 'it might be considered worthwhile to have them interrogated in the hope of obtaining information regarding Ursula BEURTON's contacts in this country'.[4] During this investigation it emerged that for the past three years the Taylors had been 'on friendly terms with Gershon Ellenbogen and his wife, Eileen. Ellenbogen, a contemporary of Hilary Wayment at King's College, Cambridge, had also been on good terms with Alan Turing. He served for six years in the RAF as a flight lieutenant in the Intelligence Branch alongside Duncan in Cairo before the latter's posting to Bletchley Park in 1944.[5] In 1951 Ellenbogen was working as a barrister sharing the same telephone number, CENtral 1984, and occupying the same chambers as D.N. Pritt.

On 17 February an HOW was taken out on the Taylors' address, 17 West Heath Road, NW3, and on Otto Hamburger's address nearby, Flat 1, Birchington Court, West End Lane, in order to discover the identities of those who wrote to Otto at his own address and those who wrote to him care of the Taylors. The association between the Taylors and Otto Hamburger was of interest partly because Otto was a cousin of Heinz London who had worked on the separation of uranium isotopes for the Tube Alloys project. In 1946 London was employed at the Atomic Energy Research Establishment, Harwell, where he had been promoted to Senior Principal Scientific Officer in 1950, and in 1958 to Deputy Chief Scientist. He remained there until his death in 1970.

In June 1951 B2 were pushing for the Taylors to be interviewed by Skardon. An interview with Barbara confined to the subject of Ursula eventually took place on 7 February 1952. Barbara was both difficult and economical with the truth, claiming that she had never been a Communist and that she didn't know anything about Ursula's activities. When told by Skardon that he had interviewed Ursula in 1947, 'she denied any knowledge of this, adding that she [Ursula] would not have told her'.[6]

After her interview with Skardon, Barbara contacted Francis and Sabine and told them what had taken place between her and Skardon. The Loefflers then telephoned Brigitte 'asking if they could come and see her for a little while as it was rather important. It was agreed that they would go round at once.'[7] Sabine also immediately contacted Bob Stewart 'and asked if she could see him for a few minutes as it was rather important'. Bob Stewart, as Sabine would have known, was a leading member of the Communist underground operating in Britain. In the 1930s he had been in charge of an underground cell that operated a clandestine transmitter in Wimbledon relaying information between the CPGB and the Comintern in Moscow. He was the CPGB's 'spymaster' (although there were plenty of other candidates) and was, at one stage, the controller of the Cambridge Five. Philby, Burgess and Blunt all 'handed over their findings to Edith Tudor Hart, who passed them on to Bob Stewart, a trusted Communist, who in turn arranged for their transmission to Moscow'.[8]

Sabine went directly to Communist Party headquarters and gave Stewart full details of Skardon's interview with Barbara, and told him that she herself expected to be interviewed in the near future. Stewart 'was pleased that she had reported it', and asked Sabine to let him know if she was interviewed by Skardon.

Not surprisingly, there were those in MI5 who wanted to take the game more forcefully to the Taylors. A.A.G. Simkins, a relative newcomer to B2a, made the point that while the Taylors had known of Ursula's espionage activities in Switzerland they had taken great care not to learn too many details of these both there and in the UK:

> I take a poor view of both TAYLORs, and I should like to apply all the pressure we can. My first impression, however, as a newcomer to this B.2.a saga, is that while Barbara (and just possibly Duncan) was perfectly well aware that Ursula was a spy in Switzerland, and continued to be one in England, she took care not to acquire any detailed knowledge of Ursula's activities.[9]

Not everyone agreed. E. McBarnet, B2b, was of the opinion that although the Kuczynski family harboured 'violent Communists', if interrogated further, the Taylors would merely conceal their views 'for reasons of discretion'. He concluded:

> I wonder if we have much to gain, from a B.2. point of view, in pursuing this case any further. We do not need confirmation of the guilt of Ursula BEURTON and Jurgen KUCZYNSKI, and even if we learned from TAYLOR that members of the KUCZYNSKI family knew what Ursula and Jurgen were doing, it does not get us much further.[10]

J.C. Robertson thought that Brigitte and Sabine both knew more about Ursula's activities than the Taylors:

> They are the least likely of the family to respond to interrogation ... their reactions since the interview with the TAYLORs (and particularly Sabine LOEFFLER's contact with Bob STEWART) have been interesting, and I should consider it well worthwhile for B.2.a. to continue to operate their checks on these individuals for a considerable further time.[11]

He also wanted to involve B1f more closely in order to probe more actively the activities of Bob Stewart.

On 8 February 1952 MI5 decided to interview Duncan separately. A tactic was agreed whereby Duncan would be wrong-footed by disclosing the extent of their knowledge regarding the movements of the Kuczynski family:

> If, for instance, he was told that Ursula BEURTON was interrogated on 13 and 14 September 1947, that we know Francis LOEFFLER visited her shortly afterwards, returning to London on the evening of 29.9.47 and that on the following evening, i.e. 30.9.47 Francis Loeffler visited the TAYLORs. It is ... quite obvious that the reason for LOEFFLER's visit to Ursula BEURTON and his visit to the TAYLORS immediately on his return was in connection with Ursula BEURTON'S interrogation.[12]

Duncan, however, remained calm throughout the entire Skardon ordeal, dismissing it as rather a 'routine thing to happen'. Sabine and Francis, on the other hand, 'took it rather seriously'.[13] The TABLE material of their conversations showed that even Tony Lewis knew what Ursula had been up to, while Duncan accused MI5 of trying to get names form them, 'leaving no stone unturned':

19.32 BARBARA and DUNCAN TAYLOR chatting …The thing that irritated DUNCAN about URSULA was that she didn't seem to do an awful lot of work.

20.01 BARBARA is speaking in rather a low voice. She thinks that 'they' have caught someone … shown them that she … I think they want to get from us, all the people she was connected with, I think that's what he was talking about.

DUNCAN: … leave no stone unturned. There might be just something that comes into your memory that you had forgotten or not thought was significant but when going over it, you might say, well, I do remember there was one …

BARBARA: That I would remember the name of this man?

DUNCAN: Not necessarily – that you know he did this or said that or – queer way of sniffing.

BARBARA: Yes, but what would that chap be?

DUNCAN: Well, it might just be that the link with – he may have a man who sniffs. (Laughter).

Duncan was convinced that MI5 suspected them of being complicit in Ursula's secret activities or were deliberately shielding Ursula and her associates from discovery:

BARBARA: I remember there was sometime someone who came to see us …

DUNCAN: No, it's not as simple as that, I mean … every little tiny bit of evidence may be important. In this case, he (she?) was very careful not to know anything so there's nothing, but MI5 aren't to know that. [MI5's emphasis] I mean there are all sorts – I mean that sort of relationship is very unlikely. It's much more likely that either you should have been in with her or that now knowing what she was doing, you should be terribly against her and wrack your brains in order to hurt her … in some way. It is equally likely from their point of view that you might have detected something at the time and …

Whatever suspicions MI5 entertained regarding the Kuczynski family's knowledge and involvement with Ursula's group it seems they had very little to go on before her escape to Berlin:

> DUNCAN: They've never been to SABINE and FRANCIS?
> BARBARA: No.
> DUNCAN: It does seem clear that they haven't bothered about her life in England, so far.
> BARBARA: FRANCIS says he thinks that they can't <u>have known, because when she left they let her get out of the country</u>. [MI5's emphasis] They can only have known that she did something here, after she left.

The conversation became increasingly anxious, with Duncan reassuring Barbara that Ursula had got out in the nick of time:

> DUNCAN: On the other hand, well – I don't know anything to speak of about it, but I thought that TONY [LEWIS] or somebody more or less hinted that they [MI5] had made it clear that they would get her pretty soon. Somebody said that things were getting a bit warm for her.
> BARBARA: Yes that's right. I think it was TONY and FRANCIS, they both said something like that …

Skardon had little doubt that both Duncan and Barbara knew 'a great deal about Ursula BEURTON's activities in the UK'; but he was unsure whether or not the Taylors subscribed 'completely to the Communist viewpoint'.[14] In fact, MI5 had very little to go on other than a vague awareness 'that their sympathies' lay 'in that direction'. Their file shows that they did not conform to accepted standards of behaviour as understood by MI5. Information obtained in 1952, for example, showed that they were readers of the *Daily Worker*. In September 1947, following Ursula's interrogation she had confessed to Sabine that, like her father, she was becoming anti-British 'but she doesn't like to say so to

DUNCAN as it hurts him'.[15] Duncan was distinctly British and upper-class, an established employee of the BBC where he was Programme Assistant in the Schools Broadcasting Department. He had a cousin, Malcolm Henderson, serving as Commercial Counsellor in the British Embassy, Lisbon. More damaging, it seems, was the observation that Barbara had only 'recently expressed annoyance that she should have been asked to wear dark clothes in view of the king's death, and added that Duncan was not going to wear a black tie'.[16]

In fact, Barbara was not quite as anti-British as she seemed and in February 1952 she attended the Coronation of Queen Elizabeth II 'as DUNCAN had been doing something on it'. She confided in Sabine that 'she had liked the Household Cavalry and all that and it was quite moving to be there when the Queen is proclaimed. After all it did not very often happen.' Sabine, however, said that she 'was sick of the whole thing'.[17] Source TABLE produced some pretty good material from the Taylor household: not the smoking gun that MI5 was looking for, but it did show that Duncan was knowledgeable and understood the spying game. It also showed that Barbara was reticent on the subject, if not uncomfortable with the whole world of spies:

DUNCAN: But in that case, if you say that 'they' [SABINE and FRANCIS], take the view that they approve of what URSULA's doing, they can't criticise the most stringent Government methods. They are always at pains to show that Communists aren't necessarily absolutely in the pocket of Russia, that one can be a patriotic Englishman and a Communist as well. Therefore if you are patriotic you can't approve of spies. If on the other hand you say that it is a good thing that Russia should have everything, then you can't blame the vast majority of the people in the country who take a different view, for not letting you take jobs where that sort of information is likely to be available, in fact, for keeping a pretty strict eye on you.

BARBARA: Yes. What they would say is ...

DUNCAN: Yes, but it's no good saying what should or should not have arisen, one's always concerned with the policy now ... As to URSULA the other (obvious?) thing she does is to make things difficult for Communists in this country. These security measures have only been clamped down because of people like FUCHS.

BARBARA: I don't know how much you can prove? on ('approve of') spies. I don't like spies very much.

DUNCAN: Well, if you want Russia to win –

BARBARA: If you don't want to have War, if you avoid a war by Russia being … You can take the line that if Russia would trust? America about the Atom, there wouldn't be a war.

DUNCAN: If you take that line or that if there is a War you want Russia to win, you're at liberty to take it, but that is such a serious difference of opinion with the majority of people that you cannot expect them not to keep a very strict eye on you.

BARBARA: I mean I'm not so (much?) good at spying, I could imagine myself being persuaded that there wouldn't be a war if Russia doesn't … much spying.

DUNCAN: But it does. That's more or less what FUCHS …

BARBARA: Yes, but I think that's …

DUNCAN: That's what attracted the attitude of the Government in tracking down Communists and being sticky about passports from and to abroad.

BARBARA: Don't you think that they are going much too far?

DUNCAN: Yes I do. But, I mean, if they have – if there are other people they've been digging up, other than FUCHS who was known … Might have been leaks.

… One or two inaudible remarks and laughter. BARBARA remarks that she has got the Daily (Worker).

20.24 Conversation turns to the King's funeral.

It is reasonable to assume from this that the Taylors had at some point casually and willingly wandered into the world of espionage during the Second World War and had known more about Ursula's activities in the UK than they were willing to admit to Skardon. However, Duncan's dilemma, which the TABLE material clearly illustrates, centred upon the central question common to many in the Taylor circle: was it possible for a patriotic Englishman to be a fervent Communist without straying into the realm of treachery?[18] Duncan's patriotism introduced him to many top civil servants whose Communism was disguised. Able to penetrate the inner reaches of the Civil Service without entering the corridors of power, Barbara and Duncan presided over the conversations of a network of fellow-travelling influential Labour Party and Communist friends who often dined at their home. Barbara was one of the four translators of the *Larousse Gastronomique* and was an extremely good cook.[19] She mixed politics and food splendidly. 'I will never eat inferior food,' she once remarked, 'unless I have a professional reason to do so. It is beyond politeness – I simply won't do it.'[20]

Among the civil servants cultivated by the Taylors were Sir Arthur Drew and his brother Henry. Arthur Drew, who had been Assistant Principal at the War Office since 1936 and was now Private Secretary to the Secretary of State for War, a position he was to hold until 1949, had known Duncan for about twenty years.[21] He was no ordinary civil servant. Those who knew him described him as possessing a 'broad administrative talent'. He was 'eminently sensible [and] charmingly devious when necessary' and 'happy to pursue his aims in a relaxed way by any one of a number of different routes. Above all, he was a good listener.'

'Behind an impassive exterior, a highly efficient system reacted to anything and everything of interest. This inscrutability was enhanced by an ironical cast of mind and a distinct taste for innocent mischief-making which meant that his real views tended to arrive in coded format ... his interest in the past was genuine, and he understood well the link between history and the present.'[22] On 15 September 1947, two days after Skardon's interview with Ursula, Duncan arranged a meeting between him and an unidentified woman friend called Vera.

The rendezvous had all the appearances of a straightforward house transaction with Barbara telephoning Vera, who was trying to buy a house in the Richmond or Twickenham area. MI5, however, who were monitoring the Taylors' phone, were not so sure. Later that day 'Duncan

... telephoned Arthur DREW of 25 Mortlake Road, Kew. Arthur DREW was apparently not in, but his wife told Duncan TAYLOR that he should ring Arthur's brother, Henry DREW (41 Ennerdale Road, Kew) as it was to him that enquiries should be made regarding the house.'[23]

NOTE: It is not possible to say whether these conversations regarding a house have any connection with information in a letter written by Karl FLEISCHER of 27 Mortlake Road, Kew, to Leon BEURTON, the husband of Ursula BEURTON in Oxford on 29.7.47. In this letter FLEISCHER tells BEURTON that 'If your brother-in-law is still without a proper house, and interested in one, he should contact me as quickly as possible after Saturday week, at 27 Mortlake Road, Kew'. So far as is known, no brother-in-law of BEURTON's was at that time looking for a house for himself. FLEISCHER was a member of the Sudeten German group of Communists in the U.K. soon after his arrival in this country in 1939. He is still resident in the U.K.[24]

There may well have been a perfectly valid reason for these contacts and MI5 may have been reading far too much into them. Fleischer was a neighbour of Arthur Drew's and the Drews were, apparently, helping him to sell his house to Vera and her husband, friends of the Taylors. Leon Beurton's brother-in-law presumably was Duncan, as Jürgen had been in Berlin for some time. Drew, who would work closely with a number of prominent politicians, among them Emmanuel Shinwell, Sir John Grigg and John Profumo, was a regular dinner party guest at the Taylors.[25] In the early 1950s their guest list extended to a number of Left-leaning alumni from the University of Cambridge, who had flirted with Communism during the war.[26]

Further investigation showed that the Taylors had a wide circle of friends linked to the CPGB, including the scientists Helen Gordon and her husband, Arthur. Arthur Gordon had been connected with Communist activities since his undergraduate days at Cambridge in 1935, and during the war he was an active member of the Leeds University group of the Communist Party. From February 1948 until early 1949 he had been working at the Carlsberg Foundation, Biological Institute, Denmark. He then worked as a biological chemist at the Karolinska Hospital, Stockholm, until May 1950 before returning to the UK. During his time in Sweden he attended the World Congress for the Defence of Peace, which was held in Stockholm in March 1950, and dined afterwards with Professor J.D. Bernal. In May 1951, when Arthur Gordon began working at the National Institute of Chemical Research, Mill Hill, the couple were regular dinner party guests of the Taylors. Both the Gordons were investigated by the security services: Arthur Gordon was the subject of PF 296798 and Helen of HS 296587.

Another interesting Taylor dinner party guest was Roger Nathaniel Quirk (PF48834) and his wife Paula. On 15 October 1947 Barbara rang them at their home at 10 Lansdowne Crescent, W11, on Park 9677 for confirmation that she and her husband were having drinks with the Taylors that evening between 7 and 7.30. Roger Quirk was then Assistant Secretary to the Minister of Fuel and Power. The Ministry of Fuel and Power had been created on 11 June 1942 from functions separated from the Board of Trade. It took charge of coal production, allocation of fuel supplies, control of energy prices and petrol rationing, and was renamed the Ministry of Power in 1957. Hugh Gaitskell had taken over as Minister from Emmanuel Shinwell on 7 October 1947.[27] Paula Quirk was the daughter of Dr August Weber, an old German Social Democrat leader living in the UK. Before her marriage Paula had worked for SIS, but this had apparently stopped at the end of 1939 when she came to this country.[28]

Also of interest were James Vernon and his wife Betty, both of whom were known to be active Party members of many years' standing and in contact with Margot and Doreen Heinemann as late as 1947. They did, however, resign their membership in 1948 owing to James's employment by the Civil Service. Margot Heinemann, also known as 'the Coal Queen' for her work with the Ministry of Fuel and Power on behalf of the mining industry was, as we have seen, an important contact of the Kuczynski family.[29]

William Scanlan Murphy, a documentary film maker, neighbour and good friend of the Taylors, spoke of the Taylors' home as 'a vital social hub for the broad Hampstead Left. What are lazily referred to as the 'chattering classes' simply thronged there. It was particularly notable that they seemed to know an extraordinary number of civil servants, who (to my, now, obviously rather naïve eye) seemed mainly to come round to moan about their political masters.'[30]

The circle included the Cambridge group of Communist sympathisers Barbara and Renate had cultivated at Cambridge and Bletchley Park during the Second World War and their partners; most notably Mary and Pat Tyler and Dorothy Gerrish, who lived opposite the Taylors' Hampstead Garden Suburb home. Mary Tyler (née Southcombe) had returned to Cambridge at the end of the war, where she had become engaged to Pat Tyler, secretary of the University of Cambridge Labour Club. She had been appointed secretary of the International Students Association and together they had attended the International Socialist Students' Conference in Czechoslovakia in 1947. They married the following year. From 1948 to 2010 they lived at 2 Corringway, Hampstead Garden Suburb, a six-bedroom house opposite the house of Barbara and Duncan Taylor, and all were members of the local Labour Party. Their close friends included such high-standing Labour Party figures as Michael Foot, Lord Howie, Anthony Crosland and Denis Healey, whom Pat Tyler had known since his Army days. They had trained together, with Healey winding up at Anzio and Pat as a beach master at the Normandy landings (on D-Day +6). They were political allies from the outset. Both stood for Parliament in the 1945 election. Pat stood for Knutsford; Healey for Pudsey and Otley, though they both lost. They remained close personal friends. The Healeys visited the Tylers' home many times between 1979 and 1985, often for dinner. The Taylors were also invited.

Another interesting member of this Hampstead dining circle was the chairman of the Labour Party's Hampstead Garden Suburb Branch,

Percy Timberlake, then in the forefront of the campaign to promote trade between British companies and Communist-controlled China. One of the so-called 'Icebreakers', Timberlake was particularly effective, along with Roland Berger, a secret member of the Communist Party, in lobbying British MPs and journalists against the US trade embargo of China, pointing out the financial losses being sustained by strict adherence to the embargo.[31] The first deal struck between British companies and China, signed in Beijing in July 1953, was worth £30 million. A year later Timberlake helped establish the 48 Group – named after the number of British firms prepared to join the venture despite the risk of being boycotted by hostile trade associations and anti-Communist Hong Kong agents. In 1953 he joined the newly established British Council for the Promotion of International Trade, which championed business links with the Communist world.[32] The impracticability of Britain's China embargo had become 'increasingly manifest' by 1957 and not long afterwards the first major Chinese technical mission came to Britain.[33]

Timberlake had also worked closely with Sabine's husband Francis as treasurer of the YRRC while working full-time at the Ministry of Information. He was drafted into the RAF as an education officer in October 1941.[34] Sabine and Brigitte, under the guidance of the resourceful Bob Stewart, were both involved in the promotion of East–West trade in the early years of the Cold War. Stewart approached Brigitte in 1952 with an offer of work from the Rumanian trade delegation that called for more than the clerical work the Rumanians appeared to be seeking:

> STEWART said that a teacher was required by the Roumanians, 'An English teacher to teach their new people.' STEWART continued – 'They also want – he called it a clerk, but it's more than a clerk. They want somebody – not out there but to work at home on questions of economics … got to show general trends and so forth and so on. Economic research work – and maybe a little more than that I think.' STEWART thought it would be a good job but he didn't know of anybody suitable at the moment.

> BETTY REID ... suggested NICHOLSON'S wife [Brigitte][35] for the jobs STEWART had in mind, and said that SABENA LOEFFLER was all right, and a very good research-worker. She thought SABENA would be a good choice.[36]

A biography form was sent to Brigitte and an appointment arranged with BOB STEWART, 'Who will explain the thing to you'.[37] At this time Brigitte was still in contact with Soviet intelligence. On 26 November 1953 F4/KM reported that Steve Boddington (John Eaton) of the London Export Corporation, who had worked for the Labour Research Department in the late 1930s, telephoned Brigitte frequently at the Rumanian Legation, where she was employed as an Economic Research Worker.[38] After the war Boddington had been involved with state planning, 'working first for the Planning Board and then the Board of Trade in which he reached a very high civil service grade'.[39] At a time when senior civil servants were being vetted and removed from the Civil Service if suspected of having Communist sympathies, Eaton began using the pseudonym Steve Boddington in order to conceal his association with the Communist Party. In Margot Heinemann's KV2 file there is a TABLE report of a conversation between her and Betty Reid mentioning Boddington and 'the trade boys' as useful sources of information:

> BETTY REID then changed the subject and asked if KLUGMANN[40] had seen Margot [HEINEMANN] lately. He saw her on Saturday and she was much better. She was at the moment working on something which would occupy her for the next few months, but after that she would be wanting something. BETTY REID thought 'the trade boys' would use her and there would be no difficulty about that. In particular BETTY mentioned STEVE [BODDINGTON].[41]

Prior to this Brigitte was listed in 1951 as being employed at the Royal Institute of International Affairs as Dr Brigitte Long, revising the Abstracts of Registration laws to be published in her father's

Demographic Survey of the British Colonial Empire, Volumes I–IV. The estate of the late Dr R.R. Kuczynski was to forego the payment of royalties in respect of the publication of the first two volumes of this Survey that, along with a grant from the Carnegie Corporation of New York, was to cover the cost of publishing further material on the British territories in Asia (Hong Kong, Borneo, Sarawak, Aden) and on St Helena and Gibraltar.[42] Brigitte had by now divorced her husband, Tony Lewis, naming Long as co-respondent, and on 25 May 1949 she married John ('Jock') Nicholson at Hampstead Registry Office with the Communist Party's blessing.[43] She had met Nicholson, a full-time Scottish Communist official from Hamilton, at a residential CPGB school in Hastings in 1948. Ten years his senior, she insisted that if his feelings for her were as strong as hers were for him, he would have to up sticks and come south to Hampstead.[44] On arrival in Scotland he asked the Party Executive to agree to his transfer to London 'for personal reasons'. They agreed but provisos were put in place:

'What is your personal reason? Is it domestic?'
'No.'
Pause.
'Is it a woman?'
'Yes'
'Don't tell me you've got yourself involved in some trouble.'
'No, it is quite straightforward and honest.'
Long pause.
'Well, you'd better put your request before the comrades on the committee. You should be prepared to give a full explanation, otherwise it will be very difficult for the comrades to understand.'[45]

With a general election only eighteen months away, Nicholson was told to remain in Scotland to work on the election campaign of William Gallacher, Communist MP for Fife. The CPGB was not backward in coming forward when it came to demanding total commitment from its members, and Nicholson soon 'understood that whom a

Communist full-timer cohabited with – and where – was almost a committee matter. He probably already knew that, if possible, one ought to marry within the faith.'[46]

In January 1951 Brigitte gave birth to a daughter that, surprisingly for such a close family, she did not disclose to other family members. Sabine was the first family member to discover the child's existence and she told Barbara over the telephone, who registered her complete surprise 'to hear this'; 'Sabine did not think she had bothered to tell anyone.'[47]

At this time Brigitte was listed as a member of the Adelaide Branch of the Hampstead Communist Party. Special Branch had launched an investigation into the Hampstead Communist Party in 1947 and had noted that it had been divided into four wards with 600 members. Adelaide had 130 members, and Brigitte was listed as Literature Secretary, a position one former Communist described as 'the practical arm of the Party's propaganda work … central to everything that an agitational organisation did. Without it the masses wouldn't even know that the Party was there, and the members would never progress into being the vanguard of the proletariat.'[48] Jock Nicholson became a railway worker and borough chairman of the CPGB's St Pancras Branch.

CHAPTER SEVENTEEN

Jürgen's Fall

In 1953, Otto Hamburger informed Skardon of a rift between himself and Barbara, who was having difficulties keeping her politics out of her 'domestic life'. This was 'altogether too much' for Otto to 'stomach' and he 'had not seen or heard of her for quite some time'.[1] He informed Skardon that Jürgen was in 'disgrace' and had come under suspicion in East Germany, having lost his position at Berlin's Humboldt University.

Following the arrest of Fuchs in England, the Operations sector of the MGB (Soviet Ministry for State Security, the forerunner of the KGB)[2] in Berlin had opened an investigation into those who had been involved in Fuchs's recruitment and subsequent attempts to contact Soviet intelligence following his return to Britain in 1946. Among those investigated were Jürgen, his former secretary Hans Siebert and Johannah Klopstock.[3] On 24 September 1946 Siebert had informed the London station of the NKGB that Fuchs had approached Jürgen's wife 'asking for help to establish contact with Sov[iet] people'. Fuchs also contacted his former lover Angela Tuckett, assistant editor of the *Daily Worker*, who relayed his request to Jimmy Shields, a member of the Central Committee of the CPGB. Moscow Centre, however, regarded a meeting between Fuchs and a Soviet agent, either through German members of the KPD or the CPGB, as 'undesirable'. It was decided, therefore, that Marguerite was not to be used to re-establish contact with Fuchs. Jürgen, who had already refused to work with the Russians in Berlin, had 'got a bad reference from the London org[anisation] of Germans', and was out of favour.[4] However, Moscow Centre's intervention came too late as Marguerite had already given Fuchs Klopstock's address and Klopstock had approached Siebert in an attempt to establish contact with Soviet intelligence. In 1947 Klopstock and Siebert went to live permanently in the Soviet-occupied zone of Berlin, where both joined the *Sozialistische Einheitspartei Deutschlands* (SED, Socialist Unity Party of Germany). At the time of Fuch's arrest Siebert had resigned from his job with the *Deutsche Demokratische Republik* (DDR)'s Ministry of Education, while Klopstock was unemployed.[5] Siebert, in the conspiracy-charged atmosphere of 1950s East Berlin, was particularly vulnerable to accusations of espionage on behalf of the West as he was related, through marriage, to the sister of Noel Field, one of the NKVD's most notorious American spies suspected by the Russians of treachery. In 1945 Siebert had married Priscilla Thornycroft, the sister of Noel Field's brother Hermann's wife, Kate Field née Thornycroft.[6]

Noel Field was arrested in Prague in 1949 on charges that he was operating as an American spymaster recruiting from dissident Left-wing groups in Czechoslovakia, East Germany and Hungary. He was handed over to the Hungarian secret police and subsequently imprisoned in Hungary. His arrest was used as the pretext for the prosecution of Tito-aligned Communists in Hungary in 1949 and 'Trotskyist–Titoist–Zionist' agents, allegedly working for US intelligence in Czechoslovakia, in 1952 during the Rajk[7] and Slánský show trials.[8] In February 1950 the Russians learnt of Siebert's personal connection with Field through an informant inside the SED:

In February of this year, the K. I. station in Berlin[9] determined the following:

At the end of 1949, the CC SED[10] received a statement from a member of the SED (whose last name is unknown to us) in which Hans Siebert is exposed for his contact with Amer. Intelligence officer Noel Field, who was a subject of Rajk's trial in Budapest. SED leadership ordered Siebert to write an explanation.

In his explanation, Siebert mentioned that in 1946, he had met with Field in England, but denied the existence of current business ties with Field.[11]

As Jürgen's London secretary, Siebert's connections with Noel and Hermann Field fed growing KPD and Russian suspicions that Jürgen's political views were suspect and that his intelligence work with the Americans was ongoing. Russian intelligence in Berlin, however, did not pursue this, preferring to shelter Jürgen from closer British and American scrutiny. In June 1950, he sub-let his house in the American Sector of Berlin and moved to Weissensee, Parkstrasse 49 in the Russian Sector. He was granted a permanent or semi-permanent interzonal pass from the authorities, permitting him to cross freely into West Berlin unnoticed by Allied intelligence.[12] In December 1950 G.T.D. Patterson, MI5's Security Liaison Officer at the British Embassy in Washington, despatched a note to London informing MI5 that the Americans 'were hoping to locate Jürgen KUCZYNSKI in the American Sector of Berlin, with a view to asking the CIA to interview him'.[13] However, MI6 had already issued instructions to Kim Philby in the hunt for Jürgen and at the time of Patterson's report Jürgen was safely ensconced in the Russian Sector.[14]

Jürgen's arrival in the Russian Sector was not welcomed by his fellow returnee from British exile, Wilhelm Koenen, who levelled the charge of 'deviation' against him.[15] Koenen's own position was far from secure, however, and only limited action was taken against Jürgen, 'aimed at decreasing his influence'. He was not expelled from the Party, merely 'discredited'. Nevertheless, his constant criticism of the way of life of leading members of the SED's Politburo as 'un-proletarian' did not endear him to comrades and he became a victim of Walter Ulbricht's anti-intellectual campaign. MI5 and MI6, who followed these events closely, identified Jürgen as a potential asset ripe for recruitment. It was hoped that he could be persuaded either to defect to Britain or to work for British intelligence inside East Germany.[16] East German counter-intelligence took precautionary measures and in 1953 Jürgen was made the subject of a major inquiry launched by the Central Party Control Committee (ZPKK) of the SED aimed at uncovering the existence of a mole operating inside the Party on behalf of the West.

The allegations against Jürgen originated in a letter sent by William Koenen to Hermann Matern, Politburo member and chairman of the ZPKK. Koenen, who had worked with the Kuczynski family in London, claimed Jürgen had been connected with the 'Jewish–Trotskyist' *Left News*, the newspaper owned by the 'anti-Soviet propagandist' Victor Gollancz.[17] Gollancz, although anti-Stalinist, could hardly be described as a 'Jewish–Trotskyist' and Koenen's accusations relied heavily on the denunciatory character of the language so peculiar to post-war Eastern European Communist Parties. The anti-Semitic nature of the show trials in Hungary, Prague and Moscow targeting alleged 'Zionist', 'Titoist' and 'Trotskyite' plotters caused considerable unease and fear in East Germany and found expression in malicious accusations.[18] The merging of 'Zionism' with the covert activities of Western imperial plotters (both real and imagined) found expression in crude anti-Semitism and Jürgen, who was Jewish, was particularly vulnerable. However, he was staunchly anti-Zionist and had argued consistently against German financial restitution to Jewish victims of Nazism living in Israel and the United States. In emigration he had accepted Zionism as a manifestation of the struggle against British imperialism in the Middle East not as an end in itself; throughout this period Jürgen never wavered in his support for Stalinism. The allegations against him in East Germany were political and had very little impact on the attempts to flush out 'a non-existent' Western spy ring in East Germany among the returning Communists from the West.[19] They centred upon three central issues: his wartime association with Paul Merker, whose Free Germany Movement in Mexico was then being investigated by the East German authorities as an alleged front for 'Zionist–US imperialist' interests; his determined stand against Vansittartism in Britain; and his opposition to the dismemberment of post-war Germany.

Merker had been cited as a co-conspirator by three of the defendants in the Slánský trial and had been arrested by the Stasi on 30 November 1952. Jürgen, who had maintained regular contact in London during the 1930s and '40s with two of the Slánský trial defendants, Otto Katz and Ludwig Freund, had confessed to meeting both men in Prague in

1949 but that was all. Koenen's accusatory letter to Matern repeatedly tried to make the Freund–Merker–Kuczynski connection appear sinister. Both Freund (a Czech-born Jew whose real name was Ludvik Frejka) and Merker (a non-Jew) were supporters of 'Zionism'.

Critical to the case against Jürgen were the conflicting attitudes of those who had been in exile during the Second World War towards the domestic German resistance to Hitler. According to Jürgen, a group around Koenen 'had adopted an overtly anti-German position' similar to Vansittartism, arguing that the entire German people, and not just the *Junker* (Prussian landed nobility) and monopoly capitalists, were responsible for Nazi crimes.[20] Jürgen, who had roundly attacked Vansittartism in April 1944 in Gollancz's *Left News*, had found himself in the opposition camp. The dispute centred upon the difficult question of how the restoration of democracy would follow from the overthrow of the Nazi regime. The DDR had proudly proclaimed itself in 1949 as an 'anti-fascist-democratic state' and that anti-Fascism legitimised the creation of a new state based upon Communist ideology.[21] Western Germany, on the other hand, had remained quasi-Fascist with Vansittartism as its defining characteristic. Only the DDR, the rightful heir to the progressive traditions of the German people, could ensure a clean break with the Nazi past:

> The founders of the DDR understood fascism to be a capitalist phenomenon. Following this logic, the establishment of socialism in the DDR had removed the roots of fascism and ensured a clean break with the Nazi past. West Germany, on the other hand, had kept both the social structure and the individuals who had made Nazism possible. Thus, underground resistance against Hitler, political activities in exile, German participation in the Allied forces, and involvement on the republican side in the Spanish Civil War were all seen as part of the prehistory of the East German state.[22]

In keeping with his attack on Vansittartism, Jürgen had argued against 'the dismemberment of Germany' and in favour of 'preserving the unity of the Reich'; Vansittartism, he maintained, did not truly represent the German people. The East German trials of 1953 set out to prove the opposite and that Nazism, owing to the nature of the German people, retained the ability to thwart the East German experiment. The case against Jürgen, therefore, was an East German- and not a Russian-led affair. As a result, the accusations against Jürgen were soon dropped by the state authorities, not least because he had retained the backing of the intelligence services of the Soviet Union. Koenen's attack on Jürgen was more symptomatic of his own personal insecurity and the weakness of the DDR, both ideologically and geopolitically, after the 1953 East German uprisings, than Jürgen's alleged 'deviations'.

CHAPTER EIGHTEEN

The Greek Civil War and the Haldane Society of Lawyers

Before the 1945 British general election, Clement Attlee had reassured Winston Churchill that there would be continuity in British foreign policy under a Labour government, which meant in practice a continuation of Britain's imperial role in global affairs, suspicion of the Soviet Union, and an acceptance of the 'special relationship' with the US. These three strategic objectives came together during the Greek Civil War (1946–49) to provide political cover for 'a sort of "parastate" of right-wing military forces' to seize power in Greece, the menace of Communism being used to eliminate all Left-wing opposition.[1] When civil war erupted in late 1946 the British police and military missions in Greece not only collaborated with the Greek authorities, tolerating Right-wing excesses against the opposition, but also adopted Fascist methods that Vansittart had once regarded as peculiar only to the German nation.[2] Francis Loeffler, having by now qualified as a lawyer, questioned the direction of Labour Party foreign policy and was placed under surveillance for covering the trials of Communists in Greece facing the death penalty for treason. The boundaries restricting the activities of MI5 were changed by the Attlee government and a number of Left-wing members of the Labour Party, lawyers and, increasingly, civil society organisations (the forerunners of non-governmental organisations or NGOs), were targeted by the security services alongside Communists. The aftermath of the Greek Civil War marked a turning point in the history of the Labour Party and its relationship with MI5. The new guidelines set out by Attlee's Cabinet in respect of subversive activities conducted by foreign actors in an independent state that threatened British imperial interests were included in MI5's remit. The Attlee Directive, initialled by the new Prime Minister on 20 April 1946, made it quite clear that MI5's responsibilities now included monitoring hostile actions 'from within or without the country, which may be judged to be subversive of the security of the State':

> Its [MI5's] task is the Defence of the Realm as a whole, from external and internal dangers arising from attempts at espionage and sabotage, or from actions of persons and organisations, whether directed *from within or without the country* [my emphasis], which may be judged to be subversive of the security of the State. In consultation with the Colonial Office you will be responsible for similar work in Colonial and other British territories overseas (para 2).[3]

The Attlee Directive was a continuation of Labour wartime thinking and was in accordance with Churchill's Second World War imperial strategy. This strategy had drawn heavily upon Hugh Dalton's 'revolutionary' conception of SOE, which had regarded subversion as a weapon capable of directly winning the war; whereas Churchill had remade SOE as 'an independent organisation for the execution of foreign policy by irregular means'.[4] Dalton, a moderate socialist, had eventually been sacked and replaced by Roundell Palmer, 3rd Earl of Selborne, known to be 'somewhere to the right of Churchill himself'.[5] The triumph of Churchill and Palmer's strategy found its hubris in subsequent SOE operations in Greece where Churchill's political views succeeded in equating guerrilla warfare and the Greek resistance movement with British interests.

In response to Fascist occupation, a broad-based resistance movement had emerged in 1941 led by the Greek Communist Party (KKE) with the National Liberation Front (EAM) and the affiliated National Popular Liberation Army (ELAS) emerging as 'the most significant opponent of the Germans and the most powerful political force inside Greece'.[6] A wide variety of anti-Fascist, republican forces joined the resistance, while EAM's Right-wing and Monarchist opponents joined the Fascist security battalions, preferring collaboration with the Nazis to the possibility of a Communist-led revolution.

Dismissing SOE reports that all the resistance groups were opposed to the return of King George II, the exiled Greek monarch, and that the Communist partisans needed to be taken more seriously, Churchill launched an offensive against the Greek Communists on 3 December 1944 when a banned EAM demonstration in Athens was fired on by police and British troops: the first military intervention against any anti-Nazi resistance movement in occupied Europe. The British, who had long regarded Greece as almost a colony, had three main strategic objectives – the containment and eventual elimination of Left-wing mass resistance to the German occupation; the restoration of the Greek monarchy backed by a Right-wing government; and the safeguarding of a major strategic lifeline to the oilfields of the Middle East and India. In pursuit of these aims British troops engaged in fierce fighting around Athens five months before the end of the war in Europe. Not surprisingly, there was considerable unease among wide sections of the British public at the use of troops to defeat a partisan movement that had fought against the Nazis. *The Times* launched a 'savage attack on Churchill and his coalition government' that 'astonished the British conservative establishment' by its severity.[7] A stalemate ensued. ELAS could not defeat the British Army in a straight fight, while the British – though able to secure Athens – lacked the resources to control all Greece.[8] A compromise truce was agreed, the so-called Treaty of Varkiza of February 1945, and preparations were made for Greece's first post-war general election under the approving eyes of the US and UK. In March 1946, after a period of 'White Terror', the Right-wing Tsaldiris government came to power with the blessing of America and Britain following an election boycotted by the Left. Attlee and his Foreign Minister Ernest Bevin's post-war intervention in Greek affairs had followed Churchill's imperialist strategy without deviation, to the consternation of the Labour press.

On 7 September 1946, six months after the election in Greece and six days after the return of the monarchy, the *New Stateman's* Kingsley Martin rounded on Attlee and Bevin, accusing them of conniving in the 'fascist' excesses of the Greek government. It was a hard-hitting piece: 'a Labour government, elected a year ago to carry out a socialist policy abroad as well as at home has ultimately connived at the restoration in Greece of a reactionary king by a government tainted with collaborationists and as repressive in its attitude to the working class in Greece as it is chauvinistic in its behaviour towards neighbouring countries.'[9]

The Allied Mission for the Observation of the Greek Elections denounced the recent elections as rigged and reported on numerous instances of fraud and harassment by government officials. A series of tough measures against the Greek Left, including the deportation of Left-wing activists and other opponents to barren Aegean islands, was followed by a ban on public meetings and the right to strike. Of particular concern was the setting up of special military courts to pass death sentences with no right of appeal. On 9 November 1946 the *New Statesman* commented, 'if instead of a positive socialist policy you make it your objective to defeat communism, you usually find yourself supporting something in the nature of fascism.'[10] The *Daily Worker* accused the Labour government of collaborating with quislings to destroy Greek independence:

Democracy in Greece has been murdered and the assassin is the Labour government in London ... Greece is no longer an independent country; it is a British colony where a ruling clique, containing a large number of quislings, has been installed in office by the occupying power.[11]

The climactic end to the Civil War in Greece took place in August 1949 when the Communist partisans suffered a major defeat in the Gramos Mountains in northern Greece and retreated into Albania. Later that year Francis Loeffler was sent to Athens by the Haldane Society of

Socialist Lawyers as an observer at the trial of a number of prominent Greek Communists sentenced to death by the military courts despite assurances given to the United Nations by the then Greek Premier that political executions in Greece had stopped. However, within a few hours of this official statement, Mr Georgiou, the elected General Secretary of the Electrical Trade Union of Greece, was executed.

On 7 November 1951 Loeffler returned to Greece as a member of the Haldane Society to attend sessions of the court martials of Ioannes Skouriotes and Menas Galeos and the Communist Solomos. Both Skouriotes and Galeos had stood as candidates for the United Democratic Left (EDA), a political party founded in July 1951 by former members of the Communist-controlled Greek People's Liberation Army (EAM-ELAS). EDA was regarded by the authorities as a substitute and political front for the banned Communist Party of Greece and had been declared illegal. Francis was refused permission to assist with the defence of the accused and protests were lodged both locally and abroad against this ruling. He attended the trial sessions until their conclusion and flew back to the UK on 22 November.[12]

MI5 took a great deal of interest in Francis upon his return and on 18 December 1951 reported that he had recently conveyed a personal message of thanks from General Stefanos Sarafis, ex-Commander-in-Chief of EAM-ELAS, to the Union of Democratic Control (UDC) for their protests against the continued detention of EDA MPs.

Founded in 1914 as the rallying point for opposition to the First World War, the UDC campaigned along similar lines during the Second World War. It could not be described as a Communist front organisation and, therefore, should have been outside MI5's remit. During the 1939–45 conflict the UDC called for a government statement of peace aims and worked with the Peace Aims Group of the Parliamentary Labour Party, the Peace Council and other pacifist bodies. In the early years of the Cold War the UDC was supporting unofficial trade union activity outside the Trades Union Congress and had assumed the role of what today would be described a non-governmental organisation (NGO). Responsibility for monitoring the

UDC and Left-wing British trade unionists supporting EDA fell to MI5's Harry Wharton, an expert in counter-terrorism. Wharton had been active in various theatres of engagement. He had been sent to the London School of Oriental Studies in June 1946 to learn Hebrew and Arabic and had been posted undercover to Palestine in mid-1947 to work with special military groups. His 'job was to get intelligence on the Jewish guerrillas of the Irgun Zvai Leumi and the "Stern Gang", who were fighting the British occupation' of Palestine. At the end of 1947 he had been posted to Egypt, to the headquarters at Fayid of Security Intelligence Middle East (SIME), run by MI6. That he should be aimed at the UDC and trade unionists was a 'most interesting' development inside MI5:

> This is most interesting. We were recently asked by F.O. for our opinion about the U.D.C's part in the recent spate of appeals against the continued detention of SARAFIS and company. Can your source tell us the extent of the U.D.C.'s influence in this campaign? The appeals were all signed by T.Us. [Trade Unions] but the U.D.C. may well have been the guiding hand behind it all.[13]

That an agent with Harry Wharton's background should be assigned to monitoring the activities of the UDC, the Haldane Society and trade unionists sympathetic to the Left in Greece was evidence that MI5's mandate had recently been expanded to include counter-terrorism as well as counter-espionage and counter-subversion in nominally independent states where Britain's imperial interests were considered to be under threat.

Francis returned to Athens in 1952 to cover the trials of Beloyannis, Ioannidou, Lazarides and twenty-six others condemned to death by the special courts the previous October. On 24 March he wrote to Theodore Dogannis, London correspondent of the exiled EAM press, expressing his horror that the men were to be executed for their political opinions 'not for any criminal acts against the State, but simply because of the fact that their political opinions were abhorrent to the Government ...

such was the strength of world opinion that the Government did not dare to carry out the executions'.[14]

Not to be thwarted, however, the Greek authorities had switched the trials of Beloyannis and his co-defendants from the special courts to the permanent Court Martial of Athens and the prisoners were charged with acts of espionage contrary to Law 375 of 1936. If found guilty, world opinion would have to accept the necessity of their executions as 'the prisoners were, in fact guilty of espionage, guilty of treachery to their Motherland'.[15] The trials were carefully staged with all evidence of police brutality in interrogations and judicial malpractice suppressed. Francis wrote:

> In its attempt to deceive the world the Government saw to it that many of the most objectionable features of former trials were missing from this one. There were no complaints on this occasion of naked police intimidation against the prisoners. There were on this occasion no confessions by prisoners obtained by the police by violence or the threat of violence, 'confessions' which were afterwards refuted in court by those who had been compelled to make them.[16]

On 18 February, the third day of the trial, the Minister of the Interior, Konstantinos Rentis, accused an opposition faction within the Greek Army of operating spy rings with funds made available from abroad. The trial was no longer directed against ideological opponents but against agents of a foreign power with wireless transmission stations and hideouts and all the paraphernalia of a spy network. The perceived threat from the Soviet Union was barely concealed and a show trial was staged to coincide with the Greek parliament's decision to ratify the North Atlantic Treaty, which Greece had joined on 22 October 1951. As Francis noted, there were a number of irregularities in the legal process:

> The court consisted of five army officers only the President having any legal qualification. At the commencement the defence lawyers applied for an adjournment on the grounds that they had been

197

unable to study the file and call witnesses for the defence owing to the early hearing of the case. Their application was rejected, and the trial was rushed through at such a speed that the defence must surely have been prejudiced.[17]

The evidence against the accused was flimsy and Francis reported on the trial's absurdities in some detail. For many months, police units and the Greek Army had been monitoring messages sent out by illegal WT transmitters operating in Greece, the whereabouts of which were said to be unknown to the authorities. According to Francis, 'the texts of the messages were also unknown as they were transmitted in code, and apparently the code had defied the efforts of the appropriate departments to break it.' The transmitters were eventually located at houses in Argyicadis in Glyfada and Kaloumenos in Kallithea. Following police raids in November 1951 and several arrests, the police found a 'carefully concealed' wireless transmitter in 'a small specially constructed cellar under the Kaloumenos house', operated by a Greek Communist named Vavoudis. During a siege lasting forty hours the police appealed to Vavoudis to give himself up, concerned that the appearance of smoke was evidence of him burning documents. Eventually Vavoudis shot himself and he died on the way to hospital. The prosecution claimed that a piece of paper torn into pieces was recovered from the cellar, 'on which was written the secret code'. This was to be the smoking gun that would condemn Beloyannis and his co-defendants to death:

> By applying this code to the monitored messages their contents became known and revealed, according to the police, that secret military information vital to Greece was being conveyed to a foreign power. It is virtually upon this melodramatic evidence that the whole of the prosecution case depends.[18]

The evidence, as Francis pointed out, was indeed melodramatic and fundamentally flawed. Common sense told Francis that something was not right:

The code is written on one single sheet of paper. One's credibility must be considerably strained to believe that a person such as Vavoudis, who shot himself rather than fall into the hands of the army and police, who had ample time to make his dispositions, would not have destroyed this most vital piece of evidence. He could have burnt it in a second, he could have chewed the pieces, one cannot understand why, if he wished to destroy it, he should have merely torn it into pieces.

A rudimentary knowledge of basic SIGINT procedure threw doubt on the entire prosecution's case:

It is quite easy to see that the whole of the messages and the code could quite easily be evidence faked by the police. In considering this aspect of the evidence, one must also give some attention to the code itself. It is a simple code in which each letter of the alphabet is represented by a number; in addition a list of names follows, of persons, places and articles of military equipment, each of which also has its distinctive number in the code.[19]

Francis was sceptical that the Soviets would have used a straightforward substitution code to transmit intelligence of this sensitivity and importance. It was very unlikely that they would be operating such a simple code and cypher system in Greece in 1951. Francis wrote:

I am no cryptographer, but I have always understood that this type of code was one of the easiest to break down, and I find my credibility strained to breaking point to believe that the Greek army would have been unable to decipher the monitored messages. But even if one accepts the document as being genuine, it is still clear that in no civilised country, could it possibly be evidence against Beloyannis and Ioannidou, who had been in prison for many months before the code was discovered.[20]

Francis continued:

> In fact, the only evidence produced against Beloyannis and Ioannidou consisted of the testimonies given by their fellow prisoners who, in order to gain their freedom, had publicly renounced their communism; while, at the same time denying having spied against their country. From a legal point of view, this evidence should not have been allowed to stand, as it was 'the evidence of accomplices', and this should not be accepted without corroboration.[21]

The Director General of Police, Panopoulos, summed up the prosecution's case: 'For me there is no Communism,' he declared, 'there is a Communist conspiracy.' In reply to the question: 'Is a Communist Party a party of spies?' he replied 'It can be nothing else.'[22]

On his return to Britain, Francis served on the Executive Committee of the League of Democracy in Greece and on 6 April 1952 addressed a meeting of the league in Hyde Park, telling the crowd that he had been 'privileged to attend the trial of Beloyannis and his three compatriots'.[23] His letter to Dogannis was read out, denouncing the Greek authorities' desire to carry out 'at all costs … the judicial murder' of the three accused.

Throughout the Athens trial Francis had stayed with the defence lawyer Minas A. Galeos at 123 Karaiskou Street, Piraeus. In September 1952 Galeos was arrested and Francis was one of the signatories of a telegram of protest sent to General Plastiras and the Left-wing Greek newspaper *Allagi* (*Change*):

> Undersigned British Lawyers gravely concerned arrest Minas Galeos defence counsel in Beloyannis and Ambatelios trials. Apparently persecution defending counsel and interference rights of political prisoners to legal representation.[24]

Surveillance of the Haldane Society and the Lawyers' Group of the Communist Party was stepped up. Francis had qualified as a solicitor in August 1953 and had begun working for 'the Communist solicitors'

W.H. Thompson and Son, 120 London Wall, EC2, soon afterwards. He later joined Garber and Vowles, which then merged with Jack Gaster's firm to become Gaster, Vowles, Turner and Loeffler.[25]

Meetings of the Central and Priory Branch of the Hampstead Communist Party were held at the Loeffler's house at Aberdare Gardens, but for some reason in 1953 Francis and Sabine began using the alias Keeling, registering as members of the Communist Party under that name.[26] It may well have been an attempt to keep his activities with the CPGB's Lawyers' Group separate from his work with the Haldane Society. But in this he was unsuccessful. He was elected a member of the Haldane Society's Executive Committee on 25 November and in 1954, 'by virtue of a mail intercept on Francis MI5 obtained the list of all the members of the Society as at 30 June 1941.'[27]

CHAPTER NINETEEN

Renate, Melita Norwood and the Rifkind Criteria

In 1950 MI5's B2a reported that Renate, the youngest sister of Ursula and Jürgen, was 'the closest in sympathy with them and probably the most ardent Party member of the family in this country'. For this reason, an HOW on the Simpsons was put in place in an attempt to obtain 'up-to-date information on the whereabouts and present activities of the BEURTONs and the KUCZYNSKIs'.[1] MI5, at the time, were unaware that both Jürgen and Ursula had crossed into the Soviet Zone of Germany.

Renate had returned to London with the National Union of Students (NUS) in February 1945 as Assistant Secretary. Her husband, Arthur, remained in Cambridge, permitting Renate to retain her links with the Cambridge Communist Party and in the 1945 general election she served as their election agent.[2] In early 1946, following Arthur's appointment as Senior Scientific Officer at the Ministry of Agriculture and Fisheries (MAF), the couple moved to 13 Marine Parade in the Suffolk coastal town of Lowestoft, where Renate presided over weekly *Daily Worker* discussion groups of ten people or more, 'a mixture of intellectuals and workers'. In November 1947 she was elected to the local Co-op Education Committee and the CPGB registered an interest in Arthur's work with MAF. The Assistant General Secretary of the Communist Party, John Gollan, approached a local Communist, W. Furnie, requesting information about scientists working in the Suffolk area. Furnie replied:

> With reference to your letter of the 18th, we have no Science contact in our district, but it may be useful if you could send the materials to Mr. A. SIMPSON, 13 Marine Parade, Lowestoft, Suffolk.

This comrade is working in the fishing industry on research work, and it may be useful if you had direct contact with him. If you are in agreement, please make sure that all correspondence is in a sealed envelope.[3]

The following month Arthur was elected Secretary of the Lowestoft Institute of Civil Servants (Trade Union), and was also made Vice-President of the United Nations Association in Lowestoft. In April 1949 he applied for the post of Director of Fisheries in Hong Kong and the Colonial Office submitted a vetting enquiry to MI5; although he was eminently qualified for the position, it was decided not to employ him owing to the security situation in Hong Kong after the war:

Personally Mr. Simpson appeared a very attractive man, thoroughly sound and capable. He has an excellent academic record. I believe SIMPSON is likely to place his career before his politics, and I do not think that there would be any objection in principle to his appointment to a post of Director of Fisheries. Present conditions in Hong Kong however are such that it would, on balance be preferable to appoint someone to whom we could give full security clearance, since there can be no guarantee that SIMPSON would not once again interest himself in Communism, to the considerable embarrassment of the authorities in Hong Kong.[4]

On 5 February 1950 an official committee on positive vetting was set up under the chairmanship of A.J.D. Winnifrith, a Treasury Under-Secretary.[5] The phrase 'positive vetting' was 'almost certainly a linguistic intervention of Winnifrith's', coined to distinguish the process from the 'Purge Procedure or 'negative vetting' that had been introduced in 1948 to keep Communists and Fascists out of the Civil Service.[6] In 1950 the Cabinet Secretary, Sir Norman Brook, quoted from Winnifrith's report:

The 'positive vetting' which the report recommends involves primarily a change of attitudes and methods on the part of the departmental establishment authority concerned who, 'having first made sure that the Security Service has no adverse record of the candidate, should itself make a conscious effort to confirm his reliability'. This is to be achieved partly by a check of personal records which will be kept in fuller form than hitherto, and partly – in a minority of cases – by specific enquiries undertaken by the Security Service.[7]

On 28 September 1950 the Chief Constable of Suffolk informed MI5 that five of the scientists employed by MAF, including Arthur, were 'believed to be Communists'.[8] Membership of the Communist Party alone was not grounds for dismissal and the only course open to MI5 was to advise that Communists be denied access to secret work. In February 1951, therefore, MI5 enquired of the Ministry 'whether SIMPSON's work entails access to any secret information'[9] and the following month recommended that on security grounds Simpson should be denied access to all information classified as secret.[10] In April MI5 wrote again to MAF on the subject of Arthur's employment and received the following reply:

> As you probably know we have discussed with the Ministry of Supply the classification of the information which they impart to our staff who are employed on the work which I described in my letter of 18th January last (PF.135568/C1a/X). We are now informed that the information given is only 'restricted' so that is the answer to your enquiry. There is no other information to which Simpson has access which is classified 'secret'.[11]

On 4 December the HOW on the Simpsons' home address was limited to correspondence from abroad. The inland correspondence addressed to a small place in Suffolk meant that all the letters sent to the Simpsons had to be copied by hand by the local postmaster, a time-consuming task and his handwriting was not good. 'Positive vetting' was finally introduced by the Churchill government in January 1952 and the HOW on all the Simpsons' correspondence was reimposed on 19 March 1952.

On 21 September 1955 MI5 again raised the question of Arthur's employment with MAF, informing the Ministry that his wife 'belongs to a family which has espionage connections'.[12] In December in a memorandum on 'positive vetting' to the Security Conference of Privy Counsellors, Winnifrith wrote: 'At the risk of being smug I would like to say in the first place that, particularly given the speed with which it has been evolved, the present system is a pretty good one.'[13] The Civil Service, however, was institutionally reluctant to be vetted by MI5 and a further letter was sent on 13 March 1956 informing the Ministry that Arthur was a member of Science for Peace, a Communist-backed organisation.[14] The reply came back:

> This officer does not have access to classified information in his present post. It is intended to transfer him to his former (permanent) official station at Lowestoft on 1st August, 1956;[15] he will not have access to classified information in his new location.[16]

Renate and Arthur's sense of loyalty, however, would soon undergo a severe test of a very different kind when Soviet tanks rolled into Budapest on 4 November 1956. The Hungarian Uprising, a nationwide revolution against the Hungarian People's Republic and its Soviet-imposed policies, reignited smouldering family tensions when both Sabine and Francis announced that they were uncomfortable with the Soviet 'invasion' and occupation of Hungary, while Renate and Arthur backed the Soviet Union's 'intervention' to the hilt. In a letter to Sabine dated 19 November, Renate condemned the rash of resignations from the British Communist Party over the issue:

> I feel very sorry for you! Having had Margaret Ryle (now Xeros [sic] and sister of Anthony who has just resigned) and her very vociferous husband for the week-end we have certainly heard a different opinion and argued 2 nights running until 2 a.m. … My position is (I say my, A's too, but he isn't writing this with me as he's at work) is this: I am open to discussion and possible doubts on Hungary – though

still inclined towards the view that all this was necessary – <u>asking for some real facts.</u> <u>But</u> I <u>utterly</u> condemn resignations of members – formation of other bodies, washing dirty linen in public, particularly the C. Press. My main object at the moment is to try and get a Congress or delegate Conference – as <u>quickly</u> as <u>possible</u> – this side of Xmas to give all these worried Gods [sic] a chance to make themselves heard, kick out the EC if the majority want to etc. etc. – Only after an attempt at a Congress and or District Conferences have failed has anyone the right to consider himself sufficiently 'stone-walled' to take drastic action. Feeling is certainly strong, and all these people should be given the opportunity to get policy changed etc. etc.[17]

Family and Party divisions were only partially resolved by discussion of the simultaneous Anglo-French-Israeli incursion into Egypt, with the question of Israeli aggression in the Middle East unsettling a number of Jewish members of the Communist Party. While the Suez Crisis demonstrated that the Israelis were prepared to engage in open warfare against Arab states alongside Britain and France, Israel continued to command a great deal of sympathy among Jewish supporters of the Labour Party and the British Communist Party. Bitter divisions of opinion within and between the Haldane Society of Socialist Lawyers and the Lawyers' Group of the Communist Party revealed an insurmountable breach between the two bodies.

The Haldane Society's Stuart Shields was 'said to be severely shaken by events in Hungary' and was 'particularly distressed' by the implications for the International Association of Democratic Lawyers (IADL).[18] He, along with Peter Pain, chairman of the Society and a member of the Labour Party, proposed a resolution at a special meeting of the Society condemning firstly 'British action in Egypt as being contrary to the principles of justice and specifically contrary to the United Nations Charter', and secondly condemning the 'Soviet action in Hungary on the same grounds'.[19] 'The first part of the motion', according to an MI5 source inside the Haldane Society, 'was entirely acceptable' to the Lawyers' Group of the British Communist Party;

but as regards the second part it was decided after much discussion to let members vote according to their conscience – a deciding factor being that to direct them to vote against the resolution would split the Haldane Society. It was proposed to put an amended version of the Shields–Pain resolution to the Society condemning Soviet intervention in Hungary but omitting all reference to the United Nations Charter. This was accepted by the Haldane Society but not by the Lawyers' Group of the Communist Party. Of those who voted for the resolution, Francis was identified as 'probably the most extreme' and was said to be 'on the verge of a breakdown. He [Francis] mentioned that, at the beginning of the last war, he had collaborated in this country with two comrades from abroad, one of whom had been hanged and the other had been imprisoned. He said everything should be done to fight against this sort of thing.'[20] Sabine was said to be 'extremely distressed by the Hungarian situation, and was especially disturbed by reports of the deportations of Hungarians to Russia. The abduction of the leader of the Hungarian Revolution, Imre Nagy, smacked too much of old familiar Nazi methods' for her 'to be able to view the situation in the accepted Party fashion'.[21]

Nagy, a member of the Hungarian Communist Party, had been elevated to the position of Prime Minister on day two of the revolution. He had immediately granted reforms that the Soviet Union found unacceptable: most notably the participation of non-Communist politicians in the Hungarian government and the unilateral withdrawal of Hungary from the Warsaw Pact. The Warsaw Pact was a particularly sensitive issue.[22] Created in May 1955 in reaction to the reintegration of West Germany into the Western defensive alliance, the Soviets feared a repeat of pre-Second World War capitalist encirclement and invasion. On 4 November 1956 the Soviets selected János Kádár, who had opposed the unilateral withdrawal, as the next leader of Hungary. The Haldane Society was unhappy with these developments and raised its concerns with the Hungarian Legation. Those Communists critical of Sabine and Francis's personal disquiet with events were upset by the lack of direction from above, with the Communist lawyer Ralph

Milner complaining that the 'Group Committee were at fault in giving no satisfactory lead' and should be censured 'for allowing comrades to vote against the Party in a broad organisation'. A majority of the Haldane Society were Labour and not Communist Party members. This posed problems of a disciplinary nature for Milner, who 'welcomed criticism inside the Party, but outside comrades must support the line'. By showing disunity, he argued, the Group Committee 'had greatly weakened the Party's position in the Haldane Society'.

Francis had wanted all references to Israeli aggression removed from any resolution to be agreed by the Haldane Society on the two crises. His colleague, Jack Gaster, offered veiled support by suggesting that there was no 'parallel between the British action in Suez and the entry of the Russians into Hungary at the request of the lawful Hungarian Government'.[23] Pritt's line was that the Society should not act rashly and that 'they should wait until they have the facts on Hungary'.[24] One view that summed up the problem facing Communists within the Society and the IADL was that 'in six months' time everybody will have forgotten the British action in Suez, because this is the sort of thing the world expects from the British, but that the Soviet Union should behave in this way is a terrible thing and will not be forgotten quickly.'[25]

In January 1957 the Executive Committee of the Haldane Society wrote to the Hungarian Legation asking them to meet a delegation from the Society to discuss the situation in their country. The Hungarians agreed to a delegation of four and the Haldane Executive Committee accepted their terms, with Shields wanting to 'make it clear to the Hungarians that they were not absolutely 'with' the KADAR government'.[26] Shields stressed the point that the Haldane Society was not 'Party minded' and that the Communists were in a minority. A special meeting of the Society was held on 23 February in the Feathers public house, Westminster, to discuss the two crises of Hungary and Suez, where the opposing factions in the Society clashed. At one point it looked as if the Society might fold, but domestic issues reunited the warring groups. On Saturday, 9 March 1957 the Haldane Society held a conference on the Rent Bill at the Conway Hall, Red Lion Square, WC1. It was an impressive gathering. There were about 400 people present, most of them delegates from tenants' and residents' associations, trade union branches, co-operative guilds and Labour Party branches. The chairman was Stephen Swingler, a backbench Labour MP, and the main speaker was William Solomon Sedley, a Communist solicitor. Francis was also on the platform and made a short speech. Normal service within the Society had been resumed, events of a domestic nature healing divisions.

Described as one of the most controversial pieces of legislation ever to be passed by a post-war Conservative government, the 1957 Rent Act was designed 'to resolve the problem of housing shortages by removing the statutory restrictions on the rents of privately let accommodation', in place since the First World War. 'The government argued that by abolishing rent controls private landlords would be encouraged to maintain, improve, and invest in private rented property and therefore increase its availability.'[27] The outcome was somewhat different: the rise of the property tycoon Perec ('Peter') Rachman, whose exploitation of tenants would be brought to national attention in 1963 during investigations into the Profumo affair.

The Rent Act had a galvanising effect on the Kuczynskis, with Bridget's husband, Jock Nicholson, making speeches from a soapbox outside Kentish Town Tube Station on Saturday mornings during the 1960 St Pancras Council Tenants' Rent Strike.[28] The public disorder that followed evictions of tenants for non-payment of rents led to the Public Order Act being imposed on the Borough of Camden. Jock, a goods checker at Camden Goods Station, had been the Communist Party candidate for St Pancras North in the general election held in May 1955, with Francis acting as his election agent. He polled 1,303 votes, 5 per cent of the winning Labour tally. Nicholson would stand as the Party candidate in St Pancras North for the next twenty years, while the ever-resourceful Bridget would help raise the money to fund his election expenses by charging tourists and others for a guided tour of Marx's and Engels' London.[29]

While Bridget and Jock took an active part in everyday Communist Party affairs, secrecy still pervaded much of Renate and Arthur's activities in Lowestoft. In January 1957 MI5 learned from a source described as 100 per cent reliable that while Arthur held a Communist Party card he was not included in the local membership figure and took no part in branch affairs. The same source reported that he was also a member of the AScW and the Communist-controlled Science for Peace.[30] On 7 February 1957 MI5's F2 also reported that Arthur was a secret Communist Party member; stating that according to the 1947 Civil Service List, Arthur was a Principal Scientific Officer earning between £1,375 and £1,950 per annum.[31] The following week F4 minuted, 'We may be able to provide some further information about SIMPSON. There is no prospect, however, of using him for F.4 purposes.'[32] On 13 March he was added to their list of Secret Communists.[33]

The Communist Party's national organiser, Peter Kerrigan, was also known to take a keen interest in Arthur's career. On 7 June 1957 Kerrigan asked Peter Thiel, East Anglia Industrial Organiser, if they had any scientists in the local Party. Simpson's name was mentioned, with Thiel informing Kerrigan that he 'was in contact with him trying to work out a policy for fisheries', prompting Kerrigan to suggest that it would be worth 'consulting with Scotland over that – (as) they had a programme'.[34]

At that time both the Polish and Russian trawler fleets were particularly active around Shetland, with Polish trawlers working between the Norwegian and British coasts. On 22 October 1957 an incident took place involving a 26-year-old Polish trawler man, Mieczyslaw Borzyskowski, and the Lowestoft constabulary that mysteriously involved the Simpsons. Borzyskowski was arrested at 1.30 a.m. in Lowestoft for being drunk and attempting to steal a car. In his possession the arresting police officer found a torn envelope with the Simpsons' address, 40 Victoria Road, Oulton Broad, Suffolk, written across it along with the address of a Mr and Mrs Unwin, Salisbury Road, Great Yarmouth, Norfolk. Mr and Mrs Unwin were known Communist Party members with Personal Files held by MI5.[35]

The Lowestoft police photographed this torn piece of paper without Borzyskowski's knowledge and returned it to his property. Another piece of paper bearing the address of John W. Gibson, 72 Heath Lane, Boughton, Chester, was found later the same morning in circumstances that highlighted the bizarre behaviour of the Pole and gave rise to suspicions that he was more than he seemed:

> Later that morning at Court, the owner of the car handed another piece of paper to P.C. Marriott which he said he had picked up in his house after BORYZSKOWSKI had been taken away by the Police. BORYZSKOWSKI was actually caught by the car owner attempting to steal his car and was taken into his house whilst the police were sent for.[36]

This new piece of paper was also photographed and copies sent to MI5 at Box 500, Parliament Street, London. But there the mysterious tale ends, with no further mention of Borzyskowski appearing in the Simpsons' MI5 file. The Kuczynski spy trail simply petered out. It would not be until the publication of the *Mitrokhin Archive* thirty-four years later under the guidance of the security and intelligence services that the Kuczynski group would make a reappearance in intelligence literature.

Vassili Mitrokhin was a KGB archivist who had been assigned responsibility for transferring files from the Lubyanka, off Gorky Street, to new headquarters situated in the woods at Yasenovo. He defected in 1992. As the historian Christopher Andrew explains in *Mitrokhin Archive*, Mitrokhin had risked his life over a period of time spanning ten years or more, compiling detailed notes from the files of the First Main Directorate (foreign intelligence) of the KGB. On the eve of the collapse of the Soviet Union, he supplied the British with files identifying a number of spies who had hitherto remained incognito. Among those exposed by Mitrokhin was Melita Norwood, an 80-year-old grandmother from Bexleyheath in Kent. Her KGB file was passed to an MI5 case officer pending a decision on whether she should be questioned about her spying activities.

During 1992 and the early months of 1993, amid growing concerns for Mitrokhin's safety and the need to keep secret the international investigations then under way into those identified agents who were still active, MI5 decided not to interview Mrs Norwood but to review her case internally. The review concluded that it was not in anybody's interest to investigate her further as she was now more than 80 years old, and her spying career had ended some time ago. When, in 1995, a decision was taken to publish Mitrokhin's material, the Conservative government of John Major insisted on a number of safeguards being put in place by the Foreign Secretary, Malcolm Rifkind, in what became known as the Rifkind criteria. Under the Rifkind criteria it was agreed that, 'The names of the people the KGB had targeted for recruitment or attempted to influence could not be made public unless they had been prosecuted and convicted or they had agreed to the release of their names.'[37] In other words, Rifkind made it quite clear that he did not want the intelligence services to decide whether names should be released into the public domain without clearance from the Foreign or Home Office. Following the election of a Labour government in May 1997 these safeguards, apparently, got lost. Since Whitehall civil servants had not worked with a Labour government since the 1970s, communication between civil servants and ministers during the first few months of the new government was not good. It was, therefore, not until 23 October 1997 that the incoming Foreign Secretary, Robin Cook, received a note from Sir John Kerr, the Parliamentary Under-Secretary in the Foreign Office, informing him about Mitrokhin's material and the publication project. Jack Straw, the incoming Home Secretary, fared little better. He was not informed of the project until 10 December 1998.

What happened next undermined the Rifkind criteria, with the Melita Norwood story sensationally hitting the headlines. The original 'objective of the publication project', under Rifkind, had been quite clear: 'to place Mr. Mitrokhin's material in the public domain in a controlled and unsensational manner'.[38] This didn't happen: 'Revealed: The Quiet Woman Who Betrayed Britain for 40 Years. The Spy Who

Came in from the Co-op', was *The Times* headline on 11 September 1999. 'The Mole Who Came into the Garden', was preferred by the *Independent*. The *Independent on Sunday* described her story as 'classically British … in more ways than one':

> The 87-year-old great-grandmother, whose wispy grey-haired exterior masks a life of studied betrayal, was for 40 years one of Russia's most effective Cold War spies. There has been a characteristically British touch of ambivalence in the reaction to the news: the old lady is simultaneously dubbed a 'great' spy to rank with the 'Magnificient Five' of Burgess, Maclean, Philby, Blunt and Cairncross, and yet there are calls for her prosecution on the grounds that 'treachery is never forgivable'.[39]

Foremost among those calling for her prosecution was the shadow Home Secretary, Ann Widdecombe. To those who knew Melita Norwood at this time, the psychological pressures upon her were immense and she needed the support of family and friends. In September 1999, when media interest in Mrs Norwood was at fever pitch, she received a copy of Ursula's autobiography, *Sonya's Report*, from Renate through the post; inside was a photo of Rosa Luxemburg bearing the simple inscription:

> To Letty
> 'Sonya' salutes you and 'Reni' sends her love. Enjoy the pictures and captions and lend it to your family – ask them to give you a summary!!

Ursula would die in Berlin on 7 July 2003 at the age of 93. In 1999, she was one of the few people capable of commenting on Norwood's life as a spy, apart from Renate and Mrs Norwood herself. At the time I was interviewing Norwood about her spying activities and whenever she spoke of her past she gave the impression that she was doing so with Ursula's tacit approval, as if the arrival of *Sonya's Report* had been one last call to arms. Mrs Norwood introduced me to Renate, who spoke very highly of her friend. The bond between the Kuczynski family and the Norwoods spanned a period of seventy years. The former head of East Germany's foreign intelligence service, Markus Wolf, once remarked that to minimise risk to agents in the field, intelligence services had to build on existing patterns of loyalty – ideological, political, geographical – that dated from childhood … the Oxford and Cambridge networks within the British secret services, and the family dynasties within Soviet intelligence were all protective mechanisms against betrayal. The secrets of the Kuczynski family in Britain and the defiance of Melita Norwood following her outing as a spy on 11 September 1999 is testimony to Wolf's sagacity.

Conclusion

It is an indisputable fact that a good secret agent needs to be more than an effective conspirator. They have to be capable of getting their bearings fast in ever-changing political situations and for this reason intelligence work is primarily political work.

The Kuczynski family were, undoubtedly, suited to this work and supplied the Soviet Union with valuable intelligence for a period greater than seventy years. From Robert and Berta's early activities with Willi Münzenberg and the Fight the Famine Council in 1920 to Renate's support for Melita Norwood in 1999, the Kuczynskis never faltered in their unswerving support for the Soviet Union. This was in harmony with a belief that worldwide Communism could only be achieved by guaranteeing the security of the Soviet State. In Renate and Melita Norwood's case this continued long after the fall of the Berlin Wall in 1989 and the collapse of the Soviet Union two years later. Norwood and the Kuczynskis were successful not simply because they were adept practitioners in the field of intelligence, but because they had a belief in the certitude of their ideology. That way, at least to themselves, their actions could not be wrong. In pursuing their aims they regarded liberalism and imperialism as twin ideological and practical enemies of Soviet Communism. This viewpoint has not entirely disappeared from modern-day Russia.

Vladimir Putin, who worked with Ursula in the DDR as a KGB agent, has often proclaimed 'the liberal idea' to be 'obsolete'. The 'liberal idea' as principal foe has a long history in Russia. Indeed, the Kuczynskis had defended the Nazi–Soviet pact in much the same way. They saw Hitler and Stalin as the gravediggers of free-market capitalism, imperialism and the protectionism underpinning the British Empire.

For many rank-and-file Communists the defeat of the British Empire would be followed by the triumph of Soviet Communism over both Nazism and the 'liberal idea'.

It would be a mistake to subject the players on the Soviet side to a crude reductionism that sees Communism and Fascism as part of the same totalitarian experience. To do so is to encourage 'fake history'. The Kuczynski network opposed Fascism throughout the lifespan of both the Nazi and Soviet systems. There can be little doubt that their anti-Fascist work opened up opportunities for Soviet intelligence in this country, with leading British Labour Party and labour movement figures successfully cultivated as sympathisers and fellow-travellers. This was political work that also involved cultural, scientific and economic work. Thus the Kuczynskis took a keen interest in Members of Parliament, high-ranking civil servants in the Board of Trade, the Ministry of Information, the Ministry of Power, the Ministry of Agriculture, Fisheries and Food, the Ministry of Economic Warfare and the Ministry of Labour and National Service. They also took an interest in the BBC, the British Council, the British Non-Ferrous Metals Research Association, the Atomic Energy Research Establishment and the legal profession.

The fact that the Soviets were able to gain access to Britain's atomic bomb secrets as well as information from fellow-travellers inside Bletchley Park is testimony to the Kuczynskis' skill and commitment. The question of treachery, however, cannot be so easily put to bed. Anybody writing about the skills of the Kuczynskis as spies confronts a thorny issue: their abilities might be manifest but their Stalinism cannot be glanced over lightly. What makes this a difficult activity is the fact that Stalinism, unless attacked with a moral vocabulary that misrepresents the true nature of the phenomenon, was a system that attracted many good people, the Kuczynskis among them. How can this be explained? Stalin may have held enormous power, but it is far too simplistic and reductionist to attribute to him every decision taken by the supporters of Communism. Such a 'puppet-master paradigm' obscures the independent capacity of those, like the Kuczynskis, who not only promoted Stalinism but elected to do so through an enemy intelligence system.

To understand the British intelligence community's contest with Soviet intelligence throughout the twentieth century, historians must take cognisance of the attractions of the Soviet Union during the widespread impoverishment, hunger and uncertainties of the interwar period and the Second World War. Jürgen's close associate in the Left Book Club, John Strachey, made the telling point that while 'the conspiratorial aspects of Communism were part of social reality during the decades in question [they] were not the only, nor the most important, aspects of Communism'.[1]

Strachey's advice holds well when it comes to explaining both the motivation of the Kuczynski family and of those who kept the family under close surveillance as spies or subversives. 'To fail to take Communism with the utmost seriousness,' Strachey wrote in 1962, 'is still almost as disastrous a mistake as to take Communism hysterically.'[2] Students of the intelligence conflict between the agents of two contradictory economic systems and ideologies during the twentieth century would do well to heed Strachey's advice.

The Evolution of the GRU and the KGB

December 1917   Cheka – All-Russian Extraordinary Commission for Combatting Counter-Revolution and Sabotage.

November 1918   GRU (*Glavnoye razvedyvatel'noye upravleniye*) refers to the Main Intelligence Directorate, that is the military intelligence division of the Red Army created in November 1918 as the Registration Directorate. Also referred to as the Fourth Department following the reorganisation of military intelligence in 1925 aimed at breaking Trotsky's hold over sections of the Red Army.

July 1921–39   OMS (*Otdel mezhdynarodnoi svyazi*), the International Liaison Department of the Communist International. The OMS undertook clandestine courier activities and work that supported underground Communist activities. Its functions often overlapped with those of the main Soviet intelligence agencies, the OGPU/NKVD and the GRU. It has also been referred to as the Comintern's Illegal Liaison Section and the Comintern's Foreign Liaison Department.

February 1922   GPU (*Gosudarstvennoye politicheskoye upravleniye*)

July 1923   OGPU (*Obyedinyonnoye gosudarstvennoye politicheskoye upravleniye pri SNK SSSR*), the Joint State Political Directorate under the Council of

	People's Commissars of the USSR, refers to the Soviet political police between 1923 and 1934.
1924	The direction of the OMS was transferred to the GRU and the OGPU.
July 1934	NKVD (*Narodnyi komissariat vnutrennekh del*), the People's Commissariat for Internal Affairs, predecessor to the KGB.
February 1941	NKGB (*Narodnyi komissariat gosudarstvennoi bezopastnosti*), People's Commissariat of State Security.
July 1941	NKVD.
April 1943	NKGB.
March 1946	MGB (*Ministerstvo gosudarstvennoi bezopastnosti*), Ministry for State Security.
October 1947– November 1951	Foreign Intelligence transferred to KI, Committee of Information (Soviet foreign intelligence agency combining the foreign directorates of the MGB and GRU).
March 1953	MVD (*Ministerstvo vnutrennikh del*), Ministry of Internal Affairs.
March 1954	KGB (*Komitet gosudarstvennoi bezopastnosti*), Committee for State Security.

The Soviet Communist Party has undergone a number of name changes during its history: 1912–18 Russian Social Democratic Labour Party (Bolsheviks); 1918–25 Russian Communist Party (Bolsheviks); 1925–52 All-Union Communist Party (Bolsheviks); 1952–91 Communist Party of the Soviet Union.

APPENDIX 2

A Note on British Intelligence

SIS, the Secret Intelligence Service, commonly known as MI6, was created in 1909 to engage in foreign intelligence gathering and was accountable to the Foreign Office. MI5, also created in 1909, had responsibility for domestic intelligence and was accountable to the Home Office. Section V (counter-espionage) was established in 1931 under Valentine Vivian to liaise with MI5.

MI5 had two Branches (also known as Divisions): A Branch, which covered administration, personnel, and records, and B Branch, which had responsibility for counter-espionage and counter-subversion, conducting 'investigations and inquiries'.

Surveillance of subversive movements in Britain by MI5 was carried out by B division, which was divided into sections.

B4 was a three-man Observation section, responsible for shadowing suspects and making 'confidential' inquiries. See Andrew, *Defence*, pp.127–8.

The section known as B4b dealt specifically with enemy espionage in industry and commerce. It was particularly concerned with the possibility of espionage inside firms that had access to government departments.

F Branch/Division handled counter-subversion.

F2(b) and F2(c) were respectively Comintern and Soviet intelligence sections within F division.

APPENDIX 3

William Scanlon Murphy to David Burke, 7 July 2016

I was a close friend of Barbara and Duncan Taylor and their son Neil in the 1980s, and saw first hand their close social contacts with senior (*very* senior) Labour Party figures (up to and including Denis Healey) and people such as Arthur Koestler and his wife. There was also a social nexus involving them both with several people who worked at Bletchley during the war; indeed, they all seem to have been at Cambridge (and in the Communist Party) early in the war or just before. One of their closest friends was a senior civil servant in Margaret Thatcher's office when she was at Education. To say the least of it, they were very unsubtle spies indeed. Literally the first thing one saw on entering their house (on Corringham Road, Hampstead Garden Suburb) was a photograph of the infant Barbara Kuczynski on the knee of Rosa Luxemburg. There were many photos on the wall of sister Ursula, always referred to as Ruth Werner …

I now have the creeping sensation that I blundered into some very dark pages of history thirty years ago, and it's time that history was written.

I was the son-in-law of Frederick ('Pat') Tyler and his wife Mary, who lived across the road from the Taylors on Corringway. The Tylers were senior figures in the local Labour Party, and – as I can now see – major social enablers for the Taylors.

APPENDIX 4

William Scanlon Murphy to David Burke, 17 July 2016

I know from a separate source that there was a Communist cell operating there (Bletchley Park). My parents-in-law were Frederick Tyler (known as Pat) and his wife Mary (née Southcombe). The two met at Cambridge at the end of the war; Mary was older than Pat, and had been in Wittgenstein's class (they detested each other, apparently). She was among the LSE people evacuated to Cambridge. She worked at Bletchley as a number cruncher from 1942, as did Pat's on/off girlfriend Dorothy White. A close friend of Pat's also worked at Bletchley – Peter Knight, who went on to become a literary agent (mine, for a while); I was once present at a lunch in London where all of these people were present together (they all kept in touch), with several others I did not know. They discussed the work of Bletchley quite openly; this was in 1980. It has been noticeable that none of them have participated in any of the TV documentaries about Bletchley that have been made since its existence was made public.

I have often wondered why Duncan Taylor was an RAF intelligence officer during the war. I would not expect this to bring him into direct contact with Bletchley (it would have been far above his clearance, surely?) but he knew (at least, and for certain) Mary and Dorothy before the end of the war. A very peculiar point (not to mention a fantastic coincidence). There was once a dinner party at the Tyler house at which the Taylors and Dorothy White were all present. The conversation turned to University romances (almost everybody but me went to Cambridge; I'm an Oxford man). I mentioned that I had been briefly engaged while at Oxford to the daughter of a Rabbinic scholar, which was thought most amusing until I mentioned his name – Hyam Maccoby – at which point an icy silence fell on the room and the conversation was frantically steered elsewhere. I learned, a full 20 years later, that Maccoby had been a 'night translator' at Bletchley – someone who actually saw the decrypts. It was obvious that they knew his name, and not in a good way. Unlike the Tyler circle, Hyam Maccoby never even faintly alluded in my hearing to having been at Bletchley – indeed, he claimed to have only rudimentary German and to have spent most of the war in Gateshead (he came from Sunderland). His wife Cynthia, however, was a fervent scholar of the Marxist classics and – odd footnote – a devout Reichian. Their house was full of Marxist literature alongside the Talmud – and contained the only Orgone Accumulator I have seen in real life. To be frank, I thought she was stark mad.

To my knowledge they (Barbara and Duncan) knew at least two Bletchley insiders directly. They knew Mary Southcombe (as she was at the time) and Dorothy White (her married name later – don't know her maiden name). Mary, I know, met Barbara through Barbara's sister Renate – as I recall it, they were both much involved in LSE student politics (your mention of Renate brought me up short rather violently!) Barbara and Mary knew each other before going to Cambridge (and, in Mary's case, Bletchley). Mary came from a well-to-do Somerset (Milborne Port) family and had the social airs to match, but was a firm Labour supporter; she became a very close friend of Barbara. Barbara, for all her Marxist heritage, was a rather haughty, even snooty woman, and the two were oddly similar.

Pat Tyler knew Denis Healey from when both were in the Army. They trained together, with Healey winding up at Anzio and Pat a beach master at the Normandy landings (on D-Day +6). However, they were also political allies from the outset. Both stood for parliament in the 1945 election (Pat stood for Knutsford) and both lost. I saw some of Pat's election literature, and it was startlingly more left-wing than his subsequent declared political position. They remained close friends for the rest of their lives. Healey visited the Tyler home many times between 1979 and 1985, often for dinner (at which the Taylors would invariably be present). Through the Tylers, the Taylors also knew senior Labour peer Lord Howie very well. I understand that Howie gave the eulogy at Pat's funeral. Healey always greeted the Taylors as old friends. Anthony Crosland was another visitor. It is important to know that Pat, despite being a self-described Socialist, was Company Secretary of Express Newspapers, which meant he had a direct line to a great deal of high-level Conservative thinking, especially under Conservative governments. He somehow combined this with running *Socialist Commentary*, which collapsed suddenly after being accused of accepting CIA funding. He was leader of the Labour group on Barnet council for several years.

There was an odd incident late in 1983 (November, I think). I was given a lift to central London by Pat Tyler one morning. Much to my surprise, he took an entirely different route from his usual rat-run down Fleet Street, choosing instead to drive through the middle of Hampstead. There, standing at the lights, was, of all people, Michael Foot. Mr Foot greeted Pat very obviously as an old friend and piled into the back of the car. Pat offered him a ride to Westminster, which was immediately accepted (he had recently lost his official car as Leader of the Opposition). The very, very first thing Mr Foot said as he got into the car was – quote – 'How is my old friend Duncan?'

The Taylors' home was a vital social hub for the broad Hampstead Left. What are lazily referred to as the chattering classes simply thronged there. It was particularly notable that they seemed to know an extraordinary number of civil servants, who (to my, now, obviously rather naïve eye) seemed mainly to come round to moan about their political masters.

An odd point to mention here is that both Taylors were highly sophisticated gourmands; Barbara was one of the four translators of the Larousse Gastronomique and was an extremely good cook. For what it is worth, my own mediocre skills with pastry were acquired in a two-day session in her kitchen, during which she said 'I will never eat inferior food unless I have a professional reason to do so, it is beyond politeness – I simply won't do it.' Mary Tyler's cooking was staggeringly bad ...

I have been absolutely scrupulous about not looking anything (e.g. political dates) up; these are my raw, unembellished memories, exactly as I remember them. Even at the time the Taylors always reminded me of the people in the attic in *Biedermann und die Brandstifter* (Max Frisch's play: *The Arsonists*) – they were so obvious that they couldn't be spies, could they?'

Notes

Introduction

1 NKVD – *Narodnyi komissariat vnutrennekh del* (People's Commissariat for Internal Affairs) created in July 1934, predecessor to the KGB.

2 GRU – *Glavnoye razvedyvatel'noye upravleniye* refers to the 'Main Intelligence Directorate', that is the military intelligence division of the Red Army created in November 1918 as the Registration Directorate. Known as the Fourth Department since 1925.

3 John Strachey on the Webbs' *Soviet Communism: A New Civilisation*; cited in Thomas, Hugh, *John Strachey* (London: Eyre Methuen, 1973), p.158.

4 Pelling, Henry, *The British Communist Party: A Historical Profile* (London: Black, 1958), p.191.

5 Merson, Allan, *Communist Resistance in Nazi Germany* (London: Lawrence & Wishart, 1985) p.2. Note the neglect of the German labour movement and the KPD in such seminal texts as Bullock, Alan, *Hitler: A Study in Tyranny* (London: Harmondsworth, 1952); Shirer, William L., *The Rise and Fall of the Third Reich: A History of Nazi Germany* (New York: Simon and Schuster, 1960; Wheeler-Bennett, John, *The Nemesis of Power: The German Army in Politics* (London: MacMillan, 1961); Grunberger, Richard, *A Social History of the Third Reich* (London: Weidenfeld & Nicolson, 1971); Prittie, Terence, *Germans Against Hitler* (London: Hutchison, 1964); Burleigh, Michael, *The Third Reich: A New History* (London: Pan Books, 2000); Kershaw, Ian, *Hitler: Hubris 1899–1936* (London: Allen Lane, 2001) and *Hitler: Nemesis 1936–1945* (London: Allen Lane, 2000).

6 These commentators rarely grapple with the thorny issue that Fascism represented the reactionary dictatorship of monopoly capitalism or, as

227

Jürgen Kuczynski characterised it in a booklet published in 1942, *The Economics of Barbarism*.

Chapter 1

1 Werner, Ruth, *Sonya's Report: The Fascinating Autobiography of One of Russia's Most Remarkable Secret Agents*, trans. Renate Simpson (London: Chatto & Windus, 1991), p.19; first published as *Sonjas Rapport* (Berlin: Verlag Neues Leben, 1977). Ursula Ruth Kuczynski ('Sonya') wrote under the pen name Ruth Werner.

2 Werner, *Sonya's Report*, fn.6 p.309. Arthur Holitscher (1869–1941) was born in Pest, Hungary. He began his writing career in Berlin in the mid-1890s. His major work, *Drei Monate in Sowjet-Rußland* (*Three Months in Soviet Russia*) was published in Berlin in 1921.

3 Robert has been described as one of the founders of modern vital statistics, an administrative system used by governments to record vital events in the lives of their populations by accumulating data on births, deaths, marriages and divorces.

4 Werner, *Sonya's Report*, p.3.

5 Ibid., p.20.

6 The National Archives Kew (hereafter TNA Kew) KV2/2932/268c/dated 12 January 1956.

7 The FFC was founded in 1918 to alleviate starvation of civilians in Germany and Austria-Hungary.

8 'To Parmoor's London house in Wilton Crescent came friends from the upper reaches of the Church and politics who were deeply interested in the "World Alliance to promote international friendship through the churches" and the "Fight the Famine Council". Stafford Cripps was drawn into these discussions ...', Estorick, Eric, *Stafford Cripps: A Biography* (London: William Heinemann Ltd, 1949), p.66; see also TNA Kew KV2/1871/H.O. Extract on THE FIGHT THE FAMINE COUNCIL FOR ECONOMIC RECONSTRUCTION, 15 August 1921.

9 Monetary and Economic Conference, *The Needs of Europe, Its Economic Reconstruction* (London: 1920).

10 Ibid.

11 Agitprop was a political strategy adopted by the Communist Party of the Soviet Union to influence and mobilise public opinion both in Russia and abroad.

12 Fischer, Ruth, *Stalin and German Communism: A Study in the Origins of the State Party* (Cambridge, MA: Harvard University Press, 1948), p.611.

13 See Caute, David, *The Fellow-Travellers: A Postcript to the Enlightenment* (London: Weidenfeld & Nicolson), p.9.

14 See Parsons, Stephen R., 'Communism in the Professions: The Organisation of the British Communist Party Among Professional Workers, 1933–1956', PhD thesis, University of Warwick, June 1990, go.warwick.ac.uk/wrap/34723, p.39.

15 For Robert Kuczynski's relation to Münzenberg see Gross, Babette, *Münzenberg* (Michigan State University Press, 1974), p.158. For 'the fellow-traveller' see Parsons, 'Communism', p.39.

16 The Communist International or Comintern was formed in March 1919 to promote the formation of Communist parties abroad and adopted the united front policy in December 1922. According to the Comintern: 'The united front tactic is simply an initiative whereby the Communists propose to join with all workers belonging to other parties and groups and all unaligned workers in a common struggle to defend the immediate basic interests of the working class against the bourgeoisie.' (Fourth Congress of the Communist International, Theses on Comintern Tactics, 5 December 1922.) Its overall aim was the infiltration and eventual capture of the 'bourgeois' parties of the Left – the SPD in Germany, the Labour Party in the UK and their counterparts worldwide.

17 The importance of the Rhine Ruhr to the German economy cannot be understated. The region provided the coal output Germany needed for her vital industries and for the purchase of necessary food supplies from Scandinavia, Denmark and Holland.

18 In Communist jargon a 'right deviation' may be defined as a departure or divergence from orthodox principles or policies towards a more capitalist or conservative one.

19 Zinoviev, G., speech to the Thirteenth Party Conference of the Russian Communist Party (Bolshevik), printed in German in *Inprekorr*, IV, 1924, no. 16, 4 February, p.168. Cited in Fowkes, Ben, *Communism in*

Germany Under the Weimar Republic (London: The Macmillan Press Ltd, 1984), p.101.

20 Degras, Jane (ed.), *The Communist International 1919–1943: Documents. Vol. II: 1923–1928* (London: Frank Cass & Co. Ltd, 1971), p.63.

21 The Chancellor was Gustav Stresemann, the leader of the *Deutsche Volkspartei* (German People's Party), a Right-wing or conservative liberal party with sixty-five seats in the Reichstag.

22 The state of emergency under which the KPD was banned was cancelled on 1 March 1924 and the party was again allowed to organise openly.

23 *Inprekorr*, 1923, no. 72, 7 November, pp.1457–60, cited in Fowkes, *Communism*, p.114.

24 The Reichswehr was Germany's small but influential regular military during the Weimar period and the first years of the Nazi regime.

25 Hans von Seeckt, Commander-in-Chief of the German Army, Reichswehr, 1920–26.

26 Alexander Kolchak, Supreme Leader and Commander-in-Chief of All Russian Land and Sea Forces of the White Forces during the Russian Civil War, 1918–21.

27 *Inprekorr*, no. 22, 18 February, p.242, cited in Fowkes, *Communism*, p.114.

28 Fischer, *Stalin*, p.504.

29 Ibid., p.505.

30 Krivitsky, Walter, *In Stalin's Secret Service* (New York: Harper Brothers, 1939), p.39, cited in Fisher, *Stalin*, p.510.

31 OGPU – *Obyedinyonnoye gosudarstvennoye politicheskoye upravleniye pri SNK SSSR* (Joint State Political Directorate under the Council of People's Commissars of the USSR) refers to the Soviet political police between 1923 and 1934. During the twentieth century Soviet state security since its foundation as the Cheka in 1917 underwent a number of changes in nomenclature. See Appendix 1.

32 Fischer, *Stalin*, p.513.

33 *Deutsche Friedenskartel – DFK*. The German Peace Cartel was an umbrella pacifist group founded in 1921. See Lütgemeier-Davin, Reinhold, *Pazifismus zwischen Kooperation und Konfrontation: Das Deutsche Friedenskartell in der Weimarer Republik* (Cologne: Pahl-Rugenstein Verlag, 1982).

34 Among its leading members were Robert Kuczynski's good friend Arthur Holitscher, Albert Einstein, Stefan Zweig, Ludwig Quidde, Helen Stöcker and the Communist Clara Zetkin.

35 TNA Kew KV2/1873/155a/dated 11 July 1941.

36 The 1926 deal was rescinded by the Soviet Union when it took control of Eastern Germany after the Second World War. See Buck, Tobias, 'Kaiser's Family Demands Palace and Spoils Seized by Soviets', *Financial Times*, 27/28 July 2019.

37 TNA Kew KV2/1873/155a/dated 11 July 1941.

38 Fischer, *Stalin*, p.523.

39 Bukharin replaced Zinoviev as head of the Communist International in January 1926. Strictly speaking, the office of President of the Comintern was abolished, releasing Zinoviev from his duties before he was replaced by Bukharin as General Secretary. The intention was to establish a collective leadership into which it would be easier to draw the non-Russian parties. See Degras, *The Communist International. Vol. II*, p.319.

40 See Fowkes, *Communism*, p.131.

41 TNA Kew KV2/1873/155a/dated 11.7.1941.

42 *Die Rote Fahne*, 19 April 1929, cited in Fowkes, *Communism*, p.153.

43 The SPD was the clear winner in the May 1928 elections to the Reichstag. The reluctance of the Centre parties to accept the result led to a coalition government of Social Democrats, *Zentrum, Deutsche Demoratische Partei* and *Deutsche Volkpartei*.

44 *Protokol des 12 Parteitages der KPD*, Berlin, 1929, pp.54–5; cited in Fowkes, *Communism*, p.154. The SPD, in fact, left the Reich government in March 1930 rather than reduce unemployment benefit as their coalition partners demanded.

Chapter 2

1 'Before 1933 the political police in German governments and county districts were a comparatively small body of (mainly) anti-Communist specialists within the broader section of the criminal police; they constituted Section 1A of a city police department which, like the rest of the city administration, was subordinate to the county government.' Merson, *Communist Resistance*, p.48.

2 Williams, Robert Chadwell, *Klaus Fuchs, Atom Spy* (Cambridge, MA: Harvard University Press, 1987), p.25.

3 TNA Kew KV4/110/13a. See also Brinson, Charmian and Dove, Richard, *A Matter of Intelligence: MI5 and The Surveillance of Anti-Nazi Refugees 1933–50* (Manchester: Manchester University Press, 2014), pp.26–7.

4 Ibid., pp.16–18.

5 In the 1920s a key part of the Labour Research Department's work looked at colonial oppression with a series of booklets on British imperialism, and a first survey of British MPs' business interests. TUC Library Collections. LMU, Old Castle Street Building, Aldgate.

6 The other contributors were Karl Radek, the British Communist W.P. Coates, the Hungarian novelist and playwright Arthur Holitscher; the American Communist Murray B. Levin, the German writer Anna Seghers and the German historian Guido Kisch, the Russian constructivist writer Sergei Tretyakov and Wiljnin.

7 Millions perished during the collectivisation of agriculture. Famine and peasant disturbances led to the extermination of the kulaks (wealthier peasants) as a class, while conditions in the factories were as bad, if not worse, than those condemned by Marx in Britain during the Industrial Revolution. Stalin's propaganda machine, however, convinced many in the West that modernisation was taking place in the Soviet Union without recourse to the worst aspects of capitalist exploitation.

8 Haslam, Jonathan, *Near and Distant Neighbours: A New History of Soviet Intelligence* (New York: Farrar, Straus and Giroux, 2015), p.50.

9 See Haslam, *Near and Distant*, p.52.

10 MI6 head of station in Berlin Frank Foley (officially the Passport Control Officer) referred to Münzenberg as 'probably the most dangerous German in existence as regards British Imperial and internal interests'. TNA Kew KV4/110/12a.

11 This World (mainly European) Congress, originally planned to be held in Geneva in July but convened in August in Amsterdam, was advertised as the World Congress against Imperialist War in Communist publications and as the World Congress against War elsewhere.

12 In 1924 the KPD claimed between 125,000 and 135,000 members. 'Class against Class', while disastrous in the struggle against Fascism, nevertheless, brought recruits into the party. See Merson, *Communist*

Resistance, p.15. Membership of the Communist Party of Great Britain, by comparison, never exceeded 17,000 during the inter-war years.

13 Löwenstein, Prince Hubertus Zu, *Towards the Further Shore* (London: Gollancz, 1968), pp.110–11.

14 Merson, *Communist Resistance*, p.31.

15 Walter Ulbricht (1893–1973) was a founder member of the KPD in 1920 serving on its Central Committee from 1923 onwards. After the Nazi takeover of Germany in 1933, Ulbricht lived in Paris and Prague between 1933 and 1937 and in the Soviet Union between 1937 and 1945. He became the first leader of the Socialist Unity Party (SED) in 1946 and leader of the DDR in 1950.

16 Franz Dahlem (1892–1981) was a member of the KPD from 1920 onwards and a Communist member of the Reichstag between 1928 and 1933. After Hitler came to power, he fled to Paris. He returned to Berlin in 1934, secretly and illegally, to carry out political work for the Communist underground. He went to Prague in 1936; and between 1936 and 1938 he was in charge of the Central Political Commission of the International Brigades in Spain. Following Franco's victory, he returned to Paris, where, following Hitler's invasion of Poland and the outlawing of the French Communist Party, he was interned in the concentration camp at Le Vernet, south-west France, where he took Soviet citizenship. He was handed over to the Gestapo in 1941 and transferred to the concentration camp at Mauthausen. He was liberated from Mauthausen by the Red Army on 7 May 1945 and taken to Moscow. He was returned to Germany on 1 July 1945 and between 1945 and 1953, played a leading role in the government of the DDR. He remained a member of the *Volkshammer* (National Parliament) until 1976. He died in 1981.

17 Wilhelm Pieck (1876–1960) was a founder member of the KPD. Following the Nazi seizure of power, he went first to Paris and then to Moscow. Pieck was Secretary of the Communist International between 1935 and 1943 and returned to Berlin in 1945 with the victorious Red Army. He served as President of the DDR until his death in 1960.

18 See Merson, *Communist Resistance*, pp.85–7.

19 A coalition of the Leftist and progressive parties to defend the interests of the working class against war and Fascism.

20 People's Commissariat for Internal Affairs.

21 Gorodetsky, Gabriel (ed.), *Maisky Diaries* (New Haven and London: Yale University Press, 2015), fn.12 p.20.

22 Brysac, Shareen Blair, *Resisting Hitler: Mildred Harnack and the Red Orchestra* (Oxford: Oxford University Press), p.217.

23 Soviet Ambassador to Berlin 1930–34, replaced by Yakov Surits who served as Ambassador 1934–37.

24 *Narodnyi Kommissariat Inostrannykh Del* – abbreviated to *Narkomindel* or NKID.

25 See Watson, Derek, 'The Politburo and Foreign Policy in the 1930s', in Rees, E.A. (ed.), *The Nature of Stalin's Dictatorship: The Politburo 1928– 1953* (Basingstoke: Palgrave MacMillan, 2004), p.150.

26 See Fischer, *Stalin*, p.198.

Chapter 3

1 Bodek, Richard, 'The Not-So-Golden Twenties: Everyday Life And Communist Agitprop in Weimar-Era Berlin', *Journal of Social History*, vol. 30, no. 1 (Autumn 1996).

2 Bodek, 'Not-So-Golden Twenties', p.65.

3 Werner, *Sonya's Report*, p.17.

4 Ibid., p.17; Bodek, 'Not-So-Golden Twenties', p.65.

5 Werner, *Sonya's Report*, p.22.

6 Powell, J.B., *My 25 Years in China* (New York: The Macmillan Company, 1945), p.332.

7 Werner, *Sonya's Report*, p.22.

8 Ibid., pp.23–4.

9 Ibid., p.24.

10 OMS – *Otdel mezhdynarodnoi svyazi* (International Liaison Department of the Communist International) 1921–39. The OMS undertook clandestine courier activities and work that supported underground Communist activities. Its functions often overlapped with those of the main Soviet intelligence agencies, the OGPU/NKVD and the GRU.

11 Pincher, Chapman, *Treachery* (Edinburgh and London: Mainstream Publishing, 2012), pp.44–6.

12 Smedley, Agnes, *China Correspondent* (London: Pandora Press, 1984), p.71; first published by Alfred A. Knopf, Inc., New York (1943).

13 See Appendix 1.

14 Knightley, Phillip, *The Second Oldest Profession: Spies and Spying in the Twentieth Century* (London: Pimlico, 2003), p.202.

15 'They called me Sonya and I gathered that Richard [Sorge] had chosen this cover name. Perhaps that is why I liked it. Whatever the reason, I immediately felt at home with my new name.' Werner, *Sonya's Report*, p.103.

16 Ibid., p.98.

17 Koch, Steven, *Double Lives: Stalin, Willi Münzenberg and the Seduction of the Intellectuals* (New York: Enigma Books, 1994), p.118. See also Krivitsky, *In Stalin's Secret Service*, pp.9–15.

18 Werner, *Sonya's Report*, p.118.

19 Ibid., p.121.

20 Ibid., p.122.

21 Ibid., pp.122–3.

22 Ibid.

23 Ibid., p.127.

24 In trigonometry and geometry, triangulation is the process of determining the location of a point by determining distances and relative positions from other known points.

25 Ibid., pp.128–9.

26 Ibid., pp.130–31.

27 Ibid., p.129.

28 Ibid., p.131.

29 Ibid., pp.133–4.

30 Ibid., p.149.

31 Ibid., p.154.

32 TNA Kew KV6/41/1x/dated 21 October 1935.

Chapter 4

1 *Passinhaber ist Auswanderer* (Passport holder is an emigrant).

2 Cladders, Lukas and Ferdinand, Ursula, 'Measuring world population at LSE – Robert René Kuczynski, an émigré scholar', LSE blog, blogs.lse.ac.uk/lsehistory/2016/09/01/kuczynski-at-lse.

3 See Burke, David, *The Spy Who Came in from the Co-op: Melita Norwood and the Ending of Cold War Espionage* (Woodbridge: Boydell, 2008).

4 TNA Kew KV2/111/146a; see also Burke, *Spy*, p.60.

5 TNA Kew KV2/111/146a.

6 Burke, *Spy*, p.68.

7 For Jack (Jacob) Miller see Burke, *Spy*, pp.68–70.

8 Robin Page Arnott to Harry Pollitt. Comintern Archives 495/100/943.

9 See Burke, David, *The Lawn Road Flats. Spies, Writers and Artists* (Suffolk: Boydell, 2014).

10 Haslam, *Near and Distant*, p.104; Tsarev, Oleg, *KGB v Anglii* (Moscow: Tsentrpoligraf, 1999).

11 TNA Kew KV2/1872/96a/dated 15.9.1938/17.9.1938.

12 Berta and Robert Kuczynski were naturalised as British citizens on 13 July 1946.

13 See TNA Kew KV2/1872/122b.

14 Thomas, *Strachey*, p.122.

15 Kuczynski, Jürgen, *Memoiren 1945–1989* (Berlin und Weimar: Aufbau-Verlag, 1992), pp.340–42.

16 Pimlott, Ben, *Hugh Dalton* (London: Harper Collins, 1985), p.30; see also Wood, N., *Communism and British Intellectuals* (London: Gollanz, 1959), p.113.

17 Thomas, *Strachey*, p.123.

18 Ibid., p.111.

19 Koch, *Double Lives*, p.218. Soviet spies working abroad in the 1930s were divided into two main categories – 'legal' and 'illegal' residents. 'Legal' residents enjoyed diplomatic immunity and held official postings at Soviet embassies or legations, and their main function was to act as live letterboxes for 'illegal' residents. They also arranged for the cyphering of reports and oversaw the general running of the Intelligence Department. 'Illegal' residents, on the other hand, did not have diplomatic status and were constantly more vulnerable to detection. They lived on the edge and possessed 'a rare combination of qualities', not least among them, 'courage'. See West, Nigel, *The Illegals: The Double Lives of the Cold War's Most Secret Agents* (London: Hodder & Stoughton, 1993)

20 See Thomas, *Strachey*, p.137.

21 Dundee election special, 18 June 1945, cited in Thomas, *Strachey*, p.137.

22 Strachey, John, *The Strangled Cry and Other Unparliamentary Papers* (London: Bodley Head, 1962), p.217; see also Neavill, Gordon Barrick, 'Victor Gollancz and the Left Book Club', *The Library Quarterly*, vol. 41, no. 3 (1971), p.198.

23 Phillip Noel-Baker, a Left-wing member of the Labour Party's National Executive Committee.

24 Brysac, *Resisting*, p.219. Brysac puts the date of this failed meeting as sometime in 1935, whereas Williams in *Fuchs* claims it took place in 1936. The latter date, given that Jürgen was known to be in Copenhagen in 1936, is the more likely.

25 Yagoda had been replaced by 'the more headstrong Yezhov' as head of the NKVD on 11 November 1936. See Haslam, *Near and Distant*, p.85. After ten gruelling months of interrogation, Bessonov finally broke down and confessed to acting in Berlin 'as a link between Trotsky and Krestinsky', declaring 'that he and Krestinsky had engaged in Trotskyist activity in Germany'. Although Krestinsky denied the allegations, he was condemned to death along with Bukharin and Yagoda, while Bessonov was sentenced to fifteen years in a labour camp. Jürgen believed in their guilt but his father, initially, did not: 'I will tell you how difficult it was. I believed in them. My father didn't believe in them – that these people were guilty. But then came the treachery of Flandin and Daladier, who surrendered France to Hitler. My father came to me and said, 'Now I believe in the trials.' It was so fantastic to him that the leaders of France would betray their country in favour of Hitler that he then thought it was possible in the Soviet Union too.' Brysac, *Resisting*, p.219.

26 TNA Kew KV2/1871/74A.

27 The word 'Trotskyite' was coined by Stalinists as a pejorative term in order to denounce the followers of Trotsky as anti-Soviet fifth columnists. To describe the supporters of Trotsky as Trotskyists was to take a more neutral stance.

28 Gannes, Harry and Repard, Theodore, *Spain in Revolt* (London: Victor Gollancz Ltd, 1936), p.126.

29 Fleay, C. and Sanders, M.L., 'The Labour Spain Committee: Labour Party Policy and the Spanish Civil War', *The Historical Journal*, vol. 28, no. 1 (March 1985), pp.187–97.

30 McLellan, Josie, *Antifascism and Memory in East Germany: Remembering the International Brigades 1945–1989* (Oxford: Clarendon Press, Oxford Historical Monographs, 2004), p.35.

31 The CPGB was particularly fervent in its condemnation of Trotsky and the POUM, equating both with Fascism: 'We will do all in our power to

support every measure taken by the Spanish Government to defeat both the fascist enemy and those foul traitors, the Trotskyists in the P.O.U.M. and those who support them in this country.'

Chapter 5

1 Werner, *Sonya's Report*, p.177.
2 Ibid., p.189.
3 Ibid., p.188.
4 There is some discrepancy over who Ursula approached for help in recruiting the two British International Brigaders: whether it was, indeed, Fred Uhlmann or the 'valiant fighter of Invergordon fame, Comrade Fred Copeman'. In her autobiography the suggestion is Uhlmann, who worked alongside Jürgen in London in the *Kulturbund*. 'In London, after some fruitless efforts, I made contact with a comrade who had fought in Spain and whom I had known in Germany. Originally he came from Austria or Czechoslovakia. I told him only the essentials. My political work was directed against fascism.' Ibid., p.189.
5 Foote, Alexander, *Handbook for Spies* (London: Museum Press 1949), p.10; see also TNA Kew KV6/42/151b; TNA Kew KV2/1612.
6 TNA Kew KV2/1613.
7 Ibid.
8 TNA Kew KV2/1568/143ab/dated 17.10.49.
9 Werner, *Sonya's Report*, p.221.
10 TNA Kew KV6/41. An 'excellent idea' that was not too far-fetched. Johann Georg Elser, a carpenter with Communist associations, made an unsuccessful assassination attempt on Hitler's life in the Munich Bürgerbräukeller on 8 November 1939. On discovery, the Nazis insisted on laying the blame at the feet of British intelligence.
11 Werner, *Sonya's Report*, p.189.
12 Ibid., p.191.
13 Ibid., p.197.
14 Ibid., p.201.
15 Ibid., p.202.
16 Ibid.
17 During the Soviet era, 23 February was celebrated as Red Army Day because it was on this day in 1918 that the Red Army celebrated its first

victory over German forces at Pskov and Narva. The marriage lasted over forty years.

18 Werner, *Sonya's Report*, p.222.

Chapter 6

1 Jordan, T.S., 'Review of *Hunger and Work*, by Jurgen Kuczynski (New York: International Publishers, 1938), *Science & Society*, vol. 4, no. 1 (Winter 1940), pp.96–8.

2 See Rowntree, Seebohm, *The Human Needs of Labour* (London: Longmans, first published 1918, revised edn, 1937).

3 'The Hitler Menace', Left Book Club leaflet. Reproduced in the *Tribune*, 23 September 1938, p.11; cited in Neavill, Gordon Barrick, 'Victor Gollancz and the Left Book Club', *The Library Quarterly*, vol. 41, no. 3 (1971), p.211.

4 Brinson and Dove, *A Matter*, p.115.

5 Ibid.

6 Johannes Fladung (1898–1982). Arrested by the Gestapo in September 1933 and sentenced to two-and-a-half years' imprisonment in November 1934, he was released from prison almost deaf in August 1936. He fled to Switzerland in 1938 and later that year to Paris and London, where he was received by representatives of the Quakers.

7 Kurt Hager (1912–98). Arrested in 1933 and after release in 1936 emigrated to Switzerland; he participated in the Spanish Civil War as a journalist. After being detained in France he emigrated to England in 1939 and wrote under the pseudonym Felix Albin.

8 Wilhelm Koenen (1886–1963) left Germany for France in 1933 on the decision of the Party leadership. From 1935 to 1938 he lived in Prague before moving to London. In 1944 he worked at the British black propaganda radio station *Soldatensender Calais* operated by the Political Warfare Executive. The station pretended to be part of the German military broadcasting network.

9 Alfred Meusel (1896–1960) was taken into protective custody by the Nazis in 1933; he emigrated with his wife Meta to the UK in 1934. A close friend and colleague of Jürgen Kuczynski.

10 Kuczynski, Jürgen, *The Condition of the Workers in Gt. Britain, Germany & the Soviet Union 1932–38* (London: Victor Gollanz Ltd, 1939), p.9.

11 Kuczynski, *Condition*, p.22.

12 Ibid., p.15.

13 [Royal Institute of International Affairs], *Documents on International Affairs, 1939–1946* (London: Oxford University Press, 1954), vol. 1, p.865. See also Govrin, Yosef, *The Jewish Factor in the Relations between Nazi Germany and the Soviet Union, 1933–1941* (London: Vallentine Mitchell, 2009), pp.32–6.

14 Molotov n.d. cited in Watson, 'Politburo', p.157.

15 *Documents on International Affairs, 1939–1946*, p.446. See also 'Trade negotiations eventually led to political ones, and attempts at a "gradual normalization" led to a political-military conspiracy', cited in Klemens von Klemperer, *German Resistance Against Hitler: The Search for Allies Abroad 1938–1945* (Oxford: Clarendon Press, 1992), p.129; Sontag, Raymond James and Beddie, James Stuart, *Nazi–Soviet Relations 1939–1941: Documents from the Archives of the German Foreign Office for the U.S. Department of State* (New York: 1948), p.14.

16 Degras, Jane, *The Communist International 1919–1943: Documents. Vol. III: 1929–1943* (London: Frank Cass & Co. Ltd, 1971). p.440.

17 TNA Kew KV2 1873/149s/n.d.

18 Thomas, *Strachey*, p.184; see also Ceplair, Larry, *Under the Shadow of War: Fascism, Anti-Fascism and Marxists, 1918–1939* (New York: Columbia University Press, 1967) p.179.

19 Quoted in Estorick, *Cripps*, p.222.

20 Pollitt, Harry, 'How to Win the War', quoted in Labour Party, *The Communist Party and the War* (London: Transport House, 1943), p.3.

21 Dallin, Alexander and Firsov, F.I. (eds), *Dimitrov and Stalin, 1934–1943: Letters from the Soviet Archives* (New Haven and London: Yale University Press, 2000), p.151. See also, Beckett, Francis, *Enemy Within: The Rise and Fall of the British Communist Party* (London: John Murray, 1995), p.91.

22 See German–Soviet Boundary and Friendship Treaty, THE AVALON PROJECT *Documents in Law, History and Diplomacy*, Yale Law School, Lilian Goldman Law Library.

23 See Degras, *The Communist International. Vol. III*, p.442; Branson, Noreen, *History of the Communist Party of Great Britain 1927–1941* (London: Lawrence & Wishart, 1985), p.268; Mahon, John, *Harry Pollitt* (London: Lawrence & Wishart, 1976), pp.166–7.

24 TNA Kew KV2 1873/149c/Statement of Siegfried HESS/n.d.

25 TNA Kew KV2 1871/39a/23.11.39.

26 Section V (counter-espionage) was established in 1931 under Valentine Vivian to liaise with MI5. SIS, the Secret Intelligence Service, commonly known as MI6, was created in 1909 to engage in foreign intelligence gathering and was accountable to the Foreign Office. MI5, also created in 1909, had responsibility for domestic intelligence and was accountable to the Home Office. See Andrew, Christopher, *Defence of the Realm* (London: Allen Lane, 2009), p.135.

27 TNA Kew KV2/1871/35A/dated 14 October 1939.

28 See Charmian and Dove, *A Matter*.

29 B Branch conducted 'investigations and enquiries'. Also known as B Division, officers dealt with counter-espionage and counter-subversion.

Chapter 7

1 TNA Kew KV2/1871/35A/dated 14 October 1939.

2 See Grenville, Anthony (ed.), *German-Speaking Exiles in Great Britain* (Amsterdam: Editions Rodopi B.V., 2000); Bearman, Marietta, Brinson, Charmian, Dove, Richard, Grenville, Anthony and Taylor, Jennifer, *Out of Austria: The Austrian Centre in London in World War II* (London: I.B. Tauris, 2007).

3 Green, John, *A Political Family: The Kuczynskis, Fascism, Espionage and The Cold War* (Oxon: Routledge, 2017), p.124.

4 Brigitte had a total of three husbands and several lovers. The family expressed their relief when she finally settled down with one man. See Chapter 5.

5 Green, *Political Family*, p.252.

6 Jürgen and Marguerite had three children: Madeline (b. 1932), Peter (b. 1937) and Thomas (b. 1944).

7 Ibid., p.124.

8 There were two German Freedom Stations at this time broadcasting anti-Nazi speeches, one of which was run by the KPD. It claimed to be in Hamburg but was actually in Spain. See Berg, Jerome S., *On the Short Waves, 1923–1945: Broadcast Listening in the Pioneer Days of Radio* (London: McFarland & Co., 2007).

9 Strauss, a supporter of Cripps's Socialist League, was expelled from the Labour Party for supporting the 'Popular Front' movement of Cripps at a time when the Labour Party had banned all contacts with Communists.

10 See Brinson and Dove, *A Matter*, p.118; TNA Kew KV2/1010/minute 97. Heartfield rented a room from Dr Otto Manasse, a 'German Jewish refugee with communist sympathies' and the Kuczynski family doctor in Highgate. See TNA Kew KV2/1010/minute 107.

11 See the *New Statesman and Nation*, March 1940. See also Kapp, Yvonne and Mynatt, Margaret, *British Policy and the Refugees, 1933–1941* (London: Frank Cass & Co. Ltd, 1997).

12 The Society was founded in 1868 to counter the Manchester School of Economists' campaign in favour of the disintegration of the British Empire.

13 Hugh Richard Lawrie Sheppard, founder of the Peace Pledge Union, popularly known as 'Dick' Sheppard, known for his philanthropic work in the East End of London. Author of *We Say 'No!': The Plain Man's Guide to Pacifism*, he founded the Peace Pledge Union in May 1936 with ex-Labour Party leader George Lansbury.

14 Other speaking engagements included the Welwyn Garden City group of the Left Book Club; and Wye College Socialist League. Sam Aaronovich invited him to speak to the Stepney Young Communist League, guaranteeing an audience of at least ninety.

15 TNA Kew KV2/1871/45ax/dated 5/12/1939.

16 TNA Kew KV2/1871/74A. Extract from pamphlets issued by KUCZYNSKI.

17 Ibid.

18 TNA Kew KV2/1871/74A.

19 *New Statesman and Nation*, March 1940.

20 TNA Kew KV2/1872/96a/dated 22.1.1940.

21 TNA Kew KV2/1872/96a/dated 22.1.1940;/9.2.40;/15/2/40;/ 11/7/40.

22 TNA Kew KV2/1872/96a/dated11/7/40.

23 Elizabeth Angela Marguerite Bowes-Lyon was the wife of King George VI and the mother of Queen Elizabeth II and Princess Margaret of Snowdon. She was queen of the United Kingdom and Dominions from her husband's accession to the throne in 1936 until his death in

1952, when she became known as Queen Elizabeth The Queen Mother, to avoid being confused with her daughter, Elizabeth II.

24 The security services' principal expert on Soviet Communism.

25 TNA Kew KV2/1871/68a/dated 19 February 1940.

26 TNA Kew KV2/1871/52/dated 6 February 1940. It was not until 3 February 1941 that MI5 began to take a serious interest in Rose Schecter. 'This woman, who is an active member of the C.P.G.B. and is now employed at the Soviet Embassy, worked until recently at the Office of "Inside Nazi Germany Publications Ltd", and the "Friends of the German People's Front", and in that capacity has been in close touch with […] Dr. Jürgen KUCZYNSKI.' TNA Kew KV2/1872/125a.

27 The Ministry of Information was formed on 4 September 1939, the day after Britain's declaration of war, and the first minister, Lord MacMillan, was sworn into office on 5 September. He was replaced by Sir John Reith on 5 January 1940. Reith was replaced by Duff Cooper on 10 May 1940 following the appointment of Winston Churchill as Prime Minister. Cooper, in turn, was replaced by Brendan Bracken on 17 July 1941.

28 TNA Kew KV2/1871/69b/dated 20 February 1940.

29 For Eichler, see Brinson and Dove, *A Matter*, p.150.

30 TNA Kew KV2/1871/73A.

31 The creation of Dr Heinrich Laufenberg and Fritz Wolffheim, the leaders of the Hamburg Communist Party in 1919, National Bolshevism was an attempt to unite the forces of both Right and Left around the contradictory concepts of nationalism and Marxism: a German understanding of Marxism that would unite Bismarckian nationalism with Lenin's proletarian dictatorship and 'rouse up Germany armed to the teeth from the Baltic to Lake Constance'. Fischer, *Stalin*, p.92.

32 TNA Kew KV2/1872/81a/dated 22.4.1940.

33 TNA Kew KV2/1871/76/dated 6 February 1940.

34 TNA Kew KV2/1871/77a/dated 9 April 1940.

35 Marguerite had moved into the Lawn Road Flats in March.

36 TNA Kew KV2/1872/85ab/n.d.

37 TNA Kew KV2/1872/82A/dated 1.5.1940.

38 TNA Kew KV2/1873/156B/dated 10.8.41; TNA Kew KV2/1873/140a/dated 5.4.41.

39 TNA Kew KV2/1873/142a/dated 11.4.41; TNA Kew KV2/1872/129a/ dated 31 January 1941.
40 TNA Kew KV2/1872/87a/dated 8.5.1940.
41 TNA Kew KV2/1872/86a/dated 8.5.1940. At this point there were only four daughters in the UK: Ursula had yet to arrive.
42 TNA Kew KV2/1872/87a/n.d.
43 TNA Kew KV2/1873/142a/dated 11.4.41.
44 TNA Kew KV2/1872/129a/122c/dated 5 March 1941/dated 122c.
45 TNA Kew KV2/1872/132/dated 17 March 1941. £200,000 equates to roughly £6 million today.
46 TNA Kew KV2/1561/44b.
47 MI5 had two Branches (also known as Divisions): A Branch, which covered administration, personnel, and records, and B Branch, which had responsibility for counter-espionage and counter-subversion, conducting 'investigations and inquiries'. B4 was a three-man Observation section, responsible for shadowing suspects and making 'confidential' inquiries. See Andrew, *Defence*, pp.127–8.
48 TNA Kew KV2/1872/85d/dated 7.5.1940.
49 Maxwell Knight was MI5's chief agent-handler, his 'M' section (so-styled because Knight always signed himself as 'M') became B5b in 1937, and was responsible for monitoring political subversion.
50 TNA Kew KV2/1872/Memo 114/dated 13.1.1941.
51 See Charmian and Dove, Richard, *A Matter*, p.71.
52 German military intelligence.
53 See Andrew, *Defence*, p.124.
54 'How was the KPD actually financed? Not just through the contributions of its members, certainly. The point is shrouded in mystery, owing to the unwillingness of KPD members to play into the hands of bourgeois and Social Democratic politicians, who claimed that the communists were paid agents of Moscow. [...] The existence of subventions from Soviet sources is not in doubt, although the exact amount is uncertain. [...] Comintern funds provided a useful supplementary income, but no more. The main sources of income were within Germany. Contributions from party members came to 4.5 million marks in 1927, and rents received from buildings owned by the party's newspaper holding company, the *PEUVAG*, made up another million. The party could thus have existed

comfortably without financial support from Russia.' Fowkes, *Communism*, pp.196–7.

55 TNA Kew KV2/1872/Minute 121/dated 26.1.1941.

56 See Brinson and Dove, *A Matter*, p.146.

57 TNA Kew KV2/1872/128a/dated 12 February 1941.

58 TNA Kew KV2/1872/128x/dated 25 February 1941.

59 The *Daily Worker* had condemned the laying of mines in Norwegian waters by the British Navy as an atrocity while virtually ignoring the Nazi invasions of Norway and Denmark.

60 The books full title was *The Betrayal of the Left: An Examination & Refutation of Communist Policy from October 1939 to January 1941 With Suggestions for an Alternative & an Epilogue on Political Morality* and included articles by George Orwell and John Strachey.

61 TNA Kew KV2/1872/127b/dated 20 February 1941.

62 TNA Kew KV2/1611/63a.

63 Vassiliev, Alexander, 'Report on Jürgen Kuczynski "Karo"', *Yellow Notebook #1*, Wilson Center Digitial Archive, p.78.

64 TNA Kew KV2/1872/85ab/n.d.

65 TNA Kew KV2/1873/185a/dated 5 March 1942; KV2/1873/148B/dated 14 May 1941.

66 Pimlott, *Hugh Dalton*, p.318.

67 Foot, M.R.D., *S.O.E. The Special Operations Executive 1940–1946* (London: Pimlico, 1999), p.x.

Chapter 8

1 Werner, *Sonya's Report*, p.228.

2 Radó, Sandor, *Codename Dora* (London: Abelard 1976), pp.44–5; TNA Kew KV2/1625/66.

3 TNA Kew KV6/41/119/'Extract from interrogation report by M.I.6. re Alexander FOOTE ment. BEURTON/dated 20 July 1947.

4 TNA Kew KV6/43/234A.

5 TNA Kew KV6/41/Minute 116.

6 *Entsiklopediya voennoi razvedki Roccii (Russian Military Intelligence Encyclopedia)* (Moscow: ACT-ACTREL, 2004), p.175.

7 For the Woolwich Arsenal case see Burke, *Spy*, pp.84–104.

8 See Haslam's discussion of the Cambridge Five in *Near and Distant*, p.73.

9 TNA Kew KV2/1611/54a.

10 TNA Kew KV6/41/Minute 15.

11 Werner, *Sonya's Report*, p.242.

12 Ibid., pp.240–2.

13 Ibid., p.240.

14 Haslam, *Near and Distant*, p.139.

15 *Entsiklopediya voennoi*, p.176.

16 See Aaronovitch, David, *Party Animals: My Family and Other Communists* (London: Jonathan Cape, 2015), pp.203–24.

17 It was published by the Oxford University Press in 1938 and ran to 1,837 pages; it was subsequently republished in several revised editions and paved the way for the 1940 Colonial Development and Welfare Act.

18 TNA Kew KV2/1567/4a/B.4a re Bridget LEWIS/dated 17.5.1938.

19 TNA Kew KV2/1567/3a.

20 TNA Kew KV2/1567/5a/B.4a (Miss Sissmore and Mr. Younger) re Bridget LEWIS.

21 TNA Kew KV2/1567/13a/M.K. (B.5b) to B.4a/Bridget LEWIS, 4 Lawn Road Flats, Lawn Road, N.W.3./dated 19.6.1940.

22 TNA Kew KV2/1567/14a/Letter from Hollis to Poynton, Colonial Office/dated 20 July 1940.

23 KV2/1567/15a /Colonial Office to Hollis/25.7.1940.

24 Founded in 1909 to combat Indian nationalism across Europe, Indian Political Intelligence, with its headquarters in London, was officially part of the India Office.

25 Leader of the Labour Party group on Oxford City Council before the war.

26 Carritt had to make do with a 'reasonable good second class'. He was: '"One of the golden boys" … this was said with a sort of paternal sarcasm by Dick Crossman, in the days of his political elevation, to describe the associates of his student days – a group of radical intellectuals at Oxford among whom were my brother, Wystan Auden and Stephen Spender. By this phrase he meant to imply that it was easy (and rather laughable) for the sons of comfortable upper middle class families like ours to be noisy advocates of the socialist society of the future … [Crossman] was a regular visitor at our big house on Boar's Hill … joining our summer holiday by the sea in Wales. My father greatly admired him for his

intellect; my mother for his good looks.' (Carritt, Michael, *A Mole in the Crown*, published privately by Michael Carritt, 1985), p.7.

27 Ibid., p.67.

28 Ibid., pp.66–7.

29 The 'specially appointed senior Judge who confirmed or reviewed orders of detention – privately in his chambers – only knew the code numbers of the informers, and their information was not written or signed by them but was the police resumé of their oral statements'. Ibid., p.79.

30 Ibid., p.77. From the early 1930s laws in India began to target terrorism as a separate category of crime, in legislation such as the Suppression of Terrorism Outrages Act of 1932.

31 Ibid., p.142.

32 Ibid., p.147.

33 Ibid., p.174.

34 Ibid.

35 TNA Kew KV2/1567/16a/ To Michael CARRITT From 'Bridgett'/ undated letter.

36 The affair with Carritt would have rendered this impossible.

37 TNA Kew KV2/1567/19a/Mr. Hollis. M.I.5.B.4a/dated 27.11.40.

38 TNA Kew KV2/1567/23c/W. Ogilvie to I.P.I./dated 4.1.1941. Surveillance of subversive movements in Britain by MI5 was carried out by B division, which was divided into sections. The section known as B4b dealt specifically with enemy espionage in industry and commerce. It was particularly concerned with the possibility of espionage inside firms that had access to government departments and were either supplying or servicing goods to naval, military, or air establishments and factories engaged in government work.

39 TNA Kew KV2/1567/17b/undated letter Brigitte to Marguerite.

40 Bridget was known to have visited 4 Lawn Road Flats between 14–16 October and 12–13 November 1939. See TNA Kew KV2/1567/23c/W. Ogilvie. B.4.a.3. to B.6. [J.H. Hunter]/dated 23.12.40.

41 Mrs Lewis came to London once a month 'to settle obligations there, and no doubt to visit her parents. Any communication from Mr. LEWIS [to the management] is always headed:- 4, Lawn Road Flats.' KV2/1567/22a/ Mrs. Bridget Lewis/dated 2 January 1941.

42 TNA Kew KV2/1567/25a/DVW/I.P.I. to M.I.5. B4a. Miss Ogilvie, dated 7.1.1941.

43 A Home Office Warrant (HOW) allowed for the interception of telephone and postal interceptions.

44 TNA Kew KV2/1567/29a/G.P.O./dated 5 February 1951;KV2/1567/31a/ M.I.5. B.4.a. Mr Hollis/dated 27.2.1941.

45 Ibid.

46 TNA Kew KV2/1567/20a/Mr. Hollis/dated 10.12.1940.

47 An earlier report said that she was also propaganda secretary to the St Pancras Branch. KV2/1567/26c/dated 14 January 1941.

48 TNA Kew KV2/1567/27a/Brigadier O.A. Harker to C.G. Maby/dated 4 February 1941.

49 TNA Kew KV2/1567/34a/Bristol Constabulary Report/dated 12 March 1941.

50 TNA Kew KV2/1567/37a/Bristol Constabulary Report/dated 7 April 1941.

51 Ibid.

52 TNA Kew KV2/1567/44a /LEWIS, Mrs. Bridget @ Brigitte/dated 10.10.41.

53 Ibid.

54 In Nuffield College Library. Introduction, p.1.

55 Papers of the Nuffield College Social Reconstruction Survey 1941–1955, p.13.

56 Ibid.

57 The Education Department, for example, courted the Arts Department of Dartington Hall in undertaking a study of the organisation of the arts in the United Kingdom. 'This inquiry into the arts was staffed and financed by the Arts department of Dartington Hall in undertaking a study of the organization of the arts in the United Kingdom.' Papers of the Nuffield College Social Reconstruction Survey 1941–1955, p.20.

'In February 1943, the Treasury, which had proved increasingly obstructive, announced that it would not be renewing its grant beyond the end of March' and the Survey was brought to a close on 31 January 1944.

Chapter 9

1 Werner, *Sonya's Report*, p.154.
2 Brown, Andrew, *J.D. Bernal: The Sage of Science* (Oxford: Oxford University Press, 2005), p.327.
3 Cornford, John, *Collected Writings*, ed. Galassi, Jonathan (Manchester: Carcanet Press Ltd; new edition, 1986).
4 TNA Kew KV2/2530/Copy of letter to BURGESS from Margot HEINEMANN found at Courtald Institute of Art in November, 1951/ dated November 1951.
5 Ibid.
6 Federman, Adam, *Fasting and Feasting: The Life of Visionary Food Writer Patience Gray* (London: Chelsea Green Publishing, 2017), p.1.
7 TNA Kew KV2/2935/1Za/dated 17.8.1939.
8 See Federman, *Fasting*, p.16; see also Davenport, Nicholas, *Memoirs of a City Radical* (London: Weidenfeld & Nicolson 1974).
9 Federman, *Fasting*, p.19; Obituary Patience Gray, *The Observer*, 18 October 1987.
10 The notorious spy Kim Philby described Harker 'as filling his position in MI5 with handsome grace, but little else'. Walton, Calder, *Empire of Secrets: British Intelligence, the Cold War and the Twilight of Empire* (London: Harper Press, 2013), p. 26.
11 Federman, *Fasting*, p.20.
12 Ibid.
13 Ibid., p.23.
14 Ibid., p.24.
15 Levy, Paul, 'Gray [*née* Stanham], Patience Jean', *Oxford Dictionary of National Biography*, 7 March 2013.
16 Federman, *Fasting*, p.28. TNA Kew KV2/2937/170a/Duncan and Barbara TAYLOR/dated 29.5.1951.
17 The Old Philologians, www.marylebonegrammar.co.uk.
18 TNA Kew KV2/2935/5a. The Winter War began with the Soviet invasion of Finland on 30 November 1939. The League of Nations deemed the attack to be illegal and expelled the Soviet Union from the organisation. Hostilities ceased on 13 March 1940 with the signing of the Moscow

Peace Treaty. Soviet gains were minimal and the Red Army suffered heavy casualties.

19 TNA Kew KV2/2935/7a.

20 TNA Kew KV2/2935/8a.

21 TNA Kew KV2/2935/8b.

22 *Entsiklopediya voennoi*, p.175.

23 Werner, *Sonya's Report*, p.153.

24 TNA Kew KV2/1873/152x/dated 17 June 1941.

25 Blumenau, Ralph, *Students and the Cold War* (Basingstoke and London: Macmillan Press, 1996), cited in fn.12 p.47.

26 TNA Kew KV2/2927/19a/dated 6 December 1941.

27 The Isobar was designed by the furniture designer Marcel Breuer, who furnished the restaurant with some of his best-known pieces of Isokon experimental furniture, including the dining chairs and tables, stools, nesting and occasional tables and the short chair. See Burke, *Lawn Road Flats*, Chapter 5: 'The Isobar, Half Hundred Club and the Arrival of Sonya'; see also Green, *Political Family*, p.289.

28 TNA Kew KV2/2927/48a/dated 26 August 1947.

29 TNA Kew KV2/2927/20a/dated 15 December 1941.

30 TNA Kew KV2/1872/137/Letter Jurgen to Hans Grafton/dated 27 March 1941.

31 TNA Kew KV2/2927/7a/dated 22 June 1941.

32 Fladung, a prominent Communist, journalist and former member of the Prussian parliament, had arrived in England in 1938 following his release from Oranienburg concentration camp.

33 Roberts, Sian, 'Education, Art and Exile: Cultural Activists and Exhibitions of Refugee Children's Art in the UK during the Second World War', *Paedagogica Historica*, vol. 53, no. 3 (April 2017), p.304.

34 TNA Kew KV2/2927/1a/dated 2 December 1940.

35 Brinson and Dove, *A Matter*, p.164.

36 TNA Kew KV2/2927/3a/dated 6 May 1941.

37 Blumenau, *Students*, p.47.

38 *The Times*, 23 June 1941.

39 Werner, *Sonya's Report*, p.241.

40 Ibid., p.129.

Chapter 10

1 TNA Kew KV2/1879/548a/dated 13 Dec. 1950.

2 Vassiliev, Alexander, 'Memorandum on K.F. from the GRU', *Yellow Notebook #1*, p.67.

3 TNA Kew KV2/2527/Minute 29/D.G.S.S. (through B.4.)/dated 2.4.1941.

4 Ibid.

5 *Daily Worker*, 30 May 1939 contains her life story.

6 TNA Kew KV2/2527/33a/dated 1 May 1941.

7 TNA Kew KV2/2527/46c/dated 13 November 1942.

8 Andrew, Christopher and Mitrokhin, Vasili, *Mitrokhin Archive* (London: Allen Lane, 1999), p.152.

9 Vassiliev, *Yellow Notebook #1*, p.86

10 Vassiliev, 'Memorandum on K.F. from the GRU', p.86.

11 See Burke, *Spy*.

12 The production of 1kg per day of U-235 involved the manufacture of between 450 and 650kg per day of UF_6.

13 TNA Kew AB/1/682.

14 Vassiliev, *Yellow Notebook #1*, p.25. 'En-s' = 'Enormous', Soviet code name for the atomic bomb.

15 Those between Norwood and Ursula would usually take place in London. BN-FMRA had been moved from its offices in Praed Street, Euston, to Cheshunt, Herts.

16 Werner, *Sonya's Report*, p.252.

17 MI5 moved its wartime headquarters first to Wormwood Scrubs Prison in London and then, following a direct hit on the prison by the Luftwaffe in 1940, to Blenheim Palace.

18 Wolf, Markus and McElvoy, Anne, *Memoirs of a Spymaster* (London: Pimlico, 1998), p.229.

19 TNA Kew KV2/1567/45b/Letter Brigitte to Jurgen/dated 1 December 1941.

20 Ibid.

21 TNA Kew KV2/2883/30a/Attempted Control by Alien Communists in U.K. of B.B.C. Continental Transmissions/dated 1 March 1942.

22 TNA Kew KV2/1567/47c/Letter R. Jardine-Brown, BBC/dated 4 December 1941.

23 Ibid.; TNA Kew KV2/1567/48a/BBC to D.L.R. Osborn, Box No. 500, Oxford/dated 17 December 1941.

24 TNA Kew KV2/1567/49a/dated 11 March 1942.

25 Interestingly, one of the founders of Mass Observation, Charles Madge, was a near neighbour of Bridget and Tony Lewis in the Lawn Road Flats. See Burke, *Lawn Road Flats*, p.119.

26 TNA Kew KV2/1567/50a/F.2.a/DKC/dated 11.3.42.

27 TNA Kew KV2/1567/51a /Intercepted letter from 'Tony' to J. KUCZYNSKI, 10, South Sq. London N.W.11; Primrose 2315 was the general line owned by the Lawn Road Flats and used by all the residents of the block. See KV2/1567/18a.

28 TNA Kew KV2/1873/163y/dated 28 August 1941.

29 TNA Kew KV2/1873/189b/dated 15 March 1942.

30 Vassiliev, 'Report on Jürgen Kuczynski "Karo"', p.78.

31 Brinson and Dove, *A Matter*, p.116.

32 TNA Kew KV2/1873/180c/dated 2 February 1942.

33 Priestley, *Postscripts* (London: William Heinemann Ltd, 1940), p.36.

34 TNA Kew KV2/1874/202a/dated 4 June 1942. In fact, in 1941 J.B. Priestley and other members of the 1941 Committee established the Common Wealth Party later in the year. It was dissolved in 1945 and most of its members joined the Labour Party.

35 Priestley, J.B., *Postscripts*, p.43.

36 See Brinson and Dove, *A Matter*, p.179.

37 Kuczynski, J. & Witt, M., *The Economics of Barbarism: Hitler's New Economic Order in Europe* (London: Frederick Muller Ltd, 1942), p.8.

38 The AScW registered as a trade union in 1942 and joined the TUC.

39 TNA Kew KV2/1874/201a/dated 21 May 1942.

40 In 1937 the AScW had 900 members on the books and one member of staff. By the end of the war it had 20,000 members and twenty on the staff.

41 Reinet Fremlin, née Maasdorp, was a physicist at the Cavendish Laboratory, University of Cambridge, and a member of the Cambridge Scientists Anti-War Group (CSA-WG). At Cambridge she joined the CPGB and married John Fremlin, also a member of the Communist

Party and CSA-WG who was working on how to gas-proof your house against poison gas, and how to deal with incendiary bombs.

42 TNA Kew KV2/1874/203a/dated 10 June 1942.

43 Ibid.

44 Ibid.

45 Smith, Richard Harris, *OSS: The Secret History of America's First Central Intelligence Agency* (California: University of California Press 1972), p.10; Gould, Jonathan S., *German Anti-Nazi Espionage in the Second World War: The OSS and the Men of the TOOL Mission* (Oxon: Routledge, 2018).

46 TNA Kew KV2/1874/203y/dated 11 June 1942; KV2/1874/204a/dated 19 June 1942.

47 'This period witnessed a dramatic growth in the membership of the Association of Scientific Workers: 513 in 1935 to 1,319 in July 1939 to 11,000 by mid-1943, and its re-registration as a trade union'. See 'The Professor takes a Union Card', *Tribune*, 21 November 1941, cited in Parsons, 'Communism', p.221.

48 A German Jew, Kamnitzer arrived in the UK in October 1933 aged 16. An official of the Communist Youth Organisation in Germany, he was brought to MI5's attention in November 1939 as editor of *Inside Nazi Germany*. He was interned in May 1940.

49 See Hemming, Henry, *Churchill's Iceman: The True Story of Geoffrey Pyke: Genius, Fugitive, Spy* (London: Preface Publishing, 2014), pp.223–5. Hemming suggests that Pyke's interest in Kamnitzer came about from the intervention of an unknown German with interesting connections and asks the question: 'Who would want to see ... Kamnitzer released?', p.225. That this was Jürgen seems to be borne out by the fact that while Pyke offered Kamnitzer work in his offices in St James's Square, he declined his offer in order to work with Jürgen at the offices of the AScW. Moreover, Jürgen had control of KPD funds and the legal costs to secure an internee's release averaged £20 per day, a considerable sum in those days. See TNA Kew KV2/2883/31a.

50 TNA Kew KV2/2883/47a.

51 TNA Kew KV2/2883/31a.

52 TNA Kew KV2/2883/35a/dated 19 April 1942.

53 TNA Kew KV2/2883/47a/dated 23 June 1942.

54 TNA Kew KV2/2883/56A/Ministry of Information referred to Miss Bagot.

55 Hemming, *Churchill's Iceman*, p.222.

56 Ibid., p.3.

57 TNA Kew KV2/3039/72a/n.d.

58 Hemming, *Churchill's Iceman*, p.416.

59 Percy Timberlake, who pioneered trade relations with Mao Zedong's China following the Chinese Revolution of 1949, remained a close friend of the Loefflers throughout his life.

60 TNA Kew KV2/3039/76a/Intercepted letter from Elvin THORGERSEN 2/Lt., Trowbridge Barracks, to Francis LOEFLER, 4d, Belsize Grove, N.W.3./dated 6.8.42.

61 TNA Kew KV2/3039/72a/n.d.

62 Vernon Bartlett was elected as an Independent Progressive MP on a Popular Front ticket in a by-election at Bridgewater, Somerset, on 18 November 1938.

63 Vansittart was then collecting material for his Germanophobic book, *Black Record: Germans Past and Present*, published in 1941.

64 Miles, Jonathan, *The Nine Lives of Otto Katz* (London: Bantam Books, 2010), p.20.

65 TNA Kew KV2/3039/72a/n.d.

66 Hemming, *Churchill's Iceman*, p.291.

67 TNA Kew KV2/3039/75a/dated 1 August 1942. N-Apparat – *N-Dienst* the intelligence service of the KPD in exile in Britain.

68 TNA Kew KV2/2927/Minute 30/dated 26 May 1942.

69 TNA Kew KV2/2927/Minute 30/dated 26 May 1942. Sgd. M.J.E. Bagot.

70 TNA Kew KV2/3040/107a/dated 25 August 1944; see Hemming, *Churchill's Henchman*, pp.408, 413.

71 TNA Kew KV2/3039/72a/n.d.

72 TNA Kew KV2/3040/107a/dated 25 August 1944.

73 Hemming, *Churchill's Iceman*, p.274.

74 Ibid.

75 Ibid.

76 Ibid., pp.251–2.

Chapter 11

1 The British atomic bomb project code-named Tube Alloys was moved to the USA in November 1943, where the two bombs that would be dropped on Hiroshima and Nagasaki were designed and built.

2 Vassiliev, 'Report on Jürgen Kuczynski "Karo"', p.78.

3 Vassiliev, Alexander, 'Goose's report on a meeting with Rest on Saturday, 5.02.44.', *Yellow Notebook #1*, p.68.

4 For Long and the GRU, see *Entsiklopediya voennoi*, p.167.

5 TNA Kew KV2/1873/172a/dated 17 November 1942.

6 Werner, *Sonya's Report*, pp.242–3.

7 Ibid., p.243.

8 TNA Kew KV6/41/32b/dated 20 July 1942.

9 TNA Kew KV6/41/55a/dated 21 January 1943.

10 Werner, *Sonya's Report*, p.250.

11 TNA Kew KV6/41/58a/dated May 1943.

12 The letter in question was post-marked Oxford, 22 May 1942 and sent to Jürgen's London address, which was then 10 South Square, Golders Green.

13 Ibid.

14 TNA Kew KV2/2395/13a/dated 3 July 1942.

15 TNA Kew KV2/2935/22a/Pilot Officer Duncan Burnett TAYLOR/ dated 10.11.1942.

16 TNA Kew KV2/2936/139a B.5. Mr. Storrier/dated 6.3.51. Bletchley Park's Roll of Honour lists an RAF Sgt Taylor working at Bletchley Park from 1942 in Block A. Air Section.

17 TNA Kew KV2/2935/38b/dated 16 February 1944.

18 Wayment had by this time left the Taylors and had returned to Cambridge.

19 TNA Kew KV2/2935/33c/dated 5 September 1944.

20 Koch, *Double Lives*, p.11.

21 RAF Instruction Unit: Control Commission School (Air), formed at Regent's Park, London, August 1944; disbanded May 1945.

22 Hinsley, Harold, *British Intelligence*, vol. II (London: Her Majesty's Stationery Office, 1990), pp.618–19.

23 Aldrich, Richard J., *GCHQ: The Uncensored Story of Britain's Most Secret Intelligence Agency* (London: HarperPress, 2010), p.30.

24 TNA Kew HW14/3.

25 For Helen Lunn see Burke, David, *Russia and the British Left: From the 1848 Revolutions to the General Strike* (London: I.B. Tauris, 2018), pp.194–7.

26 TNA Kew KV2/777/79A/80A/82; see also Burke, *Spy*, p.67.

27 Aldrich, *GCHQ*, p.36.

28 Haslam, *Near and Distant*, p.119.

29 Carter, Miranda, *Anthony Blunt: His Lives* (London: Macmillan, 2001), p.287.

30 *Entsiklopediya voennoi*, p.175.

31 Mary Caroline Tyler (née Southcombe) 1921–2016, *Hampstead Garden Suburb News*, 2016.

32 Personal correspondence, Murphy to Burke, June 2017.

33 See Verrier, Anthony, *Through the Looking Glass* (London: W.W. Norton & Company Ltd, 1983), pp.42–3.

34 Haslam, *Near and Distant*, p.161.

35 Ibid.

36 Ibid., p.98.

37 Ibid., p.161.

38 TNA Kew KV2/2935/32a/Ministry of Labour and National Service to Box 500, Oxford/dated 31 May 1943; TNA Kew KV2/2935/31a/ Ministry of Economic Warfare to Box 500, Oxford/dated 26 May 1943.

39 For Hans Gaffron see above, pp.60–61.

40 TNA Kew KV2/1876/316a/dated 9 October 1943.

41 TNA Kew KV6/41/68a.

42 TNA Kew KV2/1610/31b.

Chapter 12

1 TNA Kew KV2/1874/211b/dated 24 July 1942.

2 Kuczynski, Jürgen, *British Trade Unionism: A Short Course for Scientific Workers* (London: F.W. Bull & Co., Ltd, 1943), p.41.

3 Association of Scientific Workers, *Science and the Nation* (Middlesex: Harmondsworth, 1947), p.162.

4 Hans Siebert joined the KPD in 1931 and emigrated to England in 1936; he worked as a secretary for the Committee for Spanish Refugee Children from May 1937 to April 1940; he was briefly interned on the Isle of Man. A member of the *Kulturbund*, he headed the Free University of Applied

Sciences in London together with Alfred Meusel; from 1945 he led what remained of the KPD in the UK. In September 1947 he returned to Berlin and became the education secretary in the Central Secretariat, forerunner of the Central Committee of the SED.

5 TNA Kew KV2/1874/237a/dated 21 September 1942; TNA Kew KV2/1874 KV2/1875/300y/dated 14 July 1943.

6 See Marrack, John, 'A National Food Policy', *Labour Monthly*, vol. 20 (1938), pp.502–7; 'Food in Wartime: Free Basic Ration – or Higher Wages', *Medicine Today & Tomorrow*, vol. 2 (1940), pp.2–9; *Food and Planning* (London: Gollancz, 1942).

7 See 'Marrack, John Richardson', *Encyclopedia.com*, 13 May 2019, www.encyclopedia.com/science/dictionaries-thesauruses-pictures-and-press-releases/marrack-john-richardson.

8 A United Nations Conference on Food and Agriculture was held on the initiative of United States President Franklin D. Roosevelt at the Homestead Hotel, Hot Springs, Virginia, from 18 May to 3 June 1943. Representatives of forty-four nations participated and signed the final Act leading to the foundation of the United Nations Food and Agriculture Organisation.

9 TNA Kew KV2/1875/293b.

10 TNA Kew KV2/1874/257a/dated 23 December 1942.

11 Alexander Abusch (1902–82). A German journalist, non-fiction writer and politician and founder member of the KPD. In 1937 he became part of the exiled KPD leadership in Paris, later in Toulouse. In 1941, he moved to Mexico, where he became a member of the Free German Movement. Between 1948 and 1950 he was part of the party leadership of the Socialist Unity Party of Germany. Between 1958 and 1961 he served as Minister of Culture of the GDR.

12 *Freies Deutschland*, founded in November 1941 by Egon Erwin Kisch, Anna Seghers and the Austrian journalist Bruno Frei, was a highly regarded political-cultural monthly, published internationally with a circulation of almost 4,000 copies.

13 These included the liberal reformer Heinrich Friedrich Karl vom und zum Stein, the military strategist Carl von Clausewitz and the poet Ernst Moritz Arndt, all of whom supported the creation of a Russo-German Legion to enable Prussians to fight in the Tsar's armies.

14 'Manifesto for the National Committee for a Free Germany to the Wehrmacht and to the German People'. First published 13 July 1943.

15 Robert and Berta had returned to London from Oxford on 23 July 1942, moving into 12 Lawn Road, directly opposite the Lawn Road Flats with its literary and spying fraternity.

16 TNA Kew KV2/1876/Minute 326/dated 25 December 1943, signed M.J.E. Bagot.

17 TNA Kew KV2/1876/Minute 331/dated 13 January 1944.

18 TNA Kew KV2/1876/Minute 332/dated 14 January 1944.

19 TNA Kew KV2/1876/Minute 333/dated 18 January 1944.

20 TNA Kew KV2/1875/305ab/dated 3 August 1943.

21 Kuczynski, Jurgen, *Left News*, no. 84, June 1943.

22 Merson, *Communist Resistance*, pp.216–17; See also Mason, T.W., 'Arbeiteropposition im nationalsozialistischen Deutschland' in Peukert, D. and Reulecke, J. (eds), *Die Reihen fast geschlossen* (Wuppertal: Peter Hammer Verlag, 1981), p.309.

23 Kuczynski, Jurgen, *Left News*, No. 84, June 1943.

24 Ibid.

25 Ibid.

26 TNA Kew KV2/1875/292a/dated 1 June 1943.

27 See Brandenberger, D., *National Bolshevism: Stalinist Mass Culture and the Formation of Modern Russian National Identity, 1931–1956* (Cambridge, MA: Harvard University Press, 2002).

28 Paul Merker (1894–1969) had been National Leader of the Revolutionary Trades Union opposition (RGO) before his dismissal from the Central Committee of the KPD in April 1930 on account of his 'extremist Left-wing deviations'. Between 1931 and 1933 he worked in the USA using the cover name 'Max Fischer'. He returned to Germany to work illegally in 1934 and in 1935 he was re-elected to the KPD Central Committee, which was now operating in Paris. Following the German invasion of France, in June 1942 he managed to escape from Marseilles to Mexico, where he became secretary of the Free Germany movement, regularly producing articles for *Freies Deutschland*.

29 TNA Kew KV2/1875/312a.

30 TNA Kew KV2/1876/320/dated 18 November 1943.

31 TNA Kew KV2/1876/320/dated 18 November 1943.

32 TNA Kew KV2/1876/335b/dated 22 January 1944.

33 TNA Kew KV2/1876/347c/dated 6 April 1944.

34 TNA Kew KV2/1876/380/dated 12 October 1944.

35 TNA Kew KV2/1876/380a/dated 12 October 1944.

36 TNA Kew KV2/1876/Minute 378/dated 14 October 1944.

37 Ibid.

38 Kuczynski, *Memoiren*, p.18.

39 Thomas, *Strachey*, p.219.

40 Crossman, R.H.S., 'The Politician as a Writer', *Guardian*, 28 September 1962, cited in Thomas, *Strachey*, p.219. The *Observer* put a slightly different spin on Strachey's broadcasts, suggesting they 'took the public mind off the receiving end of the bombing attacks, and fixed it on the courage of the crews', *Observer*, 2 June 1946.

41 Werner, *Sonya's Report*, p.160.

42 See Merson, *Communist Resistance*, p.278.

43 TNA Kew KV2/1877/406a/dated 5 February 1945.

44 TNA Kew KV2/1877/406a/dated 5 February 1945.

45 TNA Kew KV2/1877/422a/dated 7 May 1945.

46 See Werner, *Sonya's Report*, pp.260–1.

47 The first walkie-talkie ever used in ground-to-air communication. *Entsiklopediya voennoi*, p.177.

48 Ibid.; Werner, *Sonya's Report*, p.262.

49 Ibid., p.264; TNA Kew KV2/1877/422a/dated 7 May 1945; 421a/dated 31 March 1945.

50 NKGB – *Narodnyi komissariat gosudarstvennoi bezopastnosti* (People's Commissariat of State Security). See Appendix 1.

51 Vassiliev, *Yellow Notebook #1*, p.79.

52 Great Britain, the United States and the Soviet Union.

53 Vassiliev, 'Report on Jurgen Kuczynski "Karo"', p.79.

Chapter 13

1 Leon had been accepted for the RAF on 18 March 1943. See TNA Kew KV6/41/58a/dated 30 April 1943.

2 TNA Kew KV6/41/109a. Hamburger had been arrested and interrogated for espionage by the Americans and the British in July 1943 before being passed to the Soviets. See above, pp.124–5.

3 TNA Kew KV6/41/111a/dated 1 May 1946.

4 Vassiliev, 'Memorandum on K.F. from the GRU', p.86.

5 Werner, *Sonya's Report*, p.274.

6 TNA Kew KV2/1567/Mrs. Bridget Lewis/Minute 67/D.D.G., through B.1./dated 29.7.1941.

7 TNA Kew KV2/1567/Mrs. Bridget Lewis/Minute 68/J.H. Marriott 29.7.47.

8 TNA Kew KV2/1567/Mrs. Bridget Lewis/Minute 68/J.H. Marriott 29.7.47; TNA Kew KV2/1567/74a/Letter to Miss Shelmerdine BBC/ dated 1/8/1947.

9 Leigh, David, *The Wilson Plot* (London: Heinemann – Mandarin, 1989), p.7.

10 Ibid.

11 KV2/1567/61a/Deputy Assistant Commissioner, Special Branch/dated 15 August 1945.

12 Their first child, Mark Christopher, was born on 24 March 1943.

13 TNA Kew KV2/1567/91a /FILE NOTE/B.1.B./23 August 1947.

14 TNA Kew KV2/1567/85c/Primrose 2701 p.2.

15 TNA Kew KV2/1567/103/ File Note/J.H. Marriott/dated 5 September 1947.

16 Krämer, Gudrun, *The Jews in Modern Egypt, 1914–1952* (London: I.B. Tauris, 1989), pp.175–6.

17 Ibid., p.178.

18 TNA Kew KV2/1567/63z.

19 TNA Kew KV2/2935/Minute 81/J.H. Marriott to Roger Hollis/dated 20.9.1947.

20 The Middle East Committee consisted of the following (18 January 1957): R. Page Arnot (chairman), George Rudé (vice chairman), Chimen Abramsky (secretary), Alan and Serena Whittleton, Lazar Kaiman, Betty Wallace, Dave Wallis, Betty Ambetialos, Chris Kuparris, George Pefkos, Dave Green and Idris Cox.

21 TNA Kew KV2/1567/97b/Primrose 6217.

22 Commentary on Jewish illegal immigration and the '*Exodus* 1947' incident in the *Jewish Clarion* and the *Egyptian Newsletter* were diametrically opposed.

23 TNA Kew KV2/1567/102b/Primrose 6217. On the *Jewish Clarion* see Wendehorst, Stephan E.C., *British Jewry, Zionism, and the Jewish State, 1936–1956* (Oxford: Oxford University Press, 2012).

24 TNA Kew KV2/1567/102b/Primrose 6217.

25 Young, George Kennedy, *Subversion and the British Riposte* (Glasgow: Ossian Publishers Ltd, 1984), p.83; see also Leigh, *Wilson Plot*, p.10.

26 TNA Kew KV2/2935/65a.

Chapter 14

1 TNA Kew KV2/1568/135a/Special Branch Report 12 Nov. 1947.

2 Ibid.

3 During the unrest forty-seven people were killed and more than 400 injured in Trinidad and Jamaica alone; more than 1,000 were arrested.

4 In the West Indies, militant leaders were jailed during the war and more moderate leaders accepted as working-class representatives. In both Jamaica and Trinidad, in particular, labour was integrated into the existing colonial system after the initial militancy of the late 1930s. See Weiler, Peter, *British Labour and the Cold War* (California: Stanford University Press, 1988), p.44.

5 Werner, *Sonya's Report*, p.276.

6 Ibid., p.291.

7 Andrew, *Defence*, p.334.

8 TNA Kew KV6/42/170.

9 TNA Kew KV6/41/170.

10 Ibid.

11 TNA Kew KV2/1568/114a /Primrose 6217/dated 17 September 1947.

12 TNA Kew KV2/2935/Minute 81/J.H. Marriott to Roger Hollis/dated 20.9.1947.

13 TNA Kew KV2/2927/49b/dated 30 September 1947.

14 Ferrets – technicians who do a fair bit of ferreting: installing, locating and removing hidden microphones and cameras.

15 TNA Kew KV2/2927/49c/dated 30 September 1947.

16 Ibid.

17 TNA Kew KV2/2927/60a/dated 26 January 1951.

18 TNA Kew KV2/1568/132b/Primrose 6217/dated 20 October 1947.

19 Ibid.

20 Ibid.

21 Ibid.

22 TNA Kew KV2/2936/100z.

23 Werner, *Sonya's Report*, p.280.

24 TNA Kew KV2/2891/171a/dated 10 October 1954.

25 TNA Kew KV2/2891/172a/dated 19 October 1954.

26 TNA Kew KV2/2891/173a/dated 7 November 1951.

Chapter 15

1 Vassiliev, Alexander, 'London – C 13.6.45', *Yellow Notebook #1*, p.25.

2 Vassiliev, 'Memorandum on K.F. from the GRU', p.86. See also *Entsiklopediya voennoi*, p.175.

3 TNA Kew KV2/1568/155a/Extract from interview held with Alexander Allan Foote/dated 18.5.1950.

4 Vassiliev, 'Memorandum on K.F. from the GRU', p.86.

5 Werner, *Sonya's Report*, p.288.

6 Ursula, however, was adamant that she had not been asked by Moscow Centre 'to contact anyone from MI5 and I had no contacts there … I must also spoil the speculation that I ever had anything to do with the one-time director of MI5, Roger Hollis.' Werner, *Sonya's Report*, p.289.

7 TNA Kew KV2/2890/108a/dated 4 June 1951. Was this a mischievous reference to the case of Roger Hollis?

8 Werner, *Sonya's Report*, p.290.

9 Ibid.

10 Ibid., p.291.

11 Vassiliev, *Yellow Notebook #1*, p.88.

12 Thomas, *Strachey*, p.259; Newman, Michael, *John Strachey* (Manchester: Manchester University Press, 1989), p.120.

13 As a result of Foot's article, the *Tribune* faced a costly action in the High Court. Foot himself faced similar accusations when leader of the Labour Party.

14 Vassiliev, Alexander, 'Addendum to the plan of oper. measures with regard to Ch-s's case', *Yellow Notebook #1*, p.93.

15 Vassiliev, Alexander, '8.03.1950 the "Refutation of TASS" is published', *Yellow Notebook #1*, p.87.

16 Vassiliev, Alexander, 'Report to S.R. Savchenko', *Yellow Notebook #1*, p.89.

17 Werner, *Sonya's Report*, p.296.

18 TNA Kew KV2/1256.

Chapter 16

1 Federman, *Fasting and Feasting*, p.311.

2 Ibid.

3 TNA Kew KV2/2936/Minute 130 D.D.G. (Through D.B.)/dated 17.2.1951.

4 Ibid.

5 TNA Kew KV2/2936/139a B.5. Mr. Storrier/dated 6 March 1951.

6 TNA Kew KV2/2937/Minute 199/dated 18 February 1952.

7 Ibid.

8 Haslam, *Near and Distant*, fn.11 p.104, Blunt's testimony: Tsarev, Oleg, *KGB v Anglii*, p.67.

9 TNA Kew KV2/2937/Minute 200/dated 20 February 1952.

10 Ibid.

11 Ibid.

12 Ibid.

13 Ibid.

14 Ibid..

15 TNA Kew KV2/2936/83a.

16 Ibid.

17 TNA Kew KV2/2937/198b/dated 8 February 1952.

18 TNA Kew KV2/2937/Minute 199/dated 18 February 1952.

19 One of the greatest cookbooks of all time, it introduced British readers to French dishes and cooking techniques. The other translators were Patience Gray, by now a salaried employee of the *Observer* newspaper, Nina Froud and Maud Murdoch.

20 Personal correspondence, Murphy to Burke, 17 July 2016.

21 Ibid.

22 Letts, John, 'Obituary: Sir Arthur Drew', *Independent*, 23 October 1993.

23 TNA Kew KV2/2935/118a/dated 31 January 1951.

24 Ibid.

25 Letts, 'Obituary: Sir Arthur Drew'. Between 1944 and 1949 he was on the International Staff, and at NATO, 1951–53. He married Rachel Anna Lambert on 9 January 1943. An illustrious career spanning fifty years as Deputy Under-Secretary of State, Home Office, 1961–63; last

Permanent Under-Secretary of State, War Office, 1963–64; Permanent Under-Secretary of State (Administration); Ministry of Defence 1968–72; Trustee, British Museum (Natural History) 1972–83; Trustee British Museum 1973–86; Administrator, John Paul Getty Jnr Charitable Trust 1986–88.

26 On 6 November 1968 a 'Request for Look-Up' was issued by F2/URG [Urgent] for Arthur Charles Walter Drew, 1951: Civil Service, address given for 1951 – 25 Mortlake Road, Kew. It revealed the following, that in 1951 a PF file was in operation for both Henry Herbert Drew and Arthur C.W. Drew – PF64961. The profession on Henry's passport was listed as Insurance Club; that of Arthur Drew as Private Secretary to the Secretary of State for War.

27 Emmanuel Shinwell took office on 3 August 1945 and left office on 7 October 1947; Hugh Gaitskell took office on 7 October 1947 and left office on 28 February 1950; Philip Noel-Baker took office on 28 February 1950 and left office on 31 October 1951.

28 TNA Kew KV2/2937/170a/Duncan and Barbara TAYLOR/dated 29.5.1951. Roger Quirk went on to have a very successful Civil Service career. He had read science at Cambridge and entered the Civil Service in 1931. He was appointed Under-Secretary at the Office of the Minister for Science in 1959 and became a member of the Historical Manuscripts Commission and the Council of the Society of Antiquaries. See the *New Scientist*, 21 November 1963.

29 See Andrews, Geoff, *The Shadow Man at the Heart of the Cambridge Spy Circle* (London: I.B. Tauris, 2015), p.158.

30 Personal correspondence, Murphy to Burke, 17 July 2016.

31 Roland Berger became Secretary of the British Council for the Promotion of International Trade while remaining a secret member of the GPGB. In 1962–63 his sympathies were with the Chinese in the Sino-Soviet split. See Berger's seveteen-volume secret service file, which starts at TNA Kew KV2/4235.

32 John Gittings, *Guardian*, 30 June 2004.

33 Rae, Ian, 'Review of *The Story of the Icebreakers in China* by Percy Timberlake', *China Quarterly*, vol. 144 (December 1995), pp.1232–3.

34 See Chapter 10.

35 Bridget married the Scottish Communist John 'Jock' Nicholson on 25 May 1949 at Hampstead Registry Office with the Party's blessing.

36 Betty Reid worked in the National Organisation Department of the CPGB and was responsible for Party security; TNA Kew KV2/1569/210b/dated 31 October 1952.

37 TNA Kew KV2/1569/210b/dated 31 October 1952.

38 TNA Kew KV2/1569/230a/dated 26 November 1953; KV2/1569/211a/ dated 12 November 1952.

39 TNA Kew KV2/1569/346a/dated 6 October 1953.

40 James Klugmann (1912–77) has been described as 'the (unofficial) mentor of several of the "Cambridge Five" who worked covertly for the Soviet Union'. See Andrews, *Shadow Man*.

41 TNA Kew KV2/2531/346A/dated 6 October 1953.

42 TNA Kew KV2/2928/2Z/dated 8 May 1951.

43 Unlike other members of the Kuczynski clan, Long was not considered a security risk. Special Branch reported on 12 November 1947: 'This man has not at any time come to the notice of Special Branch in connection with extremist activities.' TNA Kew KV2/1568/Minute 148/dated 22.2.1950.

44 Green, *Political Family*, p.301.

45 Nicholson, Jock, *A Turbulent Life* (London: Praxis Press, 2009) cited in Aaronovitch, *Party Animals*, p.47.

46 Ibid.

47 TNA Kew KV2/1568/179a/Note re telephone check on Duncan and Barbara Taylor/dated 9 February 1951.

48 Aaronovitch, *Party Animals*, p.40.

Chapter 17

1 TNA Kew KV2/2937/222A/dated 22 December 1953.

2 The MGB was formed in March 1946. See Appendix 1.

3 Vassiliev, Alexander, 'Possible reasons for failure February 1950', *Yellow Notebook #1*, p.87.

4 Vassiliev, Alexander, 'C – London 30 September 1946', *Yellow Notebook #1*, p.77.

5 East Germany, officially the German Democratic Republic, was established in the Soviet Zone of Germany in 1949.

6 See Field, Hermann and Kate, *Trapped in the Cold War: The Ordeal of an American Family* (Stanford: Stanford University Press, 1999).

7 Lázló Rajk (1909–1949) served as Communist Minister of the Interior and Minister of Foreign Affairs during the Second Hungarian Republic (1946–49) before his arrest and execution for Titoism in 1949.

8 Rudolf Slánský (1901–1952) was General Secretary of the Czechoslavakian Communist Party from March 1946 until his arrest for Trotskyite–Titoist–Zionist activities in November 1951. He was executed on 3 December 1952.

9 K.I. (Committee of Information), Soviet foreign intelligence agency initially combining the foreign directorates of the MGB and GRU, 1947–51.

10 Central Committee of the Socialist Unity Party.

11 Vassiliev, 'Possible reasons for failure February 1950', p.87.

12 TNA Kew KV2/1879/531a/dated 12 May 1950.

13 TNA Kew KV2/1879/559a/dated 19 January 1951.

14 TNA Kew KV2/1879/531a/dated 12 May 1950.

15 At this time Koenen was losing political influence. He was no longer Saxony party chief; although he was still a member of the SED's influential Central Secretariat. Nevertheless, 'he – like so many other former Western emigres – now had a somewhat precarious hold on power.' Epstein, Catherine, *The Last Revolutionaries: German Communists and their Century* (Cambridge, MA: Harvard University Press, 2003), p.120.

16 TNA Kew KV2/1879/543a/dated 21 September 1950.

17 Koenen to Matern, 13 January 1953, in *Stiftung Archiv der Parteien und massenorganisationen der DDR im Bundesarchiv Berlin* (henceforth SAPMO-Barch), DY 30/IV 2/4/123 Bl. 239–41; cited in Stibbe, Matthew, 'Jurgen Kuczynski and the Search for a (Non-Existent) Western Spy Ring in the East German Communist Party in 1953', *Contemporary European History*, vol. 20, no. 1 (February 2011), pp.61–79.

18 The trial of Rudolf Slánský in Prague in November 1952: eleven of fourteen leading Czechoslovakian Party functionaries accused of high treason and 'bourgeois nationalist' or 'Zionist' connections were Jewish, a fact that was mentioned repeatedly in the indictments against them. Six had lived in London for at least some of the period 1937 to 1945. Guilty verdicts were passed on all the defendants; eleven were handed death sentences, which were carried out on 3 December 1952, and the

remaining three were given life terms. The Doctors' Plot in Moscow in January 1953 involved an imagined conspiracy by a group of Jewish doctors to murder the Soviet leadership in the Kremlin.

19 Stibbe, 'Jurgen'.

20 Kuczynski, *Memoiren*, pp.375–6 and 393–8; cited in Stibbe, 'Jurgen', p.67.

21 McLellan, *Antifascism*, p.2; See also Stibbe, 'Jurgen', p.68.

22 McLellan, *Antifascism*, pp.2–3.

Chapter 18

1 Greece was seen as strategically important to the safeguarding of British lines of communication to the Eastern Mediterranean and the Near East, the oilfields of the Middle East and British India. Both the Americans and the British feared a Soviet Mediterranean strategy that, they believed, aimed at the domination of Greece, control of the Dardanelles, the collapse of the British Empire and Soviet imperial mastery of the entire Middle East.

2 Britain's military involvement in the Greek crisis began with the December events (*Dekemvriana*) of 1944, the first military intervention against any anti-Nazi resistance movement in occupied Europe.

3 The Attlee Directive, cited in Ewing, R.D., Mahoney, John and Moretta, Andrew, *MI5, the Cold War, and the Rule of Law* (Oxford: Oxford University Press, 2020), p.35.

4 Verrie, *Looking Glass*, p.37.

5 Ibid.

6 Weiler, *British Labour*, p.131.

7 Sakkas, John, '*The Times* and the British Intervention in Greece in December 1944', *The Balkan Studies*, vol. 46 (2012), p.27.

8 Weiler, *British Labour*, p.132.

9 *New Statesman*, 7 September 1946; cited in Sakkas, 'British Intervention in Greece', p.80.

10 *New Statesman*, 9 November 1946; cited in Sakkas, 'British Intervention in Greece', p.82.

11 *Daily Worker*, 3 September 1946; cited in Sakkas, 'British Intervention in Greece', p.82.

12 TNA Kew KV2/2930/194A/dated 30 May 1952.

13 TNA Kew KV2/2929/160a/Section and Officer of origin B.1.K/MK/ Action Copy to B.1.G/HDW./dated 18 December 1951.

14 TNA Kew KV2/2929/183b/dated 6[?] April 1952.

15 Ibid.

16 Ibid.

17 Ibid.

18 Ibid.

19 Ibid.

20 Ibid.

21 Ibid.

22 Ibid.

23 TNA Kew KV2/2929/189a/dated 6 April 1952.

24 TNA Kew KV2/2930/198z/dated 17 September 1952.

25 TNA Kew KV2/2930/213A.

26 Keeling was Francis's mother's maiden name.

27 See Ewing et. al, *MI5*, p.192.

Chapter 19

1 TNA Kew KV2/2889/Minute 64/dated 20 December 1950.

2 TNA Kew KV2/2889/36a/dated 20 September 1945.

3 TNA Kew KV2/2889/45b/dated 19 November 1947.

4 TNA Kew KV2/2889/54B dated 15 March 1949; KV2/2889/Minute 53/dated 9 April 1949.

5 Hennessy, Peter and Brownfield, Gail, 'Britain's Cold War Security Purge: The Origins of Positive Vetting, *The Historical Journal*, vol. 25, no. 4 (1982), pp.965–73. See also TNA Kew CAB 21/2248.

6 Negative vetting involved an inquiry into an individual's general background and record in order to ascertain their suitability for an official position.

7 Cited in Hennessy and Brownfield, 'Britain's Cold War Security Purge', p.969.

8 TNA Kew KV2/2889/63a/dated 30 September 1950.

9 TNA Kew KV2/2889/73a/dated 19 February 1951.

10 TNA Kew KV2/2889/74a/dated 19 March 1951.

11 TNA Kew KV2/2890/96A/dated 8 April 1951.

12 TNA Kew KV2/2892/Minute 186/dated 21 September 1955.

13 Winnifrith, A.J.D., 'The Evolution of the Present Security System in the Civil Service', 5 December 1955; Security Conference of Privy Counsellors, S.C.P.C. (55)4, 6 December 1955, TNA Kew CAB 134/1325, cited in Andrew, *Defence*, p.393.

14 Founded in 1951.

15 In September 1953 the Simpsons had moved to North Wales, where Arthur was employed as the Principal Naturalist at the Shell Fish Research Station, Ministry of Agriculture and Fisheries Laboratory, Castle Bank, Conway.

16 TNA Kew KV2/2892/195A/dated 9 April 1956.

17 TNA Kew KV2/2893/204a/dated 21 November 1956.

18 Four branch offices of the International Association of Democratic Jurists were to be opened in Paris, Budapest, Berlin and London. D.N. Pritt was to be in charge of the London office with Francis acting as his assistant.

19 TNA Kew KV2/2933/285a/dated 20 December 1956.

20 Ibid.

21 TNA Kew KV2/2933/282z/dated 23 November 1956.

22 The Soviets regarded the Warsaw pact as a collective defence treaty between the Soviet Union and the seven Eastern Bloc states of Poland, Czechoslovakia, the DDR, Rumania, Albania, Bulgaria and Hungary.

23 TNA Kew KV2/2932/281G/dated 21 November 1956.

24 Ibid.

25 Ibid.

26 TNA Kew KV2/2933/285b/dated 16 January 1957.

27 Simmonds, Alan G.V., 'Raising Rachman: The Origins of the Rent Act, 1957', *The Historical Journal*, vol. 45, no. 4 (2002), p.843.

28 Richards, Peter, 'The Banner Bright, the Symbol Plain, of Human Right and Human Gain', The Review, *Camden New Journal*, 4 June 2009.

29 Aaronovitch, *Party Animals*, p.71.

30 TNA Kew KV2/2983/201a/dated 15 January 1957.

31 TNA Kew KV2/2983/Minute 208/dated 7 February 1957.

32 TNA Kew KV2/2983/Minute 210/dated 14 February 1957.

33 TNA Kew KV2/2983/Minute 211/dated 13 March 1957; see also SF 494-2-3 Supp A – Index of Secret Communists.

34 TNA Kew KV2/2983/Minute 219z/dated 17 June 1957.

35 Mrs. Ruby Unwin P.F.133,818/F.I.A.; Mr. Eric Unwin P.F.133,818/E.I.C.

36 TNA Kew KV2/2983/220b/dated 23 October 1957.
37 Intelligence and Security Committee, 'The Mitrokhin Archive Report', June 2000, p.21.
38 Ibid., p.20.
39 *Independent on Sunday*, 12 September 1999.

Conclusion

1 Strachey, *Strangled Cry*, p.35.
2 Ibid., p.37.

Bibliography

Aaronovitch, David, *Party Animals: My Family and Other Communists* (London: Jonathan Cape, 2015).

Aldrich, Richard J., *GCHQ: The Uncensored Story of Britain's Most Secret Intelligence Agency* (London: HarperPress, 2010).

Andrew, Christopher, *Defence of the Realm* (London: Allen Lane, 2009).

Andrew, Christopher and Mitrokhin, Vasili, *Mitrokhin Archive* (London: Allen Lane, 1999).

Andrews, Geoff, *The Shadow Man at the Heart of the Cambridge Spy Circle* (London: I.B. Tauris, 2015).

Association of Scientific Workers, *Science and the Nation* (Middlesex: Harmondsworth, 1947).

Bearman, Marietta, Brinson, Charmian, Dove, Richard, Grenville, Anthony and Taylor, Jennifer, *Out of Austria: The Austrian Centre in London in World War II* (London: I.B. Tauris, 2007).

Beckett, Francis, *Enemy Within: The Rise and Fall of the British Communist Party* (London: John Murray, 1995).

Berg, Jerome S., *On the Short Waves, 1923–1945: Broadcast Listening in the Pioneer Days of Radio* (London: McFarland & Co., 2007).

Blok, Martin, *Gypsies: Their Life and their Customs*, trans. Barbara Kuczynski and Duncan Taylor (London: Meuthen & Co. Ltd, 1938).

Blumenau, Ralph, *Students and the Cold War* (Basingstoke and London: Macmillan Press, 1996).

Bodek, Richard, 'The Not-So-Golden Twenties: Everyday Life and Communist Agitprop in Weimar-Era Berlin', *Journal of Social History*, vol. 30, no. 1 (Autumn 1996).

Brandenberger, D., *National Bolshevism: Stalinist Mass Culture and the Formation of Modern Russian National Identity, 1931–1956* (Cambridge, MA: Harvard University Press, 2002).

Branson, Noreen, *History of the Communist Party of Great Britain 1927–1941* (London: Lawrence & Wishart, 1985).

Branson, Noreen and Heinemann, Margot, *Britain in the Nineteen Thirties* (London: Weidenfeld & Nicolson, 1971).

Brinson, Charmian and Dove, Richard, *A Matter of Intelligence: MI5 and the Surveillance of Anti-Nazi Refugees 1933–50* (Manchester: Manchester University Press, 2014).

Brinson, Charmian and Dove, Richard, *Politics by Other Means: The Free German League of Culture in London, 1939–1946* (London: Vallentine Mitchell, 2010).

Brown, Andrew, *J.D. Bernal: The Sage of Science* (Oxford: Oxford University Press, 2005).

Brysac, Shareen Blair, *Resisting Hitler: Mildred Harnack and the Red Orchestra* (Oxford: Oxford University Press, 2000).

Bullock, Alan, *Hitler: A Study in Tyranny* (London: Odhams, 1952).

Burke, David, *Russia and the British Left: From the 1848 Revolutions to the General Strike* (London: I.B. Tauris, 2018).

Burke, David, *The Lawn Road Flats: Spies, Writers and Artists* (Suffolk: Boydell, 2014).

Burke, David, *The Spy Who Came in from the Co-op: Melita Norwood and the Ending of Cold War Espionage* (Woodbridge: Boydell, 2008).

Burleigh, Michael, *The Third Reich: A New History* (London: Pan Books, 2000).

Carritt, Michael, *A Mole in the Crown* (published privately by Michael Carritt, 1985).

Carter, Miranda, *Anthony Blunt: His Lives* (London: Macmillan, 2001).

Caute, David, *The Fellow-Travellers: A Postcript to the Enlightenment* (London: Weidenfeld & Nicolson, 1973)

Ceplair, Larry, *Under the Shadow of War: Fascism, Anti-Fascism and Marxists, 1918–1939* (New York: Columbia University Press, 1967).

Cladders, Lukas and Ferdinand, Ursula, 'Measuring World Population at LSE – Robert René Kuczynski, an Émigré Scholar', *LSE History*.

Cole, G.D.H., *The People's Front* (London: Victor Gollanz Ltd, 1937).

Cornford, John, *Collected Writings*, ed. Jonathan Galassi (Manchester: Carcanet Press Ltd; new edition, 1986)

Croall, Jonathan, *Neil of Summerhill: The Permanent Rebel* (New York: Pantheon Books, 1983).

Crowley, Robert T., *The New KGB* (New York: William Morrow & Co., 1986).

Dallin, Alexander and Firsov, F.I. (eds), *Dimitrov and Stalin, 1934–1943: Letters from the Soviet Archives* (New Haven and London: Yale University Press, 2000).

Davenport, Nicholas, *Memoirs of a City Radical* (London: Weidenfeld & Nicolson, 1974).

Degras, Jane (ed.), *The Communist International 1919–1943: Documents. Vol. II: 1923–1928* (London: Frank Cass & Co. Ltd, 1971).

Degras, Jane (ed.), *The Communist International 1919–1943: Documents. Vol. III: 1929–1943* (London: Frank Cass & Co. Ltd, 1971).

Edinger, Lewis J., *German Exile Politics: The Social Democratic Executive Committee in the Nazi Era* (Berkeley: University of California Press, 1956).

Entsiklopediya voennoi razvedki Roccii (Russian Military Intelligence Encyclopedia) (Moscow: ACT-ACTREL, 2004).

Epstein, Catherine, *The Last Revolutionaries: German Communists and their Century* (Cambridge, MA: Harvard University Press, 2003).

Estorick, Eric, *Stafford Cripps: A Biography* (London: William Heinemann Ltd, 1949).

Ewing, R.D., Mahoney, John and Moretta, Andrew, *MI5, the Cold War and the Rule of Law* (Oxford: Oxford University Press, 2020).

Fair-Schulz, Axel and Kessler, Mario, *German Scholars in Exile: New Studies in Intellectual History* (Maryland: Lexington Books, 2011).

Federman, Adam, *Fasting and Feasting: The Life of Visionary Food Writer Patience Gray* (London: Chelsea Green Publishing, 2017).

Field, Hermann and Kate, *Trapped in the Cold War: The Ordeal of an American Family* (Stanford: Stanford University Press 1999).

Fischer, Louis, *Men and Politics* (New York: Duell, Sloan and Pearce, 1941).

Fischer, Ruth, *Stalin and German Communism: A Study in the Origins of the State Party* (Cambridge, MA: Harvard University Press, 1948).

Fisher, David James, *Romain Rolland and the Politics of Intellectual Engagement* (Berkeley: University of California Press, 1988).

Fleay, C. and Sanders, M.L., 'The Labour Spain Committee: Labour Party Policy and the Spanish Civil War', *The Historical Journal*, vol. 28, no. 1 (March 1985).

Foot, M.R.D., *S.O.E. The Special Operations Executive 1940–1946* (London: Pimlico, 1999).

Foote, Alexander, *Handbook for Spies* (London: Museum Press 1949).

Fowkes, Ben, *Communism in Germany Under the Weimar Republic* (London: The Macmillan Press Ltd, 1984).

Frisch, Max, *The Arsonists* (1953; London: Methuen, 2007 edn.)

Gannes, Harry and Repard, Theodore, *Spain in Revolt* (London: Victor Gollancz Ltd, 1936).

German–Soviet Boundary and Friendship Treaty, THE AVALON PROJECT *Documents in Law, History and Diplomacy*, Yale Law School, Lilian Goldman Law Library.

Goodman, Richard, 'Hitler's Next Move', *New Masses*, vol. 30, no. 11 (7 March 1939).

Gollancz, Victor, Orwell, George and Strachey, John, *The Betrayal of the Left* (London: Gollancz, Left Book Club edn, 1941).

Gorodetsky, Gabriel (ed.), *Maisky Diaries* (New Haven and London: Yale University Press, 2015).

Gould, Jonathan S., *German Anti-Nazi Espionage in the Second World War: The OSS and the Men of the TOOL Mission* (Oxon: Routledge, 2018).

Govrin, Yosef, *The Jewish Factor in the Relations between Nazi Germany and the Soviet Union, 1933–1941* (London: Vallentine Mitchell, 2009).

Green, John, *A Political Family: The Kuczynskis, Fascism, Espionage and the Cold War* (Oxon: Routledge, 2017).

Grenville, Anthony (ed.), *German-Speaking Exiles in Great Britain* (Amsterdam: Editions Rodopi B.V., 2000).

Gross, Babette, *Münzenberg* (Michigan: Michigan State University Press, 1974).

Grunberger, Richard, *A Social History of the Third Reich* (London: Weidenfeld & Nicolson, 1971).

Haslam, Jonathan, *Near and Distant Neighbours: A New History of Soviet Intelligence* (New York: Farrar, Straus and Giroux, 2015).

Hemming, Henry, *Churchill's Iceman: The True Story of Geoffrey Pyke: Genius, Fugitive, Spy* (London: Preface Publishing, 2014).

Hemmingway, Ernest, *For Whom the Bell Tolls* (New York: Charles Scribner's Sons, 1940; London: Vintage Publishing, 1999 edn.)

Hinsley, Harold, *British Intelligence,* vol. II (London: Her Majesty's Stationery Office, 1990).

Hennessy, Peter and Brownfield, Gail, 'Britain's Cold War Security Purge: The Origins of Positive Vetting', *The Historical Journal*, vol. 25, no. 4 (1982), pp.965–73.

Intelligence and Security Committee, 'The Mitrokhin Archive Report', June 2000.

Jordan, T.S., 'Review of *Hunger and Work*, by Jurgen Kuczynski. [New York: International Publishers, 1938]', *Science & Society*, vol. 4, no. 1 (Winter 1940).

Kapp, Yvonne and Mynatt, Margaret, *British Policy and the Refugees, 1933–1941* (London: Frank Cass & Co. Ltd, 1997).

Kershaw, Ian, *Hitler: Hubris 1899–1936* (London: Allen Lane, 2001).

Kershaw, Ian, *Hitler: Nemesis 1936–1945* (London: Allen Lane, 2000).

Kettler, David and Lauer, Gerhard, *Exile, Science, and Bildung: The Contested Legacies of German Émigré Intellectuals* (New York: AIAA, 2005).

Klemens von Klemperer, *German Resistance Against Hitler: The Search for Allies Abroad 1938–1945* (Oxford: Clarendon Press, 1992).

Knightley, Phillip, *The Second Oldest Profession: Spies and Spying in the Twentieth Century* (London: Pimlico, 2003).

Koch, Steven, *Double Lives: Stalin, Willi Münzenberg and the Seduction of the Intellectuals* (New York: Enigma Books, 1994).

Kotek, Joel, *Students and the Cold War*, trans. Ralph Blumenau (Basingstoke and London: Macmillan Press, 1996).

Krämer, Gudrun, *The Jews in Modern Egypt, 1914–1952* (London: I.B. Tauris, 1989).

Krivitsky, Walter, *In Stalin's Secret Service* (New York: Harper Brothers, 1939).

Kuczynski, Jürgen, *The Condition of the Workers in Gt. Britain, Germany & The Soviet Union 1932–38* (London: Victor Gollanz Ltd, 1939).

Kuczynski, Jürgen, *British Trade Unionism: A Short Course for Scientific Workers* (London: F.W. Bull & Co. Ltd, 1943).

Kuczynski, Jürgen, *Freedom Calling!: The Story of the Secret German Radio* (London: Frederick Muller Ltd, 1939).

Kuczynski, Jürgen, *Hunger and Work: Statistical Studies* (London: Lawrence & Wishart, 1938).

Kuczynski, Jürgen, *Memoiren 1945–1989* (Berlin and Weimar: Aufbau-Verlag, 1992).

Kuczynski, J. and Witt, M., *The Economics of Barbarism: Hitler's New Economic Order in Europe* (London: Frederick Muller Ltd, 1942).

Labour Party, *The Communist Party and the War* (London: Transport House, 1943).

Leigh, David, *The Wilson Plot* (London: Heinemann Mandarin, 1989).

Levy, Paul, 'Gray [née Stanham], Patience Jean' in *Oxford Dictionary of National Biography* (Oxford: Oxford University Press, 2013).

Löwenstein, Prince Hubertus zu, *Towards the Further Shore: An Autobiography* (London: Victor Gollancz Ltd, 1968).

Lütgemeier-Davin, Reinhold, *Pazifismus zwischen Kooperation und Konfrontation: Das Deutsche Friedenskartell in der Weimarer Republik* (Cologne: Pahl-Rugenstein Verlag, 1982).

Maclean, Fitzroy, *Eastern Approaches* (London: Jonathan Cape, 1949).

Mahon, John, *Harry Pollitt* (London: Lawrence & Wishart, 1976).

Marrack, John, 'A National Food Policy', *Labour Monthly*, vol. 20 (1938), pp.502–7.

Marrack, John, 'Food in Wartime: Free Basic Ration – or Higher Wages, *Medicine Today & Tomorrow*, vol. 2 (1940), pp.2–9.

Marrack, John, *Food and Planning* (London: Victor Gollancz, 1942).

Mason, T. W., 'Arbeiteropposition im nationalsozialistischen Deutschland' in Peukert, D. and Reulecke, J. (eds), *Die Reihen fast geschlossen* (Wuppertal: Peter Hammer Verlag, 1981).

McLellan, Josie, *Antifascism and Memory in East Germany: Remembering the International Brigades 1945–1989* (Oxford: Clarendon Press, Oxford Historical Monographs, 2004).

Merson, Allan, *Communist Resistance in Nazi Germany* (London: Lawrence & Wishart, 1985).

Miles, Jonathan, *The Nine Lives of Otto Katz* (London: Bantam Books, 2010).

Monetary and Economic Conference, *The Needs of Europe, Its Economic Reconstruction* (London: 1920), Classic reprint Series. Forgotten Books edn.

Neavill, Gordon Barrick, 'Victor Gollancz and the Left Book Club', *The Library Quarterly*, vol. 41, no. 3 (1971).

Newman, Michael, *John Strachey* (Manchester: Manchester University Press, 1989).

Nicholson, Jock, *A Turbulent Life* (London: Praxis Press, 2009).

Palmier, Jean-Michel, *Weimar in Exile: The Antifascist Emigration in Europe and America* (London: Verso, 1987, 2006).

Parsons, Stephen R., 'Communism in the Professions: The Organisation of the British Communist Party Among Professional Workers, 1933–1956', PhD thesis, University of Warwick, June 1990, go.warwick.ac.uk/wrap/34723.

Pelling, Henry, *The British Communist Party: A Historical Profile* (London: Black, 1958).

Pimlott, Ben, *Hugh Dalton* (London: Harper Collins, 1985).

Pincher, Chapman, *Treachery* (Edinburgh and London: Mainstream Publishing, 2012).

Pollitt, Harry, *How to Win the War* (London: Marston Printing Co., 1939).

Powell, J.B., *My 25 Years in China* (New York; The Macmillan Company, 1945).

Priestley, J.B., *Postscripts* (London: William Heinemann Ltd, 1940).

Priestley, J.B., *Out of the People* (London: Collins in association with William Heinemann Ltd, 1941).

Prittie, Terence, *Germans Against Hitler* (London: Hutchison, 1964).

Radó, Sandor, *Code Name Dora* (London: Abelard, 1976).

Rae, Ian, 'Review of *The Story of the Icebreakers in China* by Percy Timberlake', *China Quarterly*, vol. 144 (December 1995), pp. 1232–3.

Rees, E.A. (ed.), *The Nature of Stalin's Dictatorship: The Politburo 1928–1953* (Basingstoke: Palgrave MacMillan, 2004).

Regler, Gustav, *The Owl of Minerva: The Autobiography of Gustav Regler* (London: Rupert Hart-Davis, 1959).

Roberts, Sian, 'Education, Art and Exile: Cultural Activists and Exhibitions of Refugee Children's Art in the UK During the Second World War', *Paedagogica Historica*, vol. 53, no. 3 (April 2017).

Rowntree, Seebohm, *The Human Needs of Labour* (London: Longmans, first published 1918, revised edn. 1937).

Sakkas, John, '*The Times* and the British Intervention in Greece in December 1944', *The Balkan Studies*, vol. 46 (2012).

Salzmann, Stephanie, *Great Britain, Germany, and the Soviet Union: Rapallo and After, 1922–1934* (Suffolk: Boydell & Brewer, 2002).

Shelley, Rose, 'The Penumbra of Weimar Political Culture: Pacifism, Feminism, and Social Democracy' (2011), *History Faculty Publications*, engagedscholarship.csuohio.edu/clhist_facpub/88.

Sheppard, H.R.L., *We Say No!: The Plain Man's Guide to Pacifism* (London: John Murray, 1935).

Shirer, William L., *The Rise and Fall of the Third Reich: A History of Nazi Germany* (New York: Simon and Schuster, 1960).

Simmonds, Alan G.V., 'Raising Rachman: The Origins of The Rent Act, 1957', *The Historical Journal*, vol. 45, no. 4 (2002).

Smedley, Agnes, *China Correspondent* (London: Pandora Press, 1984, first published by Alfred A. Knopf, Inc., New York, 1943).

Smith, Richard Harris, *OSS: The Secret History of America's First Central Intelligence Agency* (California: University of California Press, 1972).

Sontag, Raymond James and Beddie, James Stuart, *Nazi–Soviet Relations 1939–1941: Documents from the Archives of the German Foreign Office for the U.S. Department of State* (New York: Department of State, 1948).

Stibbe, Matthew, 'Jurgen Kuczynski and the Search for a (Non-Existent) Western Spy Ring in the East German Communist Party in 1953', *Contemporary European History*, vol. 20, no. 1 (February 2011).

Strachey, John, *The Strangled Cry and Other Unparliamentary Papers* (London: Bodley Head, 1962).

Thomas, Hugh, *John Strachey* (London: Eyre Methuen, 1973).

Trotsky, Leon, *Lessons of October (1924)* (London: Union Books, 1993 edn).

Tsarev, Oleg, *KGB v Anglii* (Moscow: Tsentrpoligraf, 1999)

Vansittart, Robert, *The Mist Procession: The Autobiography of Lord Vansittart* (London: Hutchison, 1958)

Vassiliev, Alexander, *Yellow Notebook #1*, Wilson Center Digitial Archive, digitalarchive.wilsoncenter.org/document/112856.

Verrier, Anthony, *Through the Looking Glass* (London: W.W. Norton & Company Ltd, 1983).

von Klemperer, Klemens, *German Resistance Against Hitler: The Search for Allies Abroad 1938–1945* (Oxford: Clarendon Press, 1992).

Walton, Calder, *Empire of Secrets: British Intelligence, the Cold War and the Twilight of Empire* (London: Harper Press, 2013)

Watson, Derek, 'Molotov's Apprenticeship in Foreign Policy: The Triple Alliance Negotiations in 1939', *Europe-Asia Studies*, vol. 52, no. 4 (2000).

Webb, Sidney and Beatrice, *Soviet Communism: A New Civilisation* (London: Longmans, Green And Co., 1935).

Weiler, Peter, *British Labour and the Cold War* (California: Stanford University Press, 1988).

Wendehorst, Stephan E.C., *British Jewry, Zionism, and the Jewish State, 1936–1956* (Oxford: Oxford University Press, 2012).

Werner, Ruth, *Sonya's Report: The Fascinating Autobiography of One of Russia's Most Remarkable Secret Agents*, trans. Renate Simpson (London: Chatto & Windus, 1991).

West, Nigel, *The Illegals: The Double Lives of the Cold War's Most Secret Agents* (London: Hodder & Stoughton, 1993).

Wheeler-Bennett, John, *The Nemesis of Power: The German Army in Politics* (London: MacMillan, 1961).

Williams, Robert Chadwell, *Klaus Fuchs: Atom Spy* (Cambridge, MA: Harvard University Press, 1987).

Wolf, Markus with McElvoy, Anne, *Memoirs of a Spymaster* (London: Pimlico, 1998).

Wood, N., *Communism and British Intellectuals* (London: Victor Gollancz, 1959).

Young, George Kennedy, *Subversion and the British Riposte* (Glasgow: Ossian Publishers Ltd, 1984).

Journals and Newspapers

Daily Worker
Financial Times, 27/28 July 2019
Hampstead Garden Suburb News, 2016
Labour Monthly
Left News
New Statesman and Nation
The Times

Primary Documents

Comintern Archives 495/100/943.
Inprekorr, IV, 1924, no. 16, 4 February.
Inprekorr, 1923, no. 72, 7 November.
Monetary and Economic Conference, *The Needs of Europe, Its Economic Reconstruction* (1921).
Papers of the Nuffield College Social Reconstruction Survey 1941–1955.
Scottish Home department. Scottish Sea Fisheries Statistical Tables 1957. Edinburgh: Her Majesty's Stationary Office.

The National Archives Kew (hereafter TNA Kew)
TNA Kew AB/1. Department of Scientific and Industrial Research and related bodies: Directorate of Tube Alloys and related bodies: War of 1939–1945, Correspondence and Papers.
TNA Kew CAB 21/2248.
TNA Kew CAB 134/1325.
TNA Kew HW14 Government Code and Cypher School: Directorate: Second World War Policy Papers.
TNA Kew KV2 772–774 'Willi' Munzenberg.

TNA Kew KV2/777 Pyotr Leonydovitch KAPITZA.

TNA Kew KV2/988. Frederick Robert KUH.

TNA Kew KV2/1121–1123 Karl OTTEN.

TNA Kew KV2/1256 Emil Julius Klaus FUCHS.

TNA Kew KV2/1384 Otto KATZ.

TNA Kew KV2/1561–1566 Hans KAHLE.

TNA Kew KV2/1567–1569 Bridget LEWIS.

TNA Kew KV2/1610 Rudolf Albert HAMBURGER.

TNA Kew KV2/1611–1616 Alexander FOOTE.

TNA Kew KV2/1647–1648 Sandor RADO.

TNA Kew KV2/1871–1880 Jürgen and Marguerite KUCZYNSKI.

TNA Kew KV2/2527–2532 Margot Claire HEINEMANN.

TNA Kew KV2/2798–2800 Wilhelm KOENEN.

TNA Kew KV2/2883 Heinz Israel KAMNITZER.

TNA Kew KV2/2889–2893 Renate and Arthur SIMPSON.

TNA Kew KV2/2927–2933 Sabine and Francis LOEFFLER.

TNA Kew KV2/2935–2937 Barbara and Duncan Taylor.

TNA Kew KV2/3039–3040 Geoffrey PYKE.

TNA Kew KV2/3063–3067 Rose SCHECHTER.

TNA Kew KV2/3504 Helga KAMNITZER.

TNA Kew KV2/3716 Prince LOWENSTEIN.

TNA Kew KV4/110 Policy on liaison between Metropolitan Police Special Branch and the German, i.e. Prussian, Ministry of the Interior concerning Communism.

TNA Kew KV4/111 Liaison with German Political Police and Nazi Authorities 1933 – Visit of Captain Liddell to Berlin.

TNA Kew KV6/41–45 Ursula KUCZYNSKI.

Personal Correspondence

William Scanlon Murphy to David Burke, 7 July 2016; 17 July 2016.

Index